THE FRUGAL MARKETER

Smart Tips for Stretching Your Budget

J. DONALD WEINRAUCH
AND
NANCY CROFT BAKER

D1367689

amacom

American Management Association

This book is available at a special
discount when ordered in bulk quantities.
For information, contact Special Sales Department,
AMACOM, a division of American Management Association,
135 West 50th Street, New York, NY 10020.

Library of Congress Cataloging-in-Publication Data

Weinrauch, J. Donald, 1942–
   The frugal marketer.

   Includes index.
   1. Marketing—Management—Handbooks, manuals, etc.
2. Advertising—Handbooks, manuals, etc.   3. Small
business—Handbooks, manuals, etc.   I. Baker, Nancy C.
II. Title.
HF5415.13.W395   1989   658.8   88-48040
ISBN 0-8144-7714-3

Printing number

10   9   8   7   6   5   4   3   2   1

Dedication

This book is dedicated to:

- Don's wife, Rosemary, and children, Karen and William
- Nancy's mother, Peggy Ferguson Croft, and Nancy's husband, Mark Baker
- Don's parents, John and Florence Weinrauch, former small-business owners
- Business owners the world over, who inspired us to write about their dauntless spirit of enterprise

Preface

The responsibility of running a business can be overwhelming. As an entrepreneur, you face the daily challenge of getting your business on its feet and making it succeed. If you're a small, independent mom-and-pop shop or franchisee, you're worried about keeping your business afloat in a fiercely competitive marketplace of larger rivals. As a marketing manager, you're constantly expected to pull new customers out of a hat. If you're an association marketing director, you may have to recruit new members, keep current members, or generate good publicity for your organization—not to mention soliciting generous donations from people who can no longer take big tax write-offs for charitable contributions.

Marketing your product, service, or cause under these conditions is tough, whether you're a for-profit or a nonprofit entity. Most likely you're working with a limited budget and have little time to dream up savvy marketing ideas—but you need them to survive in today's marketplace. The key to success is making your product or service stand out in a sea of similar goods. But you don't have to pay a hefty consultant's fee to do it.

In our work with business owners and association marketing managers through Don's consulting and Nancy's marketing beat with *Nation's Business* magazine, the one thing we've heard over and over is that small-business owners/marketing managers/chief-cook-and-bottle-washers need a source of many low-cost ideas on how to boost sales, and they want the information fast and without a lot of trouble. They want practical and innovative marketing strategies that they can immediately plug into their individual enterprises.

That's where we can help. As marketing professor–consultant and business writer, we have been afforded the opportunity to talk with hundreds of business owners and marketing managers about their secrets of success on small budgets. Now we have hundreds of anecdotes to pass along to anyone who wants to get a bigger bang for his marketing buck.

Unlike most other marketing books, we have designed *The Frugal Marketer* to be a quick reference tool and idea generator because we know you don't have time to read lengthy textbooks and articles. If you're like us, you're probably lucky to skim through the morning paper—at 11 P.M. The entries are arranged as an encyclopedia for a quick read. Part I introduces you to the concept of marketing. Part II helps you set a foundation for solving your marketing problems before you actually make any decisions. Part III introduces you to hundreds of solutions.

Instead of weighing you down (and boring you) with every nitty-gritty detail about just a few marketing strategies, we have provided as many innovative tips as we could come up with to act as a springboard for your own ideas. Nobody knows your business better than you. Our objective is for you to select the tips that best apply to your marketing situation. Through the additional resources for further information that we try to provide with every topic, you can tailor the tips to meet your unique challenges. However, you'll probably find that you can use most of our tips as they are. See the entry Kudos in Part II for quick and easy selling ideas that you can start using right away.

We also try to stimulate your creative juices by including quizzes, questionnaires, checklists, and dos and don'ts. These provide quick diversions to help you expand on our tips.

Above all, we know you want to be inspired. In nearly every entry, our tips come alive with actual examples of business owners and association managers who have creatively and successfully marketed their products and services on tight budgets. They are people just like you. They have experienced the same worries about running a business or nonprofit organization and have found success with the tips we illustrate. After reading several of our ideas, you'll realize that coming up with creative marketing programs isn't impossible on a tight budget. Sometimes you just need to step away from the hassles of the moment to take a look at your marketing challenge from a different angle.

To get you started, here are a few exercises to consider trying before setting a foundation for your marketing solution. They'll help you loosen up your creativity muscles.

Advice From the Experts

Whether you've decided to take on the task of developing a marketing campaign yourself or you've hired an agency to do it for you, you can't begin without a strategy. A strategy, says Karen S. Kennedy, president of the Tysons Corner, Virginia, ad firm KSK Communications, Ltd., sets the foundation of everything that will follow: ads, direct mail, trade show participation, and public relations program, among others. Before developing a strategy, she says, evaluate your company's position in the marketplace in relation to your competition. Also devise a clear picture of where you want your company to go. Compare this to where you see your competitor going. A basic business plan will have most of the information you will need.

If you are working with a public relations, marketing consulting, or advertising agency, provide it with this and any additional data you have that might assist it, such as pertinent market studies, files you've kept on your competition, and records of inquiries produced by any recent promotional campaign.

If you lack experience in several areas of business, you may want to set up an advisory board. An advisory board is made up of several people who are professionals in the fields where you lack experience. They may be lawyers, accountants, public relations, marketing, or management consultants.

Nancy and Teressa Ellis, a mother-daughter team who publishes the *Washington Metropolitan Area Women's Yellow Pages*, knew they needed help promoting their publication, since neither had any marketing experience. They put together an advisory board that included the president of the American

Newswomen's Club and a magazine writer to help write press releases and get publicity. Not only did they get free advice and promotions consultation, they received a wide range of publicity—from speaking engagements to being featured in magazine articles—that they would not have gotten on their own.

Getting Started/Thinking Creatively

If hiring an agency to do the creating for you is not in your budget right now, you'll have to put your imagination to work to come up with the best way to sell your product or service. But as a small-businessperson or association marketing director with a small staff, you probably don't have time to ponder the best way to get attention for your product—or maybe you just don't know where to start.

Mark Kiefaber, program associate at the Center for Creative Leadership, Greensboro, North Carolina, shares some tips he uses in helping business leaders and managers think creatively. The first step he suggests is to define the problem and write it down. "We treat creativity as a skill that's used to solve a problem," he says. It can be anything from trying to come up with a way to attract more customers to your movie theater to how to make your furniture polish stand out on store shelves.

"It isn't always easy to know what your marketing problem is," admits Kiefaber, a former market researcher turned psychologist. It takes a lot of thinking just to define a problem, let alone solve it. Establishing the right environment to promote creative thinking helps accelerate the problem-solving process. For example, "One way to get yourself prepared to think creatively about a problem is to change the setting," he says. "Get up and take a walk, go to the park. Think about those times when you get your best ideas. If it's when you're taking a shower, then go take a shower."

Once you've defined your company's marketing challenge, the next step is what Kiefaber calls divergent thinking: "You've got to get yourself disengaged from the day-to-day hassles of what you're doing." The more you become an expert in your field, the less creative you become, he says. "You become overwhelmed by your own knowledge of solutions that won't work."

To help divert your attention from day-to-day business hassles, invite people outside your field with a fresh outlook on your marketing challenge to brainstorm with you. (See Four Rules of Brainstorming.) Talk with family, friends, groups of customers. Ask them, "What could my company do for you that would make you willing to buy our product?" "What can my professional association do to increase our visibility in the commu-

---

TIP: Four Rules of Brainstorming

The following is a brief description of group brainstorming rules taught at the Center for Creative Leadership:

1. *Suspend judgment:* "Because nutsy-boltsy people often think brainstorming is a waste of time, they want to run in and say, 'That won't work, that won't work.' If you do that, you're shooting yourself in the head. If it's not good, you can always throw it away later," says Kiefaber.
2. *Free wheel:* "Think of your head as a hamster wheel," Kiefaber suggests. Let ideas spin off in different directions even if some of the ideas seem completely irrelevant to the problem. "If you start censoring ideas, you're defeating the purpose of thinking creatively. You can always throw bad ideas out later."
3. *Cross-fertilize:* Build on each others' ideas. Allow your group's responses to swirl around in your head and then branch off on one idea.
4. *Think quantity, not quality:* "As soon as you start thinking quality, you're judging," says Kiefaber. That's breaking rule 1. The more ideas you come up with, the more likely you are to hit on a few winners.

Source: The Center for Creative Leadership, Greensboro, North Carolina

nity?" You might consider a company retreat in the country if you can persuade your top managers, marketing people, and other employees to give up a weekend. Getting away from the corporate atmosphere not only brings employees closer together socially but also stirs up a lot of creative juices. Employees who are comfortable with each other socially are also more likely to work as a team in the office.

After a brief brainstorming session—no more than ten minutes—Kiefaber's advice is to redefine the original problem: "Often you find out that the way you had it stated is not what's really going on. Very often when you start to think of the problem with other people, you start to get insight that this may not be the real problem." Once you've determined the "real" problem, brainstorm some more to come up with solutions.

Next, evaluate the solutions the group comes up with. Ask yourself: Which will reasonably work? Which are completely unrealistic? What are the advantages of this or that particular solution? What are its limitations and unique aspects? Once you've narrowed your list of solutions, ask for other opinions. Get your employees involved. Often, says Kiefaber, asking for their opinions and ideas not only improves company morale but may help you discover hidden talent in your employees as well.

The final step of the creative process is to investigate ways to implement the solution.

As you skim through this book, you will find ideas that may help you boost sales on a skinny budget. Not every idea will work for every business, but the ones we mention have been used successfully by many small and large companies. Remember, our main goal is to stimulate your creativity so you can come up with better ways to sell your product or service. Our ideas are the springboard for you to develop the marketing strategy that works best for you.

Nobody said marketing was easy. It takes time, effort, and persistence. But if you find the right strategy, your whole business—and even your life—can be transformed. Whenever you get discouraged, read the following success stories to boost your spirits. If these two successful entrepreneurs can survive and prosper, so can you.

Success Is Real

Very rarely does a new business start out as a big business. Most companies start out as half-baked ideas that are cultivated into legitimate businesses or organizations. The difference between the businesspeople who make it and those who don't is that the winners never stop believing in themselves and their product or cause, and they never allow the lack of money to be an obstacle. Above all, they never lose their persistence. Here are success stories of two women who started out with nothing and turned it into something big:

Nina Blanchard lives a pretty posh life. She has two large homes, owns a well-known talent agency under her name, and hobnobs with some of the most famous actors and models in the country. But when she started, "I didn't know the meaning of the word marketing," she says. "And I'm still not sure if I do."

After the Midas Muffler franchise that she co-owned went bankrupt, Blanchard found herself without a job, without credit, and without money. She had no business training or clerical skills. In other words, she says, "I was not equipped to do most things." But she had once run a modeling school and seemed to be good at it, so in 1961 she decided to start her own talent agency that would book models for print advertising and commercials.

An acquaintance who was representing Elizabeth Taylor and Richard Burton at the time loaned her $300 and warned, "You're not going to make it." "But I decided to go ahead anyway," Blanchard recalls. "I just took each day at a time, and I starved for a long time."

The $300 seed money went toward a $200 business license fee and a desk. That left virtually nothing for advertising. It didn't bother Blanchard that she had no ad budget, because she knew nothing about advertising anyway. "I never really had a [marketing] plan," says Blanchard. But she did know how to get attention.

After she recruited thirteen relatively unknown models to represent, Blanchard got a list of top photographers she wanted to book her models. Sending a brochure seemed the least expensive way to attract their interest. "I did the models' makeup and hair and took most of the pictures," she recalls. But she knew that just picturing her models would not incite interest. On the front of the brochure, says Blanchard, "I put something that puzzled everybody. I talked about excellence and related it to Schroeder, the Peanuts character. I thought it was terribly funny, but the photographers looked at it and said, 'What is she talking about?'" That image—however confusing—made her fledgling agency memorable.

When photographers started swamping her with calls to book her models, Blanchard realized she had made a mistake. Her untrained models were not ready for bookings; only two had ever worked professionally: "I knew I didn't dare send them out because they wouldn't know what to do. If I sent them out and they were bad, that would be the end of me. So, I told the photographers they were all booked."

Her quick thinking turned out to be a wise strategy. Word soon got around, and "I got the reputation of being the hottest agency in town," she says. (Note: Although this tactic worked for Blanchard, it is not recommended for everyone.)

Today her firm is one of the hottest agencies in town. Blanchard represents household names like Shari Belafonte-Harper, Cheryl Tiegs, Loni Anderson, Jack Scalia, Tony Franciosa, and Sharon Gless.

Looking back, Blanchard does not regret the years of struggle to build her business. "I don't know that money even helps you. If I had had $50,000 to start with, I don't think it would have made any difference, because I would have spent it in the wrong ways."

Like Nina Blanchard, Sophia Collier started a business to provide a job for herself. That job today is the American Natural Beverage Company, whose sole product, Soho Soda, grossed $20 million in revenues in 1987.

"I'm only a high school graduate with no background in the soft drink industry and nothing to qualify me for starting a company," says Collier. "But when I thought of the idea for Soho, which was on one hot August day in 1977 when I was sitting around unemployed in my living room, I knew that an alternative product that was healthful and tasted good would be quite an achievement." When she whipped up a batch of flavored soda water using natural ingredients from the grocery store, Collier knew she had a winner. But she didn't know how to start a business.

Collier took a partner, childhood companion Connie Best, who had a friend willing to donate $10,000 of IBM stock to help them start their company. They researched the industry at the library and found a bottler through the Yellow Pages. They designed their own label and sold the product out of the back of Collier's Jeep to local convenience stores. Typical of most start-up companies, "we were very poverty conscious," says Collier. "We even drove around looking for parking meters that had money in them when we delivered the product."

Finding grocery stores that would stock her product was practically impossible, says Collier. Realizing it would cost too much money to pay stocking fees (fees that manufacturers pay retailers to stock their products) to launch their product in large grocery stores—not to mention that their product was priced higher than other sodas on the shelves—Collier and Best decided to take their premium-priced soda to convenience stores, where customers are used to paying higher prices. "We literally had to build this business one bottle at a time."

Selling in this way gave Collier and Best an opportunity to learn the ins and outs of their product and business. "I recommend for anybody who's going to start a business to sell the product yourself—get to know your product, understand it. You get to hear customers' objections, and it's a way to have personal market research right from the customer," she says. "Initially we tried to get distributors and other people interested in selling our product, but because we didn't really understand it ourselves or how to sell it, we weren't able to help them or negotiate particularly favorable arrangements."

Collier, now a seasoned business executive, says money does not necessarily make a business successful: "If you don't have money, that's not an obstacle. There's always a way to do something, and money creates the ability to amplify your ideas. But the lack of money is not an absolute block."

Persistence in achieving the goal and the chutzpah to work around problems were key to Soho's success. When the company wanted to change its package design in 1982, Collier went to renowned designer Doug Johnson. But because Collier didn't have money to pay him, he politely declined to take on her project. Collier kept coming back with payment alternatives. Several visits later, when she suggested paying him on a royalty basis, Johnson agreed to design her label. (See Packaging.)

Collier is convinced that it was her tenacity that won Johnson over: "The fact that I kept coming back suggested that I would be as tenacious with other things. It gave him more faith in me."

Going back after being turned away once is a critical move for small-businesspeople. "Sometimes when you're a very small company and you get rejected by people you're trying to sell to, you might be afraid to go back," says Collier. "The idea is 'Oh, I don't want to bother them.' But the fact is that people actually admire you for your persistence, and eventually—if you're not obnoxious—you'll wear them down and they'll say, 'Okay, let's see what you have.'"

We hope that by using some of the tips mentioned in this book, you too will find that suppliers, distributors, and prospective customers will finally say, "OK. Let's see what you have."

Author's Note: Most of the people whose comments are found in this book were personally interviewed expressly for the purpose of being quoted in *The Frugal Marketer.* Additional quotes were excerpted from various business publications, as indicated in either the text or the endnotes.

Acknowledgments

Special thanks to:

- Our AMACOM editors Ron Mallis, Barbara Horowitz, and Kate Pferdner for their patience, confidence, and consideration
- From *Nation's Business* magazine, David Roe, publisher, Robert Gray, editor, and Ripley Hotch, deputy editor, for their support and encouragement
- *Nation's Business* senior editor Sharon Nelton for being an inspiring mentor and role model
- Tennessee Technology University administrators Angelo Volpe, president, and Fred E. Williams, dean of the College of Business, for creating an environment conducive to academic research for this book
- Scott Kronick for his enthusiasm for this project and for helping us get our feet in the right doors
- All those who agreed to share their business expertise with us for this book. You're an inspiration to all would-be entrepreneurs. We salute you.

Contents

PART

I

ABCs FOR SUCCESSFUL MARKETING

Marketing evokes many questions and misunderstandings. In our own work, we find that many businesspeople are unsure of what marketing really is. This self-doubt causes them to fear using sound marketing tools.

Marketing *is* a difficult concept to define or explain because it encompasses many aspects of running a business. Moreover, marketing theories are constantly changing. Marketing is, however, a necessity for building a successful business. Don't worry if you are unable to explain it fully or regurgitate the numerous terms. Many academicians who have studied marketing for years may not comprehend all of the vocabulary. There is even a book entitled *The Marketing Mystique*.[1]

In working with hundreds of small-business and association executives, we find some who can't explain basic college marketing terms. Yet they are extremely successful and creative in building their businesses. Says one association executive: "I didn't know I was following good marketing strategy until someone filled in the vocabulary and told me that I was actually doing marketing."

Don't let the semantic jungle scare you. Jay Lauer, president

1

of the Milwaukee, Wisconsin, firm of Event Coordinators, Inc., has probably summed up marketing best: "Marketing is a lot of common sense. You read the market, know what the market wants, know how to react to it, and know how to produce the sales."

A word of caution: Marketing is a complex and broad area. However, some people have a narrow image of marketing, and they don't appreciate the many available options for achieving success. Be wary of consultants who offer quick-fix solutions. They usually come at a high price—in dollars and by not solving the problem for the long run.

Marketing is more than just increasing your advertising dollars. A quick fix may be wrong or expensive or result in a lingering and deeper problem. Advertising is only one part of your marketing arsenal. The key is knowing which weapons are most appropriate for smart selling.

Pick strategies that give you the most value. To separate the wheat from the chaff, be aware of the many different ways to sell your products or services successfully. This rule could be one of your first steps for applying our shoestring tips.

Building and selling an enterprise can encompass many different avenues and sequences of events. For example, don't feel you are in error if you decide to look first at your current services or products or other marketing areas before you embark on additional promotion. Again, avoid a narrow marketing approach. This is the very first step for following our ABCs to success.

1

Auditing

Every enterprise—small business, association, or nonprofit organization—needs to know how well it is doing. We constantly use accounting and financial indicators for measuring profitability, costs, assets, liabilities, and net worth. These numbers provide a report card of performance. By totaling the "grading periods," you are given valuable financial trends, as well as strengths and weaknesses.

A periodic audit is also wise for marketing. The environment is constantly changing, so you must stay abreast to succeed. A successful marketing campaign can easily become outdated because of changes in competition, business cycles, and interest rates.

An ongoing review of your marketing efforts will formalize accountability. The self-examination should appraise your marketing goals, strengths and weaknesses, strategies, potential problems, and, most of all, *opportunities*. A marketing audit can be beneficial for businesses and associations of all sizes and success levels and for those that are either new or experienced at marketing. No business is too small to take an intermittent temperature.

Getting Started

There are no constraining rules, required forms, or certain formats. However, a wise principle is that your audit should be objective, orderly, and comprehensive.

Eschew a threatening approach with anyone within your organization. The audit is a strengthening tool, not a device for laying blame on anyone. Otherwise employees will dread—and, in worst cases, sabotage—your audit.

To help you get started, the following sections provide some brief answers to common questions on doing an audit.

Who Should Do It

If you are a one-person operation, find someone with business acumen who can still play devil's advocate—perhaps a reliable supplier, retailer, wholesaler, banker, or social friend who is well versed in marketing. An outside eye may find glitches that you've overlooked.

If you have a larger operation, try to select people in-house, or do the audit yourself to save precious marketing dollars. However, stress the need for honesty and a candid approach. Some employees may feel uncomfortable leveling with the boss, so it's important to emphasize objectivity from both sides. If you're a business owner, don't get angry with the auditor over the results. And try to select someone who is not particularly close to your product or service.

An in-house marketing audit serves as an informative and communicative experience. Certain key questions, such as who really are your best customers or most profitable products, may be addressed. Your introspection can be the beginning process for developing and implementing your road map to success. The marketing self-examination serves as a necessary diagnostic and prescriptive device for enhancing shoestring marketing techniques.

Finally, by doing the task in-house, you will often have more conviction on which techniques to emphasize or deemphasize. Time and dollars can then be properly allocated.

What to Include

Your marketplace, including the size and type of business, will determine the areas you'll want to evaluate. In basic terms, ask yourself some essential questions:

- Where have we been?
- Where are we now?
- Where do we want to go?
- How do we get there?

The audit will be especially useful in answering the last question. The self-analysis will shed light on your realistic capabilities regarding where you'd like to be in the future.

You may wonder how you can do a marketing audit if you lack marketing expertise or have limited time. There are a few books available with canned questions that guide you through a good marketing audit. Remember, it is often harder to ask the right questions than to find the right answers. Although some of the published questions may not apply to your situation, you're further ahead than if you did no audit at all.

How Often Should You Do an Audit?

At the risk of sounding glib, the stability of your business environment will dictate the frequency of doing an audit. Ideally, you should try for an audit once a year. But that could be time-consuming, costly, and take you away from the daily operations of building revenues. You may get away with an audit about every three years if you're in a stable environment. But you should still follow marketing intelligence tactics more frequently, using periodic customer surveys, and sales force feedback, or you can seek trends published by your industry's associations. These types of fact-finding activities should be ongoing, since they help you in day-to-day decisions and yearly plans.

Keep in mind that once you complete the first audit and a complementary marketing plan, future ones are much easier. We all learn from our experiences, and sometimes simply getting started is the hardest part of formalizing a marketing audit practice.

At first, a periodic audit sounds expensive and idealistic for small businesses or associations. But in the long run, it may be the most inexpensive route. You will better spot the best areas for spending your limited budget.

To get your audit going, we offer two marketing audit worksheets. Worksheet 1 identifies some general areas to analyze. It will show how to evaluate your own current marketing program and carry out a situation analysis. Worksheet 2 covers some specific questions to consider. It will enable you to expand on Worksheet 1. The two worksheets give you a sharper focus for doing an audit.

Inexpensive Sources for Doing an Audit

Although you may feel insecure about doing your own audit, there are several good, inexpensive publications and key groups to tap. The following list includes three sources that are likely to be cheapest for you.

1. *Your own internal secondary reports:* Sometimes by either modifying in-house forms or merely summarizing the data, you can uncover a wealth of marketing information for your audit. You may find that sales invoices, customer correspondence, credit applications, and warranty cards offer an abundance of customer data on who, where, when, why, and how. To follow through, you may merely have to tabulate the data from these forms. These summaries will provide tremendous background information for decision making.

2. *Outside published data:* The government and trade associations offer good, inexpensive market data, as well as trends for particular industries. Three good sources are *The Encyclopedia of Associations*, the *National Trade and Professional Associations of the United States* directory, and the federal government index, *The Monthly Catalog of U.S. Government Publications* (available from

WORKSHEET 1

Rate the Effectiveness of Your Marketing Program

Marketing Areas	Current Strength			
	Excellent	Average	Weak	Not Sure
Customer base	____	____	____	____
Share of served market	____	____	____	____
Product quality	____	____	____	____
Service effectiveness	____	____	____	____
Breadth of product line	____	____	____	____
Depth of product line	____	____	____	____
Business image	____	____	____	____
Customer satisfaction	____	____	____	____
Distribution	____	____	____	____
Middlemen support	____	____	____	____
Future sales growth	____	____	____	____
Development of new offerings	____	____	____	____
Sales force	____	____	____	____
Competitive strength	____	____	____	____
Advertising program	____	____	____	____
Publicity	____	____	____	____
Perceived as having fair prices	____	____	____	____

the Superintendent of Documents, U.S. Government Printing Office, Washington, D.C. 20402). This catalog provides a bibliography of publications issued by all branches of the government.

Marketing information from computerized data base services is also readily available. For less than $100, you could find important answers to your audit. The American Marketing Association (AMA), for instance, provides an on-line computerized data base search. The minimum cost is $25—roughly $1 for each

(*Text continues on page 12.*)

WORKSHEET 2

Checklist for a Marketing Audit

Last Year's Performance

- What were last year's marketing objectives? How well did we achieve them?
- What parts of our marketing program were successful? Which parts did not work? Why?
- What can be done to improve our last year's results?
- How do sales/profits break down within product/service markets, region, and the like?

Markets

- Who are our current customers?
- How can we segment our customers?
- What is our market share? Potential? What trends are developing in our market segments?
- What, when, how, and why do our customers buy from us?
- How would we segment the potential markets? Do we have the capabilities to reach these segments?
- Which market segments seem to be the most profitable? The most loyal?
- How do our current customers rate us in terms of service, quality, image, prices, distribution, and promotion? What is our image to potential customers?
- Can we break down different market segments by sales, profits, costs, regions, product/services, and preferences?
- How are we perceived by our market segments? Do their perceptions match our own?
- What are the attitudes of the many publics of our agency?
- To what market segments/publics do we wish to market?
- Who makes the buying decision?

Product/Service

- Which products or services are the most successful? Unsuccessful?

- Do our products and services meet our shop's objectives?
- Should our offerings be expanded? Deleted?
- How successful have we been in introducing new products or services? What can be done to be more successful?
- What areas need improvement?
- Do the products and services meet our desired image?
- How profitable are our individual products or services? What is our future profits potential?
- Do we package or brand our products acceptably?
- Are there any modifications we can make to better serve our markets?
- Do we have product "dogs" that should be eliminated?
- Is the level of customer service good?
- What makes our products or services different or unique? Do we have strong, competitive advantages with our products or services?
- What are some product and service trends?
- Can we reposition any of the products or services? Can we find new applications or markets? Can we increase frequency of their use?
- What should be the breadth and depth of our product or service mix?

Pricing

- How do our prices compare with those of the competition?
- Is the price list current and justifiable?
- How do we set prices?
- Do we consider costs, competition, and consumer preferences when we set prices?
- Have we matched cost data with individual products and services?
- What impact have price changes had on our various market segments?
- What was the organization's strategy? What should it be in the future?
- What impact do credit, rebates, discounts, and transportation changes have on our sales?
- How can we improve our strategy for pricing? Have we tried different prices for different markets?
- How sensitive are our markets to prices?
- Do customers think our prices are fair and realistic?

(Continued)

WORKSHEET 2 (*continued*)

Distribution and Channel Management

- What are the buying habits and preferences of different middle-men suppliers?
- Who are our most successful and helpful middlemen? Why? Most unsuccessful? Why?
- Do we provide adequate market coverage and service?
- How should we choose our middlemen? What are the most important factors?
- Should we make any distribution/channel changes? improvements?
- Do we deliver the goods and services in a reasonable amount of time according to our market segments?
- How should we transport the goods or services?
- What can be done to keep costs down and at the same time give good service in distribution?
- How are we perceived by our middlemen suppliers?

Promotion

- Do we carefully integrate the different types of promotion so that they are supportive of each other?
- What are our objectives in promoting products or services?
- How well are we doing with our advertising? How much should we spend? What is the best media mix (e.g., newspaper, radio, etc.)? Ad themes and copy?
- Do we have ongoing and effective promotion (samples, coupons, displays, contests, premiums, etc.)? What can we do to make sales promotion better?
- Are we doing enough in the area of public relations/publicity?
- Do we have an adequate sales organization?

Competition

- Who are our major competitors?
- What are their strengths and weaknesses?
- How successful is the competition?

- Are there any new competitors out there?
- What trends will affect future competition?
- Are there any substitutes for their products? Our products?
- How do our market segments perceive the competition as compared with how they perceive us?

Management's Attitude Toward Planning

- Do we have backing for the marketing program by the managers? Top manager? Board members?
- Does the marketing manager have adequate authority and responsibility?
- Is there a good working relationship between the marketing manager and the other managers?
- Do we set marketing plans and controls?
- Do we analyze marketing costs as related to sales revenue? Do we measure efficiency by the marketing units (e.g., personnel, product lines, regions, etc.)?
- Are all marketing functions under the umbrella of one manager? Does the marketing manager report to top management?
- How can we develop managers to be better marketers?
- Do we talk and think marketing?
- How do we measure and reward good marketing people?
- What can be done to make marketing management better and to develop marketing muscle?

bibliographic citation and abstract retrieved. Some questions the AMA data base can answer are: How are commodities marketed and promoted? What is the demand for health care services? The AMA's information center in Chicago can provide you with more details. (See Further Resources in the back of this book.)

3. *Helpful groups:* Accountants, advertising people, consultants, and other professionals can be quite helpful. But be careful: some professionals can be expensive. Some are more reasonable when they are beginning their practices, often working on a percentage of the revenue produced or the costs saved from their advice. This will keep your fixed costs down while only incurring out-of-pocket expenses if they produce results. There are other useful people who can help for little or no cost. Volunteers, retailers, wholesalers, manufacturers' reps, chambers of commerce, government officials, the state offices of the Small Business Administration (usually located in state capitals), and university business classes could be of service (see Universities).

How to Follow Through on the Audit

Your marketing audit can be quite expensive and a useless exercise if there is no follow-through. This is true even if your self-examination was brief and informal. Shoestring marketers cannot afford the luxury of not following up.

In looking at your marketing program, you may see a number of problems and opportunities. Some of them could require quick action. Since this is a normal outcome, don't despair. You are already reaping the benefits. You have now spotted some areas that need your attention before it's too late.

The following steps are useful in dealing with problem-solving opportunities and starting a course of action:

1. Call a meeting to deal only with the issues in question.
2. Carefully structure the agenda for clear focus. Avoid extemporaneous discussion.

3. Place priorities on which marketing problems or opportunities are to be covered first.
4. Welcome brainstorming ideas on how to translate solutions into opportunities (see Preface, "Four Rules of Brainstorming").
5. Evaluate the pros and cons of each brainstorming idea.
6. Obtain some commitments from everyone.
7. Assign someone a specific time deadline for completing the marketing task.
8. Follow through to see if tasks are completed and successful. Keep a goal schedule and check up on it periodically.

Although these steps may appear to be too theoretical, they are a good way to close your marketing audit. Some businesses get bogged down with step 2. Avoid the common error of calling a number of time-consuming meetings with little execution. Quick action to pressing problems—identified from the marketing audit—will build confidence, especially with those new to marketing.

One more benefit of a marketing audit should be noted: It will help you decide which shoestring tips in Part II have been or could be the most productive. Without any type of follow-through, how can you know if one idea actually worked?

2

Budgeting

You should have a marketing budget—even if your financial resources are limited. Otherwise you could spend funds on nonnecessities while bypassing attractive ways to sell your organization. You might overspend and not be able to take advantage of unexpected opportunities. Suppliers, for example, may suddenly offer you some extra matching advertising dollars to move some slow-moving merchandise. This supplier incentive could stretch available advertising dollars more than 100 percent.

A good marketing budget allows for better planning and timing of expenditures. It forces you to think about the amount of money you need and when you should spend it. Some businesses run out of money before they do any marketing. Because they lack a planned budget, they overspend in such areas as staffing, production, operations, inventory, rent, and capital improvements. Little money is left to promote the business that brings in the much-needed revenues.

A sound budget can:

1. Keep track of your costs and revenues
2. Evaluate where you are getting the best mileage from different marketing efforts

3. Help implement your marketing plan by itemizing and prioritizing the things you want done

The marketing items to include in your budget will depend on your own situation. Such general line items might include advertising, personal selling, trade shows, direct mail, public relations, and telemarketing. Some of the tips in this book might even be budgeted line items. As you formalize the budgeting process, you will learn which marketing efforts need budgeted amounts.

In deciding where and by how much to commit your valuable marketing dollars, think about these essential dos and don'ts:

Do	*Don't*
Allow enough money and time to complete the task	Hide your budget from employees
Get a feel for the costs and benefits of each task	Allow automatic yearly expenditures ("sacred cows") without asking if benefits really occur
Try to match marketing goals to budgeted line items	
Start comparing last year's budgeted amounts and actual expenditures	Be biased or overkill with one marketing idea
Encourage employees and board members (if applicable) to offer some suggestions	Follow the crowd and try to match the competition (especially large businesses)
Analyze your budget and cost trends over a period of time Set aside a certain amount of contingency money (10–15 percent) in case of modifications, emergencies, or unexpected opportunities	Be afraid to be different and creative with a marketing idea; creativity and successful low-cost strategies go hand in hand

In a nutshell, we are trying to save you money by offering low-cost marketing tips. But you still need a budget to get the full value of the spendable marketing dollars.

Budgeting also helps you in planning. It defines what you want and expect from your marketing efforts. When you combine budgeting, objectives, strategies, and time deadlines, you develop a powerful blueprint for knowing what must be done to build your business.

3

Controls:
Cash Flow and Costs

Cash Flow

Smart managers initiate some controls on their marketing programs. If you don't have checks and balances, you'll be experiencing nagging self-doubt as you spend money: Am I getting my money's worth? you'll wonder.

As you well know, there are countless cash demands on your business. Growing businesses—especially small businesses, associations, and nonprofit organizations—frequently experience cash crises. No matter how much you may plan, it's tough to predict downturns or needed modifications. Unfortunately uncertainties are even more pronounced in the marketing area.

Your ABCs of shoestring marketing moxie should therefore encompass progress reports, checklists, and control forms. You should also be sensitive to those marketing areas that can rob you of much-needed cash or bottom line results.

A joint study by three universities concluded that cash management is frequently cited (61 percent of the time) as the chief problem by owners of private enterprises. This concern surpassed pricing (53 percent) and cost reduction (47 percent) problems.[1]

You must spend your precious marketing dollars cautiously. To achieve greater efficiency, carefully monitor these ever-present five common cash robbers:

1. *Inventories:* Some small businesses (e.g., retailers) may have 70 percent of their assets in their stock. Watch your inventory turnover by comparing it to your own industry standards.
2. *Accounts payable:* Whenever possible, take advantage of your discounts for early payment.
3. *Accounts receivable:* Gauge your accounts to watch deadbeats. Also, set up a billing system that immediately bills customers after a credit sale. Don't make the common error of waiting until the end of the month or billing cycle.
4. *Noninterest-bearing accounts:* For your idle cash reserve, be sure to have good but safe and liquid interest-bearing accounts, such as an insured money market account.
5. *Overhead and fixed assets tied to a volatile prime lending rate:* A highly leveraged firm (one that borrows long-term debt on a variable interest rate) is at the mercy of uncontrollable fluctuating interest rates.

Beware of these five cash robbers. Because at times you will need some unexpected cash to capitalize on different marketing ventures, you must watch your revenues versus disbursements. A cash-poor situation spawns a Catch-22 situation. Inadequate cash could prevent investment in marketing, which results in low future cash revenues and thus increases the cash-poor dilemma.

Take the self-test, Worksheet 3, on cash management. It may help you spot a red herring that needs closer attention.

Cost

According to Ted Frost, president of the accounting firm Frost & Tallman, Inc., cost accounting among small businesses is often

WORKSHEET 3

Self-Test Worksheet: Cash Management

Read the following statements and answer a "yes" or "no." See how many of them you can answer with a "yes" for your business. Skip the ones that may not apply to your situation. If you are unable to answer some, you may need to consult an accountant.

Our stock turnover is comparable to firms of our size within our industry. _____

We age our accounts receivable monthly. _____

Credit customers are billed right after the sale instead of waiting for monthly billings. _____

We follow aggressive collection practices for very late accounts. _____

Cash flow analysis is done on a monthly basis (use SBA Form 1100 if guideline is needed). _____

We time our purchases for when cash flow is the strongest. _____

We try to forecast monthly cash needs. _____

We make comparisons between cash holdings for different periods. _____

We've used discounts to encourage prompt customer payment. _____

Our inventory system keeps track of receipt dates and the shelf-life of our stock. _____

We use cash discounts by paying early [assuming it's of benefit compared to using the cash for other matters, e.g., interest on savings]. _____

(Continued)

WORKSHEET 3 (*continued*)

We get a good interest rate on our cash reserves without forgoing safety or liquidity. ___

Some of our long-term debt is based on low interest rates. ___

We're able to get our fair share of extended credit terms from vendors and suppliers. ___

Without hurting the revenue side, before spending money we systematically see if there is a marketing alternative that is cheaper or free. ___

We invest excess cash. ___

We avoid owning equipment or other high-capital items if it's wiser to lease. ___

We carefully explore the merits of bartering our services and inventories. ___

Whenever desirable, we reduce our cash needs by deferring employee compensation through offering bonuses and other forms of equity. ___

We avoid paying excessive transportation charges for goods, caused by lack of distribution planning. ___

We have ample controls to make sure that our purchased materials arrive on time. ___

[If applicable] We use "just-in-time" inventory management techniques to minimize our cash requirements for materials, equipment, personnel, and materials handling. ___

We plan and control our cash requirements in a professional manner. ___

the most ignored aspect of an already neglected area known as general accounting. Yet cost controls are as necessary as a compass on a stormy sea.[2]

James Howard, a small-business consultant and chairman of Symbax Group Ltd., stresses even further the need for cost management. He notes that most entrepreneurs worry about sales, but if sales are the sine qua non of a firm, cost controls are the key to survival. He believes most business deaths result from excessive costs and inadequate capital, not lack of sales.[3]

Since the role of sales to any organization is significant, you may not agree with Howard's last point. But keep in mind that if you carefully watch your costs, you'll be able to give more money to increasing your revenues. Efficient cost management is the other part of the equation for stretching your marketing dollars.

Sound cost control is a culture that can be learned in small businesses or associations. The budget and control process will help you to spot vital signs on where costs might be reduced.

Arnold Goldstein, a successful entrepreneur and author of *Starting on a Shoestring,* believes that small-business owners may often accurately predict product demand but overlook the capital needed to push the products. He advises drawing up a detailed list of what you *think* you need and then reduce it to what you *actually* need, with an emphasis on inventory and working capital. Heavy fixed asset expenditures (such as equipment and building) drain a company. Current assets create the lifeblood of any shoestring operation: sales and cash flow.[4] Goldstein's comments dramatize one of the major reasons that small businesses fail: too much money tied up in fixed assets. This is why we include sections on auditing, budgeting, cash flow, and controls in this book. These activities will go a long way in controlling your costs.

Remember that the cost of marketing expenditures has risen faster than the inflation rate. They must therefore be closely watched. Read the dos and don'ts that follow to see if you can better control your own marketing costs.

Do	*Don't*
Try to see how a specific marketing expenditure makes some contribution to getting *more* sales	Become locked in to automatic yearly increases for certain expense accounts
Research all major cost areas and compare them to industry norms	Cut costs indiscriminately and hurt product quality
Prioritize cost areas with emphasis on better servicing customers and being competitive	Ignore efficient opportunities for subcontracting certain marketing projects
Analyze revenue and cost trends over various periods of time	Forget to analyze your competitors' costs
Explore ways to transform fixed to variable costs	Be afraid of acquiring a penny-pinching image with areas that have fat or waste; you'll be respected in the long run
Study various methods—such as bartering, outsourcing, and cost sharing—for decreasing your costs	Allow uncontrollable growth, which results in greater costs increases than revenue growth; eventually bankruptcy could occur if this persists
Attempt to track marketing expenditures and their impact on your corresponding revenues	
Explore the engineering approach. Study cost components of marketing efforts in more detail. A flabby marketing expenditure should not be hidden.	

PART

II

TIPS FROM A TO Z

$

Advertising: Budget Stretching

"When I write an advertisement, I don't want you to tell me that you find it creative. I want you to find it so interesting that you buy the product," says David Oglivy.[1] Cute or wasted advertising is catastrophic for financially strapped marketers. Shoestring marketers don't have the luxury of creating advertisements for art's sake or merely advertising because it's a popular communication medium.

Clearly define the purpose of your advertising. Then carefully watch to see if your dollars are being well spent. In planning and stretching your advertising budget, you should consider the following questions:

- Who should see or hear your advertising?
- What is your competition doing with its advertising?
- How much should you spend? Is there any way to save dollars and yet have a powerful advertising program?
- Where and when should you place your advertising?
- What do you want to emphasize in relation to consumer preferences?
- How effective is your advertising? Is it getting the job done?

An earnest attempt to answer these questions will greatly improve your odds for stretching your smaller budget. For example, if you don't analyze your market targets and set advertising strategies haphazardly, your limited budget will be misdirected.

Your advertising dollars should be considered an investment, not an expense. In other words, avoid using "whatever is left over" for advertising. Without enough money earmarked for advertising, your sales can snowball downward, and you can "afford" less and less for promotion.

There's no magic answer to how much you should spend on advertising. As a start, search your trade industry data or popular financial guidebooks (e.g., Dun & Bradstreet or Robert Morris Associates annual industry financial statement studies), which give ballpark figures on comparable businesses' expenditures.

The overall yardstick for advertising is usually from 1 to 5 percent of gross sales, but this amount varies because of so many circumstances. It's best to study your own industry and individual situation.

TIP: Four Basic Ingredients for a Successful Advertising Strategy

1. Your advertising must offer a consumer benefit or solve a consumer problem.
2. Your benefit or the solution promised must be wanted by the consumer.
3. Your product offerings should be tied directly to the promised benefit or solution.
4. Your benefit or problem solution must be distinctly communicated through media advertising.

If you constantly keep these four simple guidelines in mind, you'll get good mileage from your limited advertising dollars.

Source: Don S. Schultz, *Essentials of Advertising Strategy* (Chicago: Crain Books, 1981), pp. 33–34.

Tom McElligott, creative director for Scali, McCabe & Sloves and a renowned advertising critic, says that between 95 and 98 percent of advertising doesn't work or surface above all the other advertising clutter. "Either the ads are strategically stupid, or they are executed stupidly, or both," he says. A small-budget advertiser doesn't have the deep pockets to develop big programs in all aspects of marketing. "And so he can't afford to do a derivative, me-too advertising campaign," says McElligott. "If you break the rules, you're going to stand a better chance of breaking through the clutter than if you don't."[2]

The moral: Sometimes you can effectively break the "rules" to stretch your budget. Look at the earliest campaigns of Federal Express when it was a small, struggling firm. Nearly everyone still remembers its rapid-fire, motormouth spokesman.

Frugal marketers must achieve top results for their restricted dollars. Advertising is a necessary investment, but you must squeeze every penny. You cannot afford the classic comment by John Wanamaker, founder of his own major retail department store chain: "I know that half of my advertising is wasted but I don't know which half. I spent $2 million for advertising, and I don't know if that is half enough or twice too much."

Expand your advertising dollars by adopting some creative techniques. Here are twenty-five brainstorming low-cost ideas. Many of them are taken from *The Marketing Problem Solver:*[3]

1. Radio stations, newspapers, magazines, and other media specialists will frequently give free, valuable help on advertising strategy, especially for small or nonprofit businesses. Sometimes to sell their own medium, the staffs will help you create dynamic ads. Don't be shy about picking their brains about advertising strategy.
2. Ads placed during off-hours or in unusual print locations are charged cheaper rates. Sometimes you can still reach your market targets in these inexpensive unorthodox media slots.
3. Avoid a one-time, expensive splash that rapidly depletes your limited funds. Most of the time your audience needs more than one exposure to remember your business. Repeat and repeat the same successful ads. You'll also save

on production costs instead of having to reinvent the wheel.

4. See if media sellers will give last-minute discounts for unused time or space. Late fill-ins could result in discounts of up to 60 percent!

5. If appropriate, consider providing a convenient toll-free number in your ads to get immediate responses and feedback.

6. Try cheaper classified advertisements to see if their drawing power is comparable to more expensive display ads.

7. Consider bartering your products or services in exchange for the production of ads (e.g., artwork and printing) or for media time or space.

8. Use piggyback advertising material in other mailings, such as in invoices or special announcements, to save postage and other related costs.

9. Try cooperative advertising with the businesses you deal with, such as retailers, wholesalers, or manufacturers. Many vendors or manufacturers, for example, are receptive to sharing advertising costs with smaller businesses.

10. Take advantage of any media discounts you're offered by paying cash in advance.

11. Consider advertising in regional geographic editions of national publications. The costs are lower, and your core market might be in a certain region anyway.

12. Share your ad costs with neighboring, noncompeting firms that have common interests, such as retailers in a mall or shopping strip who are promoting a sidewalk sale. (Make sure your partners have a solid reputation.)

13. Try reducing the physical size of the print ad or the time of a broadcasting spot. A full page ad or sixty-second commercial, for example, is not twice as effective as a half-page or thirty-second ad. Sometimes frequency (number of times an ad appears) is more essential than the size or time of an ad.

14. Develop tight production controls to minimize the need to reject finished ads. Don't get carried away with the artistic endeavors in which production concerns outweigh your original advertising objectives.

15. Carefully aim your ads at the prospects or consumers who give the greatest returns.
16. See if your suppliers offer free point-of-purchase promotional material. Some will give away excellent promotional in-store display racks.
17. A few national firms provide stores with big outdoor signs to help promote both businesses. For example, Coca-Cola and Pepsi give signs to health clubs that allow small-business owners periodically to put letters or words on the stationary signs for special announcements. (The soft drink manufacturer retains a small permanent space to advertise its beverage.)
18. See if you can sponsor a community or civic event. Sometimes the sponsor is mentioned somewhere in the community ad. Although your business name is not prominently mentioned, the ad is repeated often, which gives favorable and frequent recognition.
19. You can't afford saturation advertising. Instead, work on carefully matching the particular medium—radio, newspaper, or whatever—with the market targets you want to go after. Poor target marketing causes advertising dollars to be wasted. Challenge the media reps to identify clearly their viewers, listeners, or readers.
20. Fully exploit the advantages of the various types of media; otherwise, you're needlessly paying for the higher costs or rates of certain media. Television ads, for example, give you the opportunity to demonstrate your offerings and allow visual impact. If your ads merely "talk" through the time slot, you might as well opt for the cheaper time slots of radio, billboard, or some other alternative.
21. Saturation and blitz advertising is very costly; therefore, carefully coordinate all forms of communication to develop a consistent, systematic, and effective image. With judicious integration of public relations, personal selling, telemarketing, and advertising, you'll develop a total, powerful synergistic impact on the marketplace—and you will better maximize your precious ad dollars. For instance, an IBM study concluded that selling time can be reduced from 9.3 to 1.3 hours with direct mail advertising

support. And a Sales & Marketing Executives International study showed that salespeople went from eight orders per 100 cold calls to thirty-eight orders per 100 cold calls when direct mail backing was used.

22. Experiment with an editorial-style format, especially in business-to-business markets. "There is no need for advertisements to look like advertisements," says David Oglivy. "If you make them look like editorial pages, you will attract 50 percent more readers."[4] You could provide informative suggestions, written in editorial style, which positions you as an expert in the reader's mind. This strategy could overcome advertising clutter and give better readership for your small budget.

23. Develop copy that appeals to your market while still being different from the big-budget marketers. You can't match them dollar for dollar. Experiment with unusual approaches, such as color, music, slogans, humor, or in media selection to attract the viewers' attention and interest.

24. Because the cost of traditional media (such as radio, newspapers, magazines, and television) is escalating, many low-cost marketers must explore new ways to advertise their goods. Many innovative marketers are finding great success by advertising on parking meters, taxi electronic billboards, balloons, blimps, and grocery shopping carts. They're also using aerial skywriter ads, trolley or other mass transit advertising, video billboards, grocery shelf talk displays, community bulletin boards, cinema advertising, in-flight advertising, and weekly newspaper shoppers. Alternative advertising may give you maximum value for your shoestring budget.

25. Keep close tabs on how well certain ads and different types of media are doing. You cannot afford to spend hard-earned dollars on advertising that is not getting the job done.

These twenty-five suggestions should give you some practical and economical ideas for advertising. Although all may not be relevant to your situation, they illustrate the importance of planning and controlling your advertising budget.

When working up your ad budget, set a few dollars aside for a rainy day. You can never accurately forecast your competition, economic downturns, or business opportunities that may suddenly surface. Smart shoestring marketers plan some contingency dollars for advertising.

You cannot afford the luxury of wasting your limited ad budget and must learn to get maximum mileage out of your ad dollars. Consider the warning of Leo Walsi, founder of a sound stereo equipment store in Fall River, Massachusetts: "When small ventures advertise, it's haphazard, with neither enough attention to expenditure, message, or media. A consistent and sound commitment to advertising is required."[5]

$

Advertising:
Co-op Advertising

If the high cost of producing and placing an ad is enough to make your hair stand on end, don't let that stop you from advertising. Ask another company to share the costs with you.

The concept is called cooperative (or co-op) advertising, and it is a combined promotional effort, usually by a retailer and a supplier or occasionally two retailers. Both parties are identified in the ads and mutually share the advertising costs. Co-op advertising is one vital option to leverage and stretch your ad budget. If carefully managed, this arrangement can develop into a positive partnership.

For small advertisers, co-op promotion builds buyer interest and traffic. Moreover, the larger advertiser frequently aids with the production costs of items such as artwork, setup, and typesetting. This assistance lowers your production costs without sacrificing quality. Most important, co-op advertising may give you more advertising frequency, larger ads, or some exposure in expensive types of media.

According to Professor Stephen Greyser of Harvard University and Professor Robert Young of Northeastern University, co-op advertising becomes much more important when (1) consumers perceive a purchase risk, such as with high-ticket items, (2) there's a strong consumer need for reassurance about a product or service, and (3) there's a substantial amount of economic interdependence between manufacturer and middlemen, especially when the middleman is given an exclusive territorial right to sell products.[1]

At some point, for instance, you may need extra promotional dollars to give consumers more information about your product to reassure them about its quality. Co-op dollars may give you that extra frequency rate while creating more consumer credibility, depending on whom you're sharing ad dollars with. One way to increase faith in your business is to produce advertising that is associated with a well-known, national corporate organization.

Despite the advantages of cooperative advertising, some disagreements may surface in a co-op ad partnership. To avoid disappointments, ask yourself the following questions to help you recognize some common areas of conflict:

- Do the advertisers have different advertising objectives? Retailers, for example, may want to build store traffic and sell as many different items as possible. Manufacturers, on the other hand, may want one or two brands pushed. This conflict could affect your specific advertising strategies, such as message, layout, and media selection.
- Where should the brand names and business names appear? Who should get top billing? How often should names be mentioned?
- Who specifically decides on media selection, message, layout, amount and type of body copy, and the merchandise display?
- What impact does the co-op advertising have on your regular ads? Are they consistent with your overall expectations and desired business image?
- How and when will the money be given for carrying out the co-op program? Will there be endless haggling and negotiating with the implementation stage and with payment procedures? (Most national companies avoid legal enforcement and are quite good about reimbursing small businesses.)[2]

See if any of your vendors, suppliers, or distributors offer co-op dollars. With a good partner, you can combine the resources of both organizations.

If you're hesitant, seek references from potential co-op ad partners. When making your decision, ask questions about the five areas of conflict. Evaluate their answers and prior experiences for minimizing disputes. Talk with other shoestring marketers who are participating in co-op programs about their experiences.

Remember, like anything else, a few campaigns are sometimes needed before positive results occur. Cooperative advertising has proved very effective in many cases. Be sure to give it a fair chance.

Further Resources

Standard Rate and Data Service—Co-op Source Directory
Standard Rate and Data Service, Inc.
Macmillan
3004 Glenview Road
Wilmette, Illinois 60091

Lists more than 3,700 manufacturers that offer cooperative advertising programs. Biannual, $124 for one issue or $149.40 for both.

$

Advertising: Media and Message

Where and how often to advertise is a difficult decision. You don't want your limited dollars scattered among too many types of media. Part of your success therefore depends on where you successfully spend your hard-earned dollars—otherwise known as *media selection.*

One rough guide is that you'll spend 80 percent of your advertising budget for the media cost and 20 percent for producing the ad. (These percentages will vary in different circumstances, including which types of media are selected.) Because shoestring advertisers cannot afford exotic production frills, the media costs are typically higher than the 80 percent.

In both media (e.g., radio versus newspaper) and medium selection decisions (e.g., between two radio stations), you should ask yourself some important questions:

- To whom do I want to advertise?
- Where are these people?
- Which type of media are they most likely to respond to?
- How can I economically reach them?

- When is the best time to appeal to them?
- What kind of message do I want to deliver?

You must also develop certain criteria for choosing, for example:

- Total cost of placing one ad
- Cost per contact of the medium's audience members, often stated as costs per 1,000 viewers or readers (CPM)
- Market and geographic exposure of medium
- Visual and/or sound quality of medium
- Lead time (from placing the ad to seeing or hearing it)
- Amount of assistance given by medium
- Life span of the ad (e.g., a thirty-second radio spot versus a six-month run in a magazine)
- Amount of advertising clutter within a medium
- Previous performance of a medium in reaching your goals

Each type of medium has strengths and weaknesses. To illustrate, when you desire speedy action, you'll look to radio or newspapers, where turn-around time may be only twenty-four hours; magazines may take months before an ad is actually printed. Consequently, newspapers and radio are popular with small companies in household markets. On the other hand, magazines and trade journals have good credibility, visual quality, and are ideal for business-to-business markets.

Consider lesser-known types of media. Many shoestring advertisers have good luck with grocery shopping carts, balloons, transit shelters, skywriting, cinema advertising, and the like. Dollar for dollar, these types of media are becoming more useful and valuable.

After making your media decisions, you must develop your copy (message). A small budget requires a strong message clearly communicated to the targeted audience. "A common mistake that small companies make is that they don't target their consumer as precisely as they should," says Edward Vick, president of Ammirati & Puris, a mid-sized advertising agency in New York.

TIP: Using Classified Advertising

Classified advertising in newspapers, magazines, or weekly shoppers appears in special columns on pages (usually in the back of the publication) where the ads are arranged by product or service. Typeface, layout freedom, and size are usually limited.

Because of the low cost that's involved, it's a popular selection in print medium among small advertisers. You can concentrate on selling while the medium does the work. It's an inexpensive and effective way to start a modest advertising campaign. Some retailers may even get 10 to 30 percent of their sales from classified ads.

Bernard Lyons of Goreville, Illinois, editor of *Key Newsletter* for the direct marketing and mail order trade, offers some good tips on classified advertising:

- To increase response, use your name or the company name instead of a post office box.
- Use words or phrases that are "power-packed," such as *free, new, amazing, how-to, easy,* and *now.*
- When requesting money, offer money-back guarantees.
- Advertise consistently since many people respond only after seeing the ad repeatedly and becoming familiar with your name.
- Avoid charging for your sales literature.
- State the offer in twenty-five words or less. The average classified ad is twenty to twenty-five words.
- Code ads to see which ones are getting the best response rates.
- If you have a lengthy message, leave it for display ads or direct mail.

Source: Sales & Marketing Digest (November 1987 and December 1987), pp. 11 and 6R, respectively.

They try to be too many things to too many people, and they don't have the resources to do that. Even a company like BMW with gigantic revenues precisely targets its customers. And even if you have a mass appeal product, you have to somehow target it because you can't be everywhere geographically, and you can't be all things to all people. You have to concentrate your resources so you can make some kind of a dent in the consciousness of at least one small group.

Vick tells clients who have less than $5 million to spend that they should not try to tackle a national ad campaign. "Five million dollars just doesn't cover the whole country. You might as well save it and give it to your sales force." First, he says, decide precisely how to position your product or your service. "People are bombarded with so many messages, and you can't spend a very little amount of money and tell people here are eight reasons why this is a good product. You have to give them one thing to remember." To make the most of an ad message, Vick suggests using it consistently not only in advertising but on stationery, matchbook covers—anything that the public will see—to build name recognition. "It's critical to a small company," he says. "You have to use every single resource to position this product or service you're trying to sell. You can't afford to waste anything, and everything has to very clearly and consistently say the same thing about your product."

The message doesn't necessarily have to be flamboyant or even entertaining. It just has to be memorable in some way. With so few dollars to spend, a steady, appealing, and motivating message is mandatory. Admittedly, however, this is easier said than done.

Copywriting is probably more of an art than a science. Nevertheless, as a frugal marketer, you should consider some basic guidelines. Headlines are a good starting point for study, since an audience often pays more attention to headlines than to the ad's text. Among the gurus of copywriting, there's some consensus on how to write effective headlines:

1. Appeal to the audience's self-interest by promising a benefit.

2. Avoid tricky, confusing headlines. People move too fast to worry about what you're trying to say.
3. If feasible, name your target audience in the headlines.
4. Give one major idea of the goods advertised. Don't clutter the headlines with many confusing concepts.
5. Reduce prospects' potential anxieties.
6. Display your headlines prominently.

You should also keep some essential principles in mind when writing ad copy. Write the ad from the customer's point of view (called the you approach). It's critical to spell out specific facts about how your merchandise can meet the consumers' needs or solve their problems. For example, "You can cut heating costs by 50 percent," offers a specific reward for the audience.

The ad should clearly explain why your goods are better than those of the competition. Identify your competitive niche and unique selling proposition, and state them in your advertising.

If possible, make the ads believable by using testimonials, warranties, endorsements, satisfaction guarantees, business awards, or favorable publicity. Low-cost marketers must attack some consumer doubt and business credibility. Ask yourself:

- Does the business have the resources to support the post-sale services?
- Will the business still be around long after the product has been consumed? Mention your features such as warranties or customer endorsements.

Your message should spur the audience to action. Encourage purchases with such tactics as these:

- Money-back guarantees
- Coupons (*The Levinson Letter* advises placing coupons in the lower-right corner of a right-page ad. Be sure the coupon looks like a coupon to avoid confusion.)[1]
- Statement of limited quantities
- Limited time offers
- One-time-only offers
- Free estimates

- Free demonstrations
- "Bill me later" statements
- Early-bird discounts
- Discounts for the first 100 customers
- Special prices with cutoff dates
- Free trial periods
- Charter memberships

A shoestring marketer's cash flow is sometimes a problem. Therefore, consumer action messages are vital objectives. Don't be apprehensive about asking for an order.

Besides taking the you approach and matching offerings with consumer needs, remember to identify your business. Are your products and your business name noticeable at a glance? Do your

---

TIP: Top Ten Words for Compelling Advertising

The Yale University Psychology Department has developed a list of the ten most personal and persuasive words:

1. *New*—People like novelty.
2. *Save*—Everyone wants to save time, money, or energy.
3. *Safety*—This shows long-lasting quality.
4. *Proved*—People like documentation.
5. *Love*—It gives inner satisfaction.
6. *Discover*—People like excitement.
7. *Guarantee*—Consumers want some assurances.
8. *Health*—The health consciousness of the 1980s is applicable to many products.
9. *Results*—Every consumer wants some reward for the purchase.
10. *You*—This could be the most persuasive copy word of all.

Source: "The Top Ten Words," *Sales & Marketing Digest* (April 1987): 3.

ads contain information on where (phone numbers and location), when (store hours), and how (cash versus credit) consumers can buy from you?

Copy also includes such elements as photos, layout, illustrations, artwork, color, typesetting, printing, music, and visual props. These specific items will depend on the medium used, market targets, and budget. If properly done, they can make a message come alive, gain attention, and create excitement. Often your audience remembers the visual and/or sound elements more than the words themselves.

When creating and evaluating your own visual and sound elements, many advertising experts suggest keeping these important points in mind:

- Photos are remembered more than illustrations.
- Rectangular photographs are usually more effective than irregular shapes.
- Visuals and/or sound should highlight key selling points.
- One dominant picture or illustration is more effective than many pictures/illustrations in an ad.

These suggestions are illustrative points and not absolute rules. Develop the visual/sound in the same way you would the copy, such as identifying benefits, using a you approach, making it believable, and offering a reward for patronizing your business.

As you can see, it's hard to present specific advice on the exact statements or pitches to include in your own ads. However, some basic, but important, suggestions have been given for writing your advertising message. Our major point: You need not spend thousands of dollars for good copywriting services.

Many of our recommendations are just plain common sense. An awareness of them is an excellent start for low-cost marketers who are inexperienced copywriters. Interestingly, even some big-buck marketers forget some of these tips. So don't despair and feel you're unable to write good messages. Successful shoestring marketers are doing it every day. It's a matter of trying to *apply* some of the popular copywriting guidelines identified in this book.

$

Advertising: Miscellaneous Notes

"For the small-business owner, advertising is like weight lifting: If you don't do enough, you're wasting your time. And if you lose control, you can get seriously hurt," say Sandy McGlashan and John Clausen, co-owners of Wordiorights Advertising in Sacramento, California.[1]

The amount of advertising you do place depends on your own situation. Fair prices, courteous service, and solid work advertised through posters, handbills, small mailings, and a big store sign could be more than adequate. For example, if you operate the only full-service laundry near a large mobile home park and many apartment dwellings, these means of advertising may serve you quite well.[2]

Hiring an Agency

In some cases, thrifty marketers need a great deal of advertising, or as they grow, their advertising becomes more complicated and time-consuming. Eventually it's decided to explore the hiring of an advertising agency. Although agency services increase cost, they could increase advertising effectiveness.

Depending on the contractual agreement and your own needs, an agency might provide any or all of the following services:

- Analyze your business strengths and weaknesses.
- Study your industry and competition.
- Plan your advertising strategy.
- Select media plus buy space and time.
- Produce the ads, including copy, visuals, layout, and/or sound.
- Create finished ads in the physical format required by different media.
- Do record keeping of the advertising expenditures and scheduling.
- Perform research studies to measure results.

For low-cost marketers, the two most popular services are the production aspects of the ads and the liaison work with different media. Business and industry analysis and marketing research studies, on the other hand, are usually prohibitive in costs for the shoestringer.

To help minimize the time you spend in choosing an agency, develop selection criteria and standards to guide your choice. Lack of standards will result in trial and error, which is too costly.

Edward Vick, president of Ammirati & Puris, a mid-sized ad agency in New York, suggests hiring an agency whose size is comparable to your company's: "If you have a small ad budget, hire a small advertising agency. What you get in a small agency is personal attention, and a small agency is most likely to be really hungry for your business." Small agencies, he says, will typically go the extra mile to please their clients, because that, in turn, helps their businesses. How do you know if an ad agency is hungry for your business? "A lot of bigger agencies will take your money, and they'll tell you they're going to do a good job," but you often find yourself lost in the shuffle, he says. "You'll know an agency is legitimately interested in your company only after getting into a meeting with them. If they're not hungry, it will come out some way."

A big factor in choosing the right agency, he says, is the chemistry you feel between you and the people you would be working with. "The chemistry has to be good. If they're not people that you'd like to spend the weekend with, then they're probably not the right people for your campaign," Vick points out. "They have to be people you wouldn't mind working with until midnight and on the weekend."

Will there be any personality conflicts? Will you be able to get along with the agency's creative people, as well as the executive handling your account? Chemistry is a subjective but important intangible. Before committing, ask the agency to visit your business. You should visit the agency a few times as well. See how the relationships feel under different circumstances and environments.

Just as with selecting a public relations firm, look at an ad agency's work for other companies. Ask for references. "You have to be confident that the agency will be able to do the kind of work that will represent your company well," says Vick. "You have to get somebody who's really interested, who understands your company, its goals and concerns. And the hungrier they are, the more flexible they'll be."

To find ad agencies that are similar in size to your business, Vick suggests reading the annual issue of *Advertising Age,* which lists advertising agencies by rank and size. Or read through the *Standard Directory of Advertising Agencies,* which lists virtually every advertising agency of consequence. You can find both of these books at your local library.

Potential advertisers can also contact:

American Association of Advertising Agencies (AAAA)
666 Third Ave.
New York, N.Y. 10017

Someone there can give you some guidance on your advertising challenge.

To help you gauge different agencies, Worksheet 4 lists some constructive questions. In answering them, you'll have a clearer focus on picking the best ad agency for your own business. You can, of course, modify this worksheet to meet the special needs

TIP: Agency Size Is Vital Concern

As a rule of thumb, when an annual advertising budget is less than $1 million, avoid an agency with $50 million or more in annual billings. With a smaller agency, which may have billings of $10 million to $20 million or much less, your business may receive more attention from the agency owners. Smaller agencies cannot afford to lose as many shoestring marketers without hurting their businesses.

Larger agencies should not be automatically eliminated. However, if you use one, make sure your "small" account is not lost in the shuffle.

Source: "Selecting an Advertising Agency," *Small Business Report* (January 1988), pp. 62–64.

of your situation. Whatever questions you decide to ask, challenge the agency to suggest canny ways to advertise effectively with a modest budget.

Learn From Others' Mistakes

Advertising is critical, yet most of it fails, says Alec Benn, an advertising professional and author of *The 27 Most Common Mistakes in Advertising*. If you doubt this, look through recent newspaper and magazine ads. "Note how many of the advertisements that were meant to influence you had no effect upon you," says Benn. "Not only did you not read them—you didn't even notice them." However, not all the common mistakes mentioned by Benn pertain to shoestring advertisers. Therefore, only those relevant to sellers with shallow pockets are listed on pages 47–48 (the opening statements are his; we give the interpretation for shoestring marketers).[3]

WORKSHEET 4

Interviewing: Advertising Agency Questionnaire

_____

Name of agency _____

Phone _____

Title of person interviewed _____

Address _____

Who will actually work on my account? _____

Background and experience _____

_____

How long has your agency been in business? _____

Do you specialize in serving any one industry? ____

Do you have experience in serving businesses with modest budgets?

_____

If yes, what have you done successfully in your advertising for these clients? _____

_____

If there are account problems or disagreements, how do you resolve them? _____

_____

_____

Please explain all the costs that will be incurred in using your services (including any subcontracting). _____

_____

How and when will I be billed? _____

Are there any positive or negative comments that you want to make about my potential account? _____

_____

Thank you for answering my questions.

_____

1. *"Trying to do too much with too few advertising dollars."* You cannot afford to be something to everyone. Too often you may try to say too much, hit many different media or have a huge, one-time flashy ad to get "your money's worth." It could be a costly blunder. You might need a better focus, a clear niche, or just one powerful message for dealing with competitive advertising clutter.

2. *"Choosing a medium based on its low rate rather than on its cost per thousand readers, listeners, or viewers."* You should compare audience size, image, and the selling results for businesses that have advertised in various media. Don't just look at the ad rates of a medium.

3. *"Not advertising frequently enough."* You may need to run an ad several times to increase the awareness and recall of your message.

4. *"Making an advertisement bigger than it need be."* Don't sacrifice quality and repetition just for size. Sometimes attention is increased at a diminishing rate as the ad is made bigger.

5. *"Expecting too much from creativity in copy and art."* A flashy

and innovative ad will not overcome weaknesses in a business.

6. *"Imitating instead of analyzing."* A frugal seller cannot financially compete with big-buck marketers. Avoid me-tooism advertising.

7. *"Not concentrating the advertising on the reader, listener, or the viewer."* This reinforces our you-approach discussion.

8. *"Failing to fully utilize the unique advantages of the medium, especially television."* For example, if you decide on TV, then demonstrate the virtues of your products. Avoid just talking through a TV script without product demonstrations. If you use billboards, avoid copy with a number of words or statements. Passersby will not have time to read them.

9. *"Failing to capitalize on the inherent nature of the product, service, or company."* Carefully match your market's preferences with the strengths of your offerings and business.

10. *"Having no objective measure of the advertising effectiveness."* Carefully watch and evaluate your ads and the resulting campaigns to see if they're getting the job done.

11. *"Believing advertising is more powerful than it really is. Discover what it takes for advertising to succeed."* Advertising cannot overcome a structural business weakness, nor is it an automatic solution to all of your problems (e.g., prices too high, poor post-sale service, or lousy location).

Every organization and business makes mistakes. We are not immune from them, but we can learn from them or recognize the ones that others have made. If you remember these advertising mistakes and suggestions, you'll save some precious ad dollars while dramatically improving your advertising efforts.

If advertising is a major part of your total budget, you may like to start reading *Advertising Age* and *Adweek*. (Most public and university libraries subscribe to these two periodicals.) Intermittently, there are some excellent advertising articles in such publications as *Business Marketing, Entrepreneur, Inc., Inside Business, Marketing News, Small Business Report, Venture,* and

Nation's Business. Your limited time will not permit you to read all of these publications. However, by looking at them and deciding which one or two best fit your own situation, you'll begin a steady diet of learning what's the best approach to strengthen your advertising efforts.

Further Resources

For more information on advertising, see the advertising resources and associations listed in Part III—Further Resources.

$

Auctions

"Auction." The word conjures up images of a rapid-fire talker with gavel in hand, turning tugs of the ear, a thumb to the nose, and nods from members of a stone-faced audience into million-dollar bids for a crusty old antique. When the highest bid is reached, slam goes the gavel, and the objet d'art is sold.

Although those images are not far from reality, this ancient form of marketing has been growing rapidly in recent years—partly due to forced liquidations resulting from bankruptcy but also as a means of moving excess inventory.

Almost any item can be auctioned, though the most commonly auctioned items are industrial equipment, livestock, commodities—such as real estate and tobacco—and art. Whatever you want to liquidate, there are thousands of auctioneers across the country who are willing to take on the job. Nearly every state has an auctioneers' association, and if you read the classified ad section of your local newspaper, no doubt you have seen a column or two devoted to auction announcements.

If you have excess inventory that is preventing you from bringing in newer product lines, putting it up for auction may be the quickest and most profitable way to get rid of it.

Here's how the auction process works. First you contact an auctioneers' association in your area and describe the inventory you would like to move. The person handling the call will usually refer you to three or four auctioneers who specialize in your type of inventory. You then contact the auctioneers. They evaluate your inventory individually and present you with a proposal that details the auction date, location, time, cost of advertising, sales commission, and other expenses.

"A typical arrangement is that the auctioneer gets a 10 percent commission plus expenses," says Stephen Grove, president of the Los Angeles–based auction firm Kohn Megabow, as well as president of the Southern California Auctioneers' Association. Expenses include advertising the event through local newspapers, flyers, or direct mail. The auctioneer is also responsible for preparing the merchandise for the auction, which can include cleaning, painting, repairing, setting it up at the auction, and anything else needed to make the property more marketable.

Often an auctioneer will offer cash on the spot instead of a commission off the auction's sales. "We liquidate a lot of excess inventory this way," says Grove. Carl's Jr., a fast-food hamburger chain on the West Coast, sold Kohn Megabow 800 surplus tomato slicers and undercounter dishwashers for cash on the spot instead of going to auction. "A lot of people would rather get $25,000, for example, and put it in their pocket because it's a sure thing rather than take the chance of going to auction and maybe getting a little more," explains Grove. "A good auctioneer will make money off this and can buy the inventory cheaper— but not too much cheaper because a smart seller will go to three or four auctioneers and get bids."

Once you have bids from a few auctioneers, Grove says it is imperative that you check references. "Too often people get references and say, 'That's nice,' and they never check them. An auctioneer is going to handle and hold your money—possibly a great deal of money," says Grove. "Reliability and credibility of the auctioneer are extremely important, and just like all businesses, there's some bad guys out there."

It is also important to make sure that the auctioneer you choose is experienced in selling your particular type of goods.

"Even a good auctioneer might not be the best person to sell equipment he's not familiar with," says Grove.

As the seller, you have a choice of selling styles. You may decide to go with an absolute auction in which each item goes to the highest bidder regardless of the price. Or you may prefer a with-reserve auction where you, the seller, reserve the right not to accept the highest bid. Usually you and the auctioneer decide during your initial discussion. Whatever type of auction you prefer, the end result is usually instant cash that you would not normally have by conventional means of marketing.

"The number-one drawback, however, is that when you go into an auction situation, you're not sure of the price that you're going to get," says Grove. "But statistics have shown over the years that a good auctioneer who advertises properly and knows what he's doing is going to get market value for the inventory."

Selecting the Right Auctioneer

The National Auctioneers Association offers the following guidelines for selecting the professional who will make your auction a success:

1. *Motivation and initiative:* The auctioneer must approach the job with energy and enthusiasm if he or she is to generate the same enthusiasm from buyers. When you hire an auctioneer you are hiring a salesperson. The more motivated this salesperson is, the better the sale you will obtain. This personal drive should come across in the interview.

2. *Empathy and involvement:* The auctioneer must put himself in the shoes of the potential seller and evaluate that person's needs and problems. The auctioneer should demonstrate this ability in some way. Involvement in the community is often an indication that the auctioneer is concerned for the people around him.

3. *Integrity and honesty:* The auctioneer, as an intermediary between the buyer and seller, holds a position of trust. Not only is

the auctioneer going to handle your money, but he is also trusted to elicit the highest bids for your product. Checking references and credentials through a professional auctioneers' association can ensure that you will not be disappointed.

4. *Product knowledge:* The auctioneer should know the merchandise being sold, its market value, and how to best present the product to obtain the highest price at auction. Many auctioneers specialize in specific products, gaining a reputation for their knowledge, wide range of contacts in the industry, and ability to sell those products. General auctioneers, on the other hand, have knowledge of many products and may be best suited to auction a variety of items at a time. Although product knowledge is important, an auctioneer who learns quickly and researches merchandise he knows little about can overcome initial lack of specialized product knowledge.

5. *Professionalism:* This is the most important characteristic to look for in an auctioneer. You will want to select one who is dedicated to his profession and not just looking for a fast buck on the side. The auctioneer's appearance, attitudes, and actions should indicate that he or she is a thorough, knowledgeable, and professional businessperson. A certified auctioneer or one who has a membership in an auctioneers' organization will most likely fit the bill.

Further Resources

For literature on auctions and a list of state member associations, write to:

National Auctioneers Association
8880 Ballentine
Overland Park, Kansas 66214

For more information on auctions see the *Auctioneers Directory* listed in Part III—Further Resources.

(*See also* entry entitled Restaging Products.)

$

Barter

The word "barter" probably brings to mind early settlers swapping bushels of corn for a new hoe, but barter is still used frequently today by small businesses. In fact, it has developed into a $1 billion industry, increasing at a rate of about 15 percent a year, according to Paul Suplizio, executive director of the International Reciprocal Trade Association. He says that more than 100,000 businesses—mostly small companies but a growing number of well-known large firms—used the services of commercial barter exchanges in 1988.

This ancient form of trade is most commonly used to unload surplus or slow-moving inventory and concentrate instead on selling a new line of goods. It is used also by businesses, professionals, or associations that want to trade skills for a product or service they normally cannot afford with cash or because they want to conserve their liquidity for larger expenditures. Barter is particularly good, says Suplizio, for seasonal businesses. A hotel resort, for example, can finance its maintenance and other expenses during the off-season by working with barter customers.

There are many other ways to use barter to market your product or service. One common way to barter is for advertising space. Many magazines, trade and professional publications, newspapers, and periodicals will offer ad space in return for products or services they need. Many business machine companies, for instance, will swap last year's models or surplus inventory of, say, typewriters, computers, or other equipment for a year's worth of one-page ads in a magazine.

Hotels often offer a certain number of rooms overnight to reporters or publication representatives, who are doing out-of-town traveling, in exchange for ad space. These swaps are usually arranged by a barter broker.

Deciding whom you will barter with depends on the type of product or service you want to trade and what you want in exchange. You might start with a one-on-one barter exchange with suppliers or other local businesses. That is, you contact someone whose product or service you want in exchange for your product or service. A landscaper, for instance, may offer free gardening services to a local accountant for balancing the books.

Many barter swaps begin in the classified ad section of a local or regional newspaper or magazine. Barterers place ads listing the services or products they're offering and the products or services they may be looking for. Savvy barterers, however, will approach any classified advertiser with a swap offer, even if their ads do not indicate a desire to barter. A bakery owner, for example, wants to buy a new oven. He looks in the classifieds and sees an ad by a local restaurant that just bought new ovens and wants to sell its old ones. The baker does not have enough cash to purchase an oven but offers the restaurant owner the cash he has on hand, as well as a six months' supply of freshly baked bread. The restaurant owner gets free fresh bread and gets rid of an oven. The bakery owner gets a better-working oven and unloads the bread that he cannot sell each day.

If it's not your style to haggle over merchandise, a barter broker will help you unload excess inventory quickly and quietly through a large network of business contacts. You can find most barter brokers listed in the Yellow Pages. However, because brokers typically work on commission, they generally prefer to work with large companies, which offer big commissions.

Many small companies and self-employed professionals prefer

to swap through commercial barter clubs or exchanges. Participants typically pay a one-time membership fee, as well as annual renewal fees. An additional commission fee, typically a percentage of the gross value of each transaction, is also paid to the club. Most Yellow Pages directories, community organizations, bulletin boards, and local publications have information on local commercial barter exchanges.

These clubs, however, do have a drawback: the occasional (and, in some cases, frequent) limited availability of products and services offered, especially the ones in great demand. It is not unusual to be placed on a waiting list for goods and services or find yourself with barter credits (credit for a certain amount of merchandise or services) you can't use. Be sure to investigate a barter exchange thoroughly before joining. First, find out what goods and services the other members are offering; you don't want to join an exchange where the other members are offering and trying to barter for the same goods and services that you are. Second, check the financial stability of the exchange. Many are undercapitalized and go out of business, leaving members with useless credits.

An organized barter system also provides bookkeeping services to keep track of members' barter purchases for IRS purposes. The exchange records each transaction and sends members monthly statements for their personal records. At the end of the year, the club tallies each member's yearly transaction total and reports it to the IRS on Form 1099-B. Members receive a copy of this form or an equivalent document, which should be included as income when filing their own tax returns. Remember, however, that barter is *not* a way to dodge taxes; it is a marketing tool. Barter purchases must be treated the same as cash purchases.

Generally barter purchases that are business related are tax deductible; exchanges for personal use are not. And when you realize a capital gain—such as when you trade something worth $500 and gain something worth $1,000—the profit is taxable. There is a lot of gray area as to how exchanges are taxed, depending on the value of each exchange. Be sure to seek the advice of an accountant, attorney, or other tax consultant familiar with barter to determine which barter exchanges should be reported as income.

Barter can help a business through some lean times, but no company should be run strictly on barter, says Valerie Bohigian, a business writer, barter expert, and small-business owner in North Tarrytown, New York. Barter is only one of many methods of conducting business, and it should not exceed 15 to 20 percent of a business's total volume.

Further Resources

For more information about barter and barter clubs, contact:

International Reciprocal Trade Association
4012 Moss Place
Alexandria, Virginia 22304

$

Brochures and Flyers

Brochures

Brochures. You see them all the time, but how many do you actually read? The brochures that usually get the most attention are typically ones that seem to be talking directly to an individual reader and are peppered with tantalizing graphics and interesting copy. After reading an effective brochure, you feel as if you've learned something important in only a few minutes.

Brochures can be terrific marketing tools if they are carefully planned and designed. They are not a tool to brag about your company but rather a means to make readers feel that they can benefit in some way by becoming more familiar with your product or service.

Here are a few points to think about before you design your next brochure:

1. Decide what you want your brochure to do. Do you want to introduce a new product line? Stress an improved service?

Your brochure should have a format or theme that conveys your company's personality and how it is better than the competition. You might consider using the same format in future brochure literature to reinforce your company's image. This may include using a certain color, such as that of your logo, on the cover or throughout all your brochures. Remember, you want to build an association with your target audience. When they see your particular logo, color combination, or style format, they will automatically associate it with your business.

2. Determine your audience: present customers, prospective customers, the media? Prioritize the benefits you want to convey in the brochure, and don't try to include everything you do. Always think from the reader's point of view. Are you more likely to read a brochure that is wordy and cluttered or one that is streamlined, concise, and highly visual?

3. Choose a style of type that reflects your company's personality and the image you want to project. For instance, you would not use formal script if you are a country-cooking restaurant.

4. Use a writing style that fits your readers' language. Don't use technical industry jargon if your audience does not normally use it. In fact, avoid jargon in general whenever possible. If you must use it, be sure to explain it briefly. Don't assume that your audience will know it. Most important, you want your message to be communicated easily. Remind yourself that your audience receives reams of promotional literature at home and at the office. The quicker and easier your brochure is to read, the better. Choose your words wisely, and go for the short message.

5. Illustrations and photos should communicate what your company does and break up the monotony of words. They should reinforce the consumer benefits outlined in your copy. You may want to include captions to explain the photos.

6. List your company's address and phone number in a convenient and highly visible place for reader response. Provide a contact person's name or a reply card. Make it easy for the reader to respond.

7. If you plan to mail your brochures, make sure your mailing list is up to date to avoid wasted postage. Don't overlook leaving

brochures at related but noncompeting businesses. You want to distribute your brochure wherever your target market may see it. One northern Virginia woman who makes dried flower arrangements, for instance, leaves brochures in bridal shops around the Washington metropolitan area. A sideline photographer may leave brochures with local churches that provide wedding kits to engaged couples planning to marry at the church.

You may decide to design the brochure yourself with customized software for brochure production, or you may want to seek the advice of a printer or marketing consultant. Keep in mind, however, that the more professional the look you want, the more expensive the project usually becomes.

Flyers

Flyers, like brochures, also quickly tell readers how they can benefit from a special offer, product, or service. But unlike brochures, they are typically one-page handbills with one-color type and are less expensive to produce. The flyer can be an inside scoop on how consumers can take advantage of a limited offer, sale, or a coupon. The message should be short and to the point.

"The best thing I did to get my business started was having flyers printed up," says Lisa Renshaw, who runs a parking service in Baltimore. "Using flyers triggered the success of the garage." Renshaw's creation wasn't your typical, flimsy 8½-inch by 11-inch handbill. It was a heavy-stock, pocket-sized flyer that included a coupon for a free car wash. Her strategy was to appeal to Amtrak travelers at nearby Penn Station who did not have time to read a lot of promotional literature. The flyer's wording was bare-bones brief. Renshaw highlighted "Secured—Covered Parking, One Block Away, Free Car Wash" in bold block letters. "If people see a 'free' anything, they're going to read the rest of the flyer," she says. Other details, such as the garage's name, were secondary and not highlighted. "The name isn't as important—they want to know where it's located." Renshaw purposely avoided using wordy paragraphs to explain the benefits of parking at her garage:

> People don't want to read that, especially if you're catering to business people. They're on the go all the time. They read three to four newspapers every day. You don't think they read every word; they skim. That's what they're going to be doing with your flyer. I looked at it from the readers' perspective. When you're the one advertising, your inclination is to put everything down. But when you're the reader, your inclination is to toss it, regardless of what it is because you get so much of that stuff.

Marketers have to make their advertising look different from everybody else's if they are to stand out above the clutter of junk mail stuffed into consumers' mailboxes and thrust at them on street corners. Having a different look may simply mean using a different color ink or a different size flyer or brochure—though it may cost a few dollars extra. "Some people say, 'What's the difference between red ink and black ink?'" says Renshaw. "A lot, because black ink is used by everybody. If you have to pay that extra $15 to get red and blue ink, then get it, because those are minimal costs considering that you want people to read the flyer and not toss it." Renshaw used a different color ink—the same bright blue as on her signage. She also included a tickler to make sure that prospective customers would hang on to her flyer: A perforated coupon for a free car wash after five full-day visits to the garage. "The perforation was more expensive, but it made it easy for people to tear off the coupon and use it and not just toss it away," she says.

A true shoestring marketer, Renshaw designed her flyer so she could get three cut out of one standard sheet of paper. That lowered costs considerably, although the printer charged a nominal cutting fee. She found that there are so many small, independent printers and printing franchises competing for business that it was easy to find reasonable prices. Many printers are willing to negotiate the cost, she says. Renshaw cannot recall the total cost of her flyers, but she knows it was minimal compared to her return.

With flyers in hand, Renshaw stood outside the Amtrak station, smiled at passersby, handed them flyers, and asked them to park at her garage. Then she wished them a good day. She believes the personal contact helped lure them in: "I got a lot of people in that way. I think some of them felt that if I could stand out there in the cold, the least they could do was park at my garage."

Renshaw took her personal touch one step further and washed the cars herself—though partly because she had only one other employee at the time. "Do you know how you wash cars in the dead of winter? You heat the bucket of water, you keep the car running so it stays warm, you throw the water on the car, you wash it as quickly as you can, praying that it doesn't freeze and then you dry it off."

Her water costs increased considerably because she was washing so many cars, but the cost was nominal compared to the revenue generated by an influx of steady customers. "The car wash was only to bring the parker in," she says. By the fifth visit, which was required for the free car wash, customers were used to her service. "So, they came back the sixth and seventh and eighth times and started paying for the car washes, which are $6," says Renshaw. "So they'd come in at $11 a shot. And the expense for the water and the advertising was minimal compared to the response that I got back."

Although Renshaw had only one other employee, she says the time away from the business did not worry her. "What's the sense of being at the office if there's no business coming in?" she points out. "You can be there if a problem comes up, but there are no problems coming up if there's no business in there. You have to get out on the street."

In addition to "getting out on the street" with her flyers, Renshaw built up a strong referral system through local travel agencies. She sent personal letters introducing herself and her business and enclosed several flyers. The travel agencies used the discount as an added customer service for their Amtrak customers, and Renshaw did not have to pay extra to use this distribution channel. It also built a good reputation for Renshaw among the agencies. "I had a tremendous response from that," she says. "If you can get somebody else to distribute it [promotional literature] and it's good for them, then their customers are happy, I'm happy, and they are happy to be able to do it. You establish a good relationship all the way around, and that's a good way to increase your business."

Further Resources

For more information, see the *Typesetting Services Directory* listed in Part III—Further Resources.

$

Business Cards

Almost every entrepreneur, small-business owner, and executive needs business cards. Handing out business cards is a normal activity. It is an acceptable, low-cost form of communication. In fact, your contacts, prospects, and associates expect to receive your business cards. Unlike their response to other communication and promotion media, people are attentive and quite receptive to having your business card. They can easily file it away and use it at their convenience.

Frederick J. Cowie, an entrepreneur who designs business cards and brochures, says that business cards have become the forgotten stepchild of the business community. Since they are small, plentiful, inexpensive, and used frequently, one can easily be complacent about developing an effective card.[1]

Not everyone agrees on what is the best and most effective design, however. *Sales & Marketing Digest* has provided these suggestions:

1. Make your cards 1/4 inch larger than normal size.
2. Distribute your cards to both prospect and secretary. (We believe that's an excellent idea since executives will frequently rely on their secretaries to file cards.)

TIP: Suggestions for Business Card Design

David Kaltenbach, a corporate identity and packaging graphics consultant in Akron, Ohio, believes that design is influenced by the way you use the card. Will the card be used as a sales tool, a reminder for the holder, or a way to stand out from the competition? For example, if you want your card to stand out, special inks and paper or more than one color could be the solution. His additional tips are:

1. Avoid a cluttered look to your cards.
2. If you need more space than a 2- by 3.5-inch card provides, utilize a foldover design, such as a list of products or services.
3. Don't use more than one symbol or logo per card.
4. Prominently display your logo, if you have one.
5. Be consistent. All members of your firm should use the same card design.

If the card is a selling device, Kaltenbach suggests putting an incentive on the back of the card, such as a sales discount if the card is presented at your place of business. For shoestring marketers, this may be one good way to get extra mileage from your cards while creating customer loyalty.

Source: "Selling Strategies: Card Tricks," *In Business* (September–October 1986), p. 12.

3. In the presence of the prospect, add your home address and phone number in pen—you'll create a "special feeling" in the prospect's mind.
4. Place a printed calendar of a coming year on the back of your card (this will encourage prospects to keep your card and use it for future reference).[2]

Some people may feel that the third suggestion is tacky. Your own prospects and customers are really the best judge. In some professional service firms, such as law, accounting, and engineering, this may convey a shoddy image. But some customers in other markets may like the personalized approach. You may be giving them the impression that you really care and are willing to be "bothered at home." As you can see, the creation, design, and production of business cards is an art that has no simple answers.

Cowie advises marketers to perform an analysis in order to understand the experiences, skills, obstacles, goals, plans, and life-style expectations of their business, customers, and competition. Some key questions must be answered. Will you be available "24 hours" or just "9 to 5"? Are you or your business insured, licensed, bonded, factory trained or authorized, franchised, UAL, "Good Housekeeping" or offer limited warranty? How critical are such services or promises as "free delivery," "satisfaction guaranteed," or "money back"? What type of competitive image are you conveying: lowest prices, high product quality, extra services, or an innovative, distinct organization?

The answers to these questions could affect the design, color, and content of your cards. Therefore, first decide what you want your business to be, what you want it to accomplish, and how you'd like it to be perceived in your marketplace.

Cowie advises everyone to carry several dozen cards at all times and to attach a card with every company and personal letter. Letters may be trashed, but cards are often filed. Depending on the type of business you're in, Cowie says never to pass up a bulletin board without putting a card on it. You could also leave cards at complementary businesses. For example, writers and typists can leave cards with printers, and plumbers, handymen, and electricians might leave cards in real estate offices.

"Business carding" is an inexpensive form of promoting your small business or association. The right business card is part (along with your stationery, letterhead, envelopes, logo) of a total image you are trying to project.

Don't be afraid to experiment with different types of business cards, including color. You can have hundreds printed for a few dollars. In fact, once you have a card designed, it costs only a few *more* dollars to have, say, 1,000 or so printed, rather than just a couple hundred. One small job or new customer can pay for the cost of this printing.

Carefully watch to see what your customers and associates think. Based on their feedback and reactions, you'll be able to develop a business card that is best for your business.

More important, don't be stingy with your cards. They become useless when hiding in a printer's box or in your filing cabinet. Also, avoid using someone else's cards by scratching the name off and printing your name in its place. (We've seen this done by a few real estate sales people within the same firm. This presents a very unprofessional image.)

Remember, business cards are a popular way to network. They are your calling cards. You must distribute them widely and frequently. If used properly, they are an outstanding tool for shoestring marketers that deserve your attention.

$

Customer Relations

According to the federal Office of Consumer Affairs, 96 percent of all dissatisfied customers never bother to complain to the seller. They make their dissatisfaction known in other ways—90 percent of them will take their business elsewhere. Harrington Market Research in Kalamazoo, Michigan, did a survey that showed that one-third of the Michigan respondents would not go back to a business after one bad experience. Retail stores, hotels, and restaurants were cited most often as targets of customer anger. Some of the respondents' biggest gripes were poor service, apathetic or rude personnel, poor complaint handling, and the poor quality of the products themselves. Brenda Murphy, Harrington's president, believes that "all employees who are in contact with the public need to be trained in customer relations."[1]

Marketers at Ford Motor Company have discovered that if they could keep loyal customers in a lifetime relationship, Ford would realize a $140,000 profit per customer, says Ray Considine, a business consultant in Pasadena, California. As a seller, you should strive for creating a lifetime contract with your customers, he says.[2]

Although Ford is a large company with a healthy marketing budget, good customer relations affect the revenues of all businesses. The American Management Association says that an estimated 65 percent of the average company's future business comes from its present customers.

It makes good dollars and sense to keep your current customers. The marketing costs of attracting new business are usually five times greater than selling to existing customers, points out the Technical Assistance Project of Washington. And dissatisfied customers make a greater impact than just quietly taking their business elsewhere. According to the White House Office of Consumer Affairs, one dissatisfied customer will speak negatively about the company to at least nine other people.[3]

Robert Krughoff, president of the Center for the Study of Services in Washington, D.C., believes that it's much smarter and cheaper to keep customers than to spend a large part of a budget to get new ones. Earning customer loyalty does not entail marketing magic; instead, it requires an awareness of the revenue opportunities of customer retention, some basic common sense, and a solid commitment to be of service. Smart shoestring marketers don't take their customers for granted.

Carol Gold, president of her own firm and author of *Solid Gold Customer Relations*, notes that it's easy to find reasons or excuses for sloppy customer service. She cites the ten most popular excuses employees give: (1) "I am too busy"; (2) "There are too many interruptions"; (3) "People don't listen"; (4) "I am not given enough information"; (5) "People are rude to me"; (6) "The telephone keeps ringing"; (7) "I had an argument with my spouse"; (8) "I need product knowledge"; (9) "People don't read instructions"; and (10) "My office has no window."[4]

These excuses are too costly for shoestring marketers. Replacing lost customers is an expensive proposition. But most often, more attention is spent on acquiring customers than on retaining existing customers. "Retention marketing is no easier than acquisition marketing," says Laura Liswood, customer service executive and author of *50 Ways to Keep a Customer*. "The future belongs to those who can get and keep a customer."[5]

TIP: Keeping Customers Happy

John Tschol, customer service consultant and head of Better Than Money Corp., Bloomington, Minnesota, suggests the following:

- Solicit customer criticism, which allows problems to be solved. You can win back as many as 74 percent of your dissatisfied customers with this technique.
- Teach *all* employees the importance of respecting your customers.
- Identify applicants and employees who don't view customer contact work as critical.
- Constantly remind employees of the value of good customer relations.
- Evaluate all employees—even part-timers—and yourself on how well you deal with complaints.
- Treat employees as worthwhile people since this treatment is expected to be given to customers.

Source: "Unhappy Customers," *Industry Week* (September 10, 1987), p. 36.

Don't merely delegate customer contact and relations to your own salespeople or external reps. Sometimes the people who actually work on the product may be the best ones to deal directly with your accounts. For example, Hugh Vestal of Carbide Surface Company, a small machine tool business in Fraiser, Michigan, encourages buyers who need tools coated with carbide to contact his "impregnators." These coating specialists schedule the job, arrange delivery dates, perform the work, and submit job-cost forms. Vestal's customers like this system because they can ask technical questions, avoid intermediaries (especially sales reps), and save time. This practice also creates another benefit: It establishes a business culture of positive customer relations—everyone learns the need for good customer contact.

A study by Technical Assistance Research Program, Inc. (TARP), found that successfully settling a complaint will often create greater customer loyalty; 70 to 80 percent of customers whose complaints were resolved satisfactorily were willing to buy other products compared to only 10 to 20 percent of noncomplainers. Perhaps many complainers were impressed that the seller even responded to their problems. "Assuming that you can satisfy the customers on the spot," says John Goodman, TARP's president, "that's the perfect time to sell him on something else."[6]

Shoestring marketers must not only listen to complaints but expeditiously solve complainers' problems. Don't think that no news from customers is good news. Many unhappy customers will not make the effort to complain. For every one complainer, there are twenty-six who feel like complaining but don't, according to TARP's research.

When customers do call to complain, avoid keeping them on hold or giving them the runaround. Poor phone etiquette may cause your customers to call someone else—a competitor.

Have a positive attitude toward customer complaints instead of taking an adversary role. Don't assume the customers are trying to cheat you. Most complaints, product returns, and consumer concerns are quite sincere and honest.

Consumer complaints should not be seen as a threat to your business. Look at them as an opportunity to strengthen your marketing efforts. Remember, a limited marketing budget eliminates the unusual luxury of having "turned off" customers. See their problems from their point of view and offer solutions from that viewpoint—not your own.

Good marketing requires concern with every possible customer interaction: in-store, by mail, phone, collection procedures, refunds, complaint handling, product returns, or ongoing servicing of the product.

To get repeat business, encourage your customers to speak out by making it easy for them to communicate. You will learn a great deal about your marketing efforts while demonstrating your sincere efforts to ensure customer satisfaction. Depending on your own circumstances and your type of business or association, you could try any of these marketing customer relations tools:

- Customer suggestion box
- Telemarketing program with recent customers to gauge the level of satisfaction with your product or service
- Mailed surveys
- Focus groups
- One-on-one personal interviews
- Mystery shoppers (shoppers *hired* by an employer to determine how well employees are treating customers)
- Customer comment cards, such as postcards
- Toll-free numbers for out-of-town customers
- Special complaint department
- Newsletters and product use bulletins, pamphlets, or guides
- Educational seminars
- Product demonstrations
- Videotape instructions
- Follow-up sales calls whereby customers can voice concerns or problems
- Goodwill gifts to key customers to show your appreciation

Of course, your budget and time constraints won't enable you to use all of these customer retention tools—and you won't want to use all of them. You'll have to experiment to find the ones best suited to your own situation.

Although IBM has a huge marketing budget, one simple goal—good customer relations—has played a key role in making it an international business giant. F. G. "Buck" Rodgers, former vice-president of marketing for IBM and author of *The IBM Way*, says, "No magic formula or guarded secret keeps customers 'married' to IBM long after their equipment is installed and their check deposited. IBM simply approaches the customer . . . after the sale . . . with the same interest and attention as when he was the prospect being courted."[7]

In short, achieving good customer relationships is a major marketing goal and opportunity for shoestring marketers. With

---

TIP: Bringing the Customers Back Again and Again

You might consider posting the following poem (source unknown) on employees' and management's bulletin boards:

> A little bit of quality
> Will always make 'em smile;
> A little bit of courtesy
> Will bring 'em in a mile;
> A little bit of friendliness
> Will tickle 'em 'tis plain—
> And a little bit of service
> Will bring 'em back again.

---

your small size in sales or employees, you avoid the common problem of customers getting lost in the shuffle. Small businesses, associations, and nonprofit firms have a golden chance for keeping their customers and never letting them go.

Further Resources

For further help or suggestions, contact:

International Customer Service Association
111 East Walker Drive
Suite 600
Chicago, Illinois 60601

$

Direct Marketing

Like some magic spell, effective direct marketing has the power to give prospective customers an uncontrollable urge to respond to your sales message. Whether your message is low-key or an urgent plea, direct marketing is a great way to get results.

We offer several examples of direct marketing throughout this book, but many people don't really know what the term means. *Direct Marketing* magazine, a leading publication in the field, defines direct marketing as "an interactive system of marketing which uses one or more advertising media to effect a measurable response and/or transaction at any location." Within this definition, direct marketing has the following characteristics:

- It requires a data base system to:
  —Record names of customers, expires, and prospects
  —Store and measure advertising results or actual purchases
  —Continue direct communication with prospects or customers
- It demands that a response or purchase at any location (e.g., phone or mail order) be recorded on cards, mechanical equipment, or, preferably, computer.

Direct marketing, more simply, involves the use of telephone inbound or out-bound sales, mail order, promotional postcard decks, television home shopping, promotional package or bill inserts, vending machines, party plans, radio ads with toll-free numbers, or door-to-door selling to get your message across. There is no one best way to sell through direct marketing. It depends on your business or cause.

While the formal definition of direct marketing may sound like mumbo jumbo, the technique has immediate value to frugal marketers. Direct marketing makes an earnest attempt to evaluate the impact of a specific marketing effort. It may also try to stimulate sales in the short run (some general advertising may be more long-term image building). For low-cost marketers with some cash flow problems, direct marketing can become a vital tool.

One of the greatest benefits of direct marketing is that you can track your selling efforts to see if they are bearing fruit. You could, for example, count the number of returned coupons from a magazine display ad, the number of orders from a coded address of a classified magazine ad, or the number of toll-free calls received from a special promotional mail order mailing or an out-bound advertisement.

For more detailed information on direct marketing techniques, see Telemarketing, Mail Order Catalogs, and Brochures and Flyers. Our main purpose in this brief entry is to define and expose you to the term to help avoid possible confusion in case someone recommends direct marketing to you. The term is a broad, catch-all phrase that has some outstanding possibilities for frugal marketers.

Further Resources

For more information on direct marketing than is provided in this book or if you need some start-up assistance, contact:

Direct Marketing Association
6 East 43rd Street
New York, New York 10017

or **Direct Selling Association**
1776 K Street, N.W.
Suite 600
Washington, D.C. 20006

If you're an association manager and wish to drum up contributions through direct marketing, contact:

Direct Mail Fundraisers Association
1501 Broadway
Suite 610
New York, New York 10036

$

Downturns

Periodically every shoestring marketer encounters tough economic times. A financial straitjacket is often spawned by a bad business cycle, unforeseen problems, or attrition of major customers. You must take aggressive action to survive and turn around a bleak situation. Sometimes if your business just hangs tough during slow periods, you'll reap tremendous rewards when the recovery does occur.

If you could safely forecast downturns, your marketing tasks would be much easier; however, the marketplace and the general economy are quite fluid. This dynamic condition generates distasteful surprises, especially for frugal sellers.

Albert Sommers, economic counselor of the nonprofit New York City–based Conference Board, says, "We know, or at least can be reasonably sure, that the forecasters won't warn us about the next recession until it's too late. It has been a long time—like since the Peloponnesian War—since any significant number of forecasts have predicted recession until after it had actually begun."[1]

Without close attention to the basics, an organization with shallow pockets can become a struggling business. When slow periods do occur—and they do for everyone—you must be cautious with both your selling efforts and your costs of doing business. Otherwise your business may even teeter on bankruptcy.

"There is one thing that all sick and ailing businesses have in common: they are, to a greater or lesser degree, out of control," say Robert Allen and H. John Altorfer, consultants with Management Practice Consulting Partners. "The resulting lack of focus, murkiness of strategy, and uncertain management priorities are classic symptoms of outfits tailspinning into bankruptcy." Allen and Altorfer recommend reestablishing control of the key business elements. Otherwise the business should be "taken out and shot."[2]

Organizations with tight budgets are in a precarious spot. Poor controls increase your chances of failure. Smart turnaround strategies require a good accounting system, a diagnostic analysis of strengths and weaknesses in the business, and a solid plan of action to fight a sluggish environment. If things really get nasty, a business may even need a tough attorney to negotiate with unsympathetic creditors.

Dean Treptow, president of Brown Deer Bank in Brown Deer, Wisconsin, and a national authority on small-business borrowing, believes in tight internal controls, particularly in the areas of inventory management and trade credit. Much has been written about watching inventories, but too little has been covered on small businesses giving trade credit to their commercial buyers. "I think trade credit has the potential to become a far more dangerous problem for businesses," says Treptow. "Small businesses will frequently ship goods while offering customers credit of at least 90 days. Usually this credit is unsecured and lacks collateral from customers."[3]

In uncertain times with hidden perils, businesses should place emphasis on earnings coverage and cash flow related to capital investments, continues Treptow. Buying office buildings, expensive equipment, raw land, and other costly fixed assets can be quite dangerous. There must be adequate sales revenue and cash flow to cover the debt incurred from the fixed assets. Treptow stresses the importance of spending money to increase sales or reduce costs.

Frugal marketers must resist the mistake of indiscriminately slashing expenses on promotional efforts in slow periods. Besides eliminating the fat, you could be cutting into the marrow and bone. For example, certain sales promotional efforts may be necessary in moving current inventory, or additional telemarketing expenses may help in closing some key deals.

TIP: Knowing When You're Cutting Too Deeply

A. J. Magrath, author of several marketing texts and director of marketing services for a Fortune 500 manufacturer in Canada, warns businesses to be careful about creating a "lean and mean" business. "Wartime tactics backfire in peacetime, when rebuilding is called for in morale, people programs, and market development activities," says Magrath. Poor belt-tightening strategies could reduce the ability to rebound. Magrath offers six red flags that may pop up when cutbacks and productivity pressures have gone too far:

1. Loyal customers complain they see your sales representatives too infrequently and therefore have begun trying your competitors' products.
2. Communication and follow-through on marketing programs to end users or resellers are slipshod.
3. It becomes harder to motivate distribution channel members.
4. The morale among your sales and marketing people is poor.
5. There is less urge to experiment and try new ideas for sales growth.
6. There are fewer one-on-one coaching sessions to help the salespeople and marketers to improve their promotional efforts.

Source: A. J. Magrath, "Are You Overdoing 'Lean and Mean'?" *Sales & Marketing Management* (January 1988): 46–54.

A passive attitude and waiting for the economy to turn around could be detrimental to your survival. Avoid the natural instinct of squeezing the marketing budget with tough times. This will frequently compound your problems.

On the other hand, you must be merciless with nonessential or luxurious expenses. As an illustration, Chuck Ritzen of the Ritzen Group, turnaround consultants in Nashville, Tennessee, describes a remedy for one deeply troubled business. "We scooped up the books and took control of the cash flow. We parked and sold company cars, called in credit cards, stopped bonuses, fired seventeen people, changed the compensation system, changed the management system, and told every employee the company could die if we didn't work together toward salvation."[4]

The degree of bloodletting depends on the amount of hemorrhaging within your own business. Sometimes your turnaround strategy may require fast, drastic, and short-run results. You don't want to alienate your good long-term customers and vendors, yet you must be brave when cutting in such areas as nonessentials, fixed costs and overhead (land, buildings, etc.), and superfluous administrative operating costs.

Worksheet 5 can assist you with your own turnaround business strategies. It is based on sound theory, and the questions give some practical thoughts for a touchy but common problem for shoestring sellers: surviving until the good times roll around again.

Further Resources

For more information, see the following, which are listed in Part III—Further Resources:

- *Business Organizations, Agencies and Publications Directory*
- *Free Money for Small Businesses and Entrepreneurs*
- Small Business Administration
- *Small Business Sourcebook*

WORKSHEET 5

Checklist for Dealing With Downturns

	Yes	No	Not Sure
1. Have you identified key problem areas that are responsible for your losing customers?	____	____	____
2. Did you get rid of unproductive products and employees?	____	____	____
3. Are you giving more attention to your core products and/or customers?	____	____	____
4. Could product lines be consolidated to save costs?	____	____	____
5. Should you delete any vendors or middlemen who are not carrying their fair share?	____	____	____
6. Should your purchasing system be reviewed?	____	____	____
7. Can you sell off excessive inventory and equipment?	____	____	____
8. Do you have control of cash flow?	____	____	____
9. Are you analyzing cash flow more frequently—monthly, weekly, or even daily if necessary?	____	____	____
10. Can you tighten your accounts receivables and get customers to pay faster?	____	____	____

(Continued)

WORKSHEET 5 (*continued*)

	Yes	No	Not Sure
11. Is there a better way to reduce short-term debt?	___	___	___
12. Have you adequately tightened expense accounts, employee perks, and nonessential expenditures?	___	___	___
13. Should you pay only the most pressing items to keep the doors open, such as utilities, payroll, and key suppliers?	___	___	___
14. Could you be more aggressive with your "dead-beat" receivable accounts and still collect from those way-overdue accounts?	___	___	___
15. Can you better extend your own debts and accounts payable schedule?	___	___	___
16. Are there inefficient assets that are drawing cash?	___	___	___
17. Are you directing your selling efforts where you can get the fastest payback in sales?	___	___	___
18. Should you offer additional incentives to reward good selling efforts?	___	___	___
19. Is the promotion budget adequate to fight the downturn?	___	___	___
20. Could you share some promotional costs with business associates, suppliers or vendors, or middlemen?	___	___	___

	Yes	No	Not Sure
21. Should your business be reorganized?	——	——	——
22. Can you obtain a bigger line of long-term credit, find additional investment partners, or sell new stock in the public sector?	——	——	——
23. Do you have to boost public image or employee morale?	——	——	——
24. Do you have team players and the support of your employees, sales reps, and vendors to implement the turnaround successfully?	——	——	——

$

Employee Backing

As a business owner or marketing manager, you've just come up with what you think is the best marketing campaign in your company's history. You hold an employees' meeting to tell them about the plan you've developed and to let them know that they are responsible for its success. You're met with disinterested stares. After several months you realize that your socko marketing campaign isn't succeeding like it did on paper when you devised it.

What's wrong?

Perhaps your employees aren't enthusiastically backing your campaign because you neglected to ask for their input. Although you may think the campaign is the best ever, maybe your employees could have given you a different viewpoint on the basis of their dealings with customers. "The most elaborate business plan, the most innovative product, the best-conceived marketing strategy will come to little if the people responsible for its realization fail to perform the way a computer model predicts they will," says Bradford F. Spencer, president of Spencer, Shenk & Associates, Inc., a behavioral consulting firm based in Los Angeles. His company provides research-based business information and development assistance primarily designed to optimize human resources.

Although your employees aren't embracing your marketing campaign, everything may not be lost. Perhaps a simple morale boost is all your employees need. "American companies with a history of high employee morale often tend to outperform their competition," says Spencer.

Morale plays a major role in how employees react to new procedures and strategies. "If a change in routine is perceived by the employees as burdensome or disruptive, their commitment to the program's success is likely to be less than total," says Spencer. "There may be compliance, but it is often perfunctory and ineffectual."

To ensure that employees accept their roles in any new marketing or management procedure, managers must create a psychological sense of ownership of the new concepts, he says. If you involve employees in the development of company goals and make them responsible for achieving and determining the best means of obtaining those goals, employees will be more likely to perform beyond management's expectations, says Spencer.

"Workers are more likely to adopt a new program if they feel some responsibilty for its creation," he says. "In several instances, applying this technique in marketing and sales has produced results that surprised management, because the input of the front-line sales staffs allowed the companies to realize results in excess of their projections and goals."

For example, Omnivest, a direct-sales company specializing in investment-grade coins, faced an erratic performance level by its sales force. Quotas were rarely met and sales tended to fluctuate near the desired level, but usually fell somewhat short of management's goals.

A three-month experimental program was implemented that allowed sales representatives to establish their own quotas. Management first conducted a training program in goal setting that focused on the need for establishing realistic standards, and representatives were shown the importance of setting goals that were achievable but that required some extra effort. During the experimental period, management held weekly meetings with the sales reps to help keep the program in focus.

Several positive results emerged. The sales reps set significantly higher goals for themselves than management had. And, although the majority of reps did not achieve the ambitious goals they set for themselves, they did surpass both management's expectations and their previous performance levels. In the end both the company and the reps benefited. The company's revenues increased, and the sales reps' commissions were substantially higher.

"The process proved successful because management avoided the temptation to sell the workers on a predetermined set of goals," says Spencer. "By giving the employees genuine ownership of the results, the companies were able to take full advantage of the desire by the workers to prove the worth of their input, and to reap greater rewards than their own projections would have led them to expect."

Barbara Fine, who owns the Map Store, Inc., in Washington, D.C., says she, too, notices that employees perform better when they are given greater autonomy. Fine, who is well known around Washington for her innovative window displays, frequently encourages employees to test their creativity by designing displays, too. "It gives them a new curiosity about the company they work for, because the display says something about the company's image," says Fine. Employees frequently comment that when they tell people where they work, people immediately mention the festive window displays. "That gets them involved, and they take pride in the store's public image," she says.

However, Fine notes that if employers give their employees this freedom, they should not be overly critical of the results. "I've had some really imaginative displays from some people on staff, and I've had some bad ones, too," she says. "But I don't mind because they're having fun. And they know I'll pretty much accept anything."

Most important, be sure to praise employees for a job well done. Let them know their input and participation are valued. Form special committees of exceptional employees for ongoing input on various aspects of the business. Recognize all outstanding employees in a company newsletter or offer a small reward, such as a plaque or bonus. Departments that churn out exceptional work at CareerTrack, a business seminar company in Boulder, Colorado, for instance, are chauffeured to lunch in the company's limousine. As a business owner or manager, your appreciation will motivate employees to become more productive.

The lesson seems obvious, says Spencer. "Allowing employee ownership of marketing results can be as successful as employee participation in other areas of a company's business."

$

Ethics

At times, we all wonder if we're being fairly treated in the marketplace. Did the seller do us right, and was he honest in the process? Are we getting a fair deal? Will the seller stand behind his products, services, or warranties?

The subject of ethics periodically concerns potential buyers. Consumers who have been previously mistreated may be afraid to make a future purchase or patronize an establishment. They may have been burned by a business within a certain industry and now—rightly or wrongly—are afraid of all firms within this industry. This fear must be eliminated before a sale can be made.

The buying process entails some natural risk. This uncertainty is compounded with high-priced items (like autos, homes, and appliances) or with hard-to-measure professional services, such as with doctors, lawyers, dentists, and consultants.

Shoestring marketers cannot afford any consumer doubt about ethical practices. Prospective buyers must have complete faith and confidence in you and your offerings. Spending money to convince people of your integrity may be extremely costly.

High ethical standards do not guarantee business success, but low standards will eventually cause failure. Once a tarnished image is created, it's difficult to increase sales and turn the business around.

To help you identify and prevent any misunderstandings, the American Marketing Association (AMA) has developed a code of

---

TIP: Communicating Your Code of Ethics to Your Customers

By letting your own customers or prospects know that you're sensitive to their needs and adhere to strict professional morals, you can put them at ease—and increase your odds of making a sale. In our own work, we have developed a list that is germane to business consulting, writing, and investigative reporting. Here is our personal code of ethics:

It is our sincere desire and practice to always strive for the highest professional and moral standards. The following points are our own self-imposed rules and regulations:

1. Work to the best of our abilities to meet the client's needs.
2. Avoid the client's organizational politics and minimize threatening situations to the organization's employees.
3. Always respect the confidentiality of the client's proprietary information.
4. Never pad the expense account or increase the "load" time.
5. Perform our assignments in an objective, candid, and honest manner.
6. Eschew tasks beyond our capabilities.
7. Refuse work that results in a conflict of interest by advising clients' competitors.
8. Earnestly try to meet reasonable deadlines that are mutually agreed upon.
9. Initiate a follow-up on a completed assignment to determine if the clients' needs have been met.
10. *Primum non nocere*, above all, not knowingly to do harm.

ethics, which offers a clear focus and some guidelines on ways to deal fairly with customers, organizations, and in general, with society.

If you are confused about a complex question or customer issue, the AMA code serves as a handy reference point. The answer to what is ethical is not always so simple; therefore, the AMA's definitions provide a good beginning for making judgment calls.

Since the AMA's specific list of suggestions is quite long (you can contact AMA in Chicago if you want the full list), we won't enumerate all of them. Their suggestions are classified by the areas of:

- Honesty and fairness
- Product development and management
- Promotions
- Distribution
- Pricing
- Organizational relationships

This entry is not intended to imply that you're unethical or engage in questionable business practices. Remember, some skepticism in the marketplace is normal.

As a shoestring marketer, you must put potential buyers at ease. A good way is to post your own and/or association rules and regulations at the office, store, waiting room, or any other place buyers may likely see them. You may even include your ethical standards on stationery, brochures, sales letters, or some other customer communication medium. We've found this practice to be appreciated by customers, and it makes a nice contribution to selling our professional services.

In sum, two things can be done about the subject of ethics: (1) identify the rules and ethical issues that are of interest and concern to your customers, association, and yourself, and (2) let everyone know about your high standards of conduct so that there is no hesitation to buy from you.

$

Exporting

Surprisingly, foreign markets offer good revenue opportunities for many low-cost marketers. The size of your business or association should not preclude you from exporting. According to the U.S. Department of Commerce, three of every five U.S. exporters have fewer than 100 employees. It's a misconception to believe that exporting entails big bucks and a complex marketing plan.

Commerce Department experts say that if your firm is successful in domestic markets, there's a likelihood that you can sell your products to foreign customers. Advanced planning, market research, attention to detail, and simple hard work are the keys to success.

Yet small- and medium-sized businesses in the United States export only about 6 to 7 percent of what they produce. In one recent Commerce study, it was concluded that there were roughly 11,000 U.S. manufacturers with export potential that were not exporting.[1] Another study conducted by the Department of Commerce and Judd Kessler, an export attorney in Washington, D.C., estimates that about 35,000 small- to me-

dium-sized companies are sophisticated enough to export but
never get around to starting a program.[2]

Where to Start

How do you get started? Or, if you're already selling abroad, how
do you expand your modest export program?

Luckily for low-cost marketers, a wealth of free or inexpensive
services is available. Since governments want economic growth
and a positive foreign exchange, they are aggressive in providing
exporting advice.

Your own state agency is a good starting point. Look in the
Yellow Pages of the state capital; many state agencies even have
in-state toll-free numbers. Don't get discouraged if you're unable
to locate the correct governmental official and department right
away. After a few referrals, you'll be switched to the right people.
We have personally found state governmental officials who are
very dedicated and helpful consultants to exporters.

Many state governments also publish their own comprehensive guides to aid your exporting endeavors. Here are some examples:

> *Florida Export Guide*
> *Wisconsin's International Trade*
> *Exporter's Guide for Maine Manufacturers*
> *Exporter's Assistance Guide, Minnesota*
> *Tennessee Export Guide & Services Directory*

These guides, which are either free or very modestly priced,
provide a wealth of information on starting an exporting business. For example, the Tennessee guide contains detailed information on:

- Organizing for export and six tenets of professional exporting
- Exporters' service contacts

- Preparing for the international market
- Financing the export sale
- Getting the export sale
- Processing the order
- Appendixes (documentation advice, common exporting mistakes to avoid, building your own export library and professional sources)

Many state governments will also provide specific information about foreign countries or businesses that are looking for particular products or services to buy and export intermediaries that could facilitate export sales. One state offers a free computer printout called a "country-risk survey" with data on types of economy, Export-Import Bank coverage, market opportunities, transfer position and trends, remarks, and recommendations for exporting. It also gives a free computer printout on data about individual overseas importers and other foreign businesses looking for certain products or services.

As a shoestring marketer, you would be making a grave mistake if you ignore your own state government. Eleven states now spend more than $1 million a year just to stimulate exports in their states. (California, $5.7 million; New York, $3 million; and Minnesota, $2.6 million are the biggest spenders.)

The federal government also has a wealth of free or low-cost information and advice about exporting. Its *A Basic Guide to Exporting* (available from any government bookstore or from the Superintendent of Documents, Washington, D.C. 20402) is an excellent source. It details the decisions you must make, the knowledge you need for profitable exporting, as well as where you can get additional information on specific exporting questions. The guide contains numerous references to persons and organizations who can assist you—often at little cost. For example, the U.S. and Foreign Commercial Service of the Commerce Department's International Trade Administration has offices in seventy U.S. cities with trade specialists who are knowledgeable about exporting.[3]

Other popular, helpful and low-cost sources on exporting include:

- Local or regional World Trade clubs
- Export management companies
- Export trading companies
- Chambers of commerce
- Trade associations
- International trade consultants
- Commercial banks with international banking specialists

Another way to get assistance is by talking to neighboring businesses already exporting. Since you're not competing, they may be quite cooperative. They may offer some solid suggestions and names of people who may assist you. Also, if you're narrowing your choice to one or two countries, invite foreign students (high school or college) from these countries into your homes. Learn about their cultures and offer to help them adjust to the United States. While improving international relations in a small way, you'll have a better feeling for doing business abroad. This is a frequently used bare-bones approach to building a network of overseas contacts.

Finding a Product or Foreign Market Match

Can your business offerings be exported? Naturally you'll have to look for a product or a foreign market match. Interestingly, "studies indicate that a technical product with price advantages and proven acceptability in the domestic market has strong export potential."[4] However, businesses and associations with all types of products and services are finding opportunities in foreign markets.

One economical method for testing your own export potential is to look at international trade shows (also known as fairs)— inexpensive state-sponsored catalog booths for overseas shows. Sometimes you can display your catalogs, promotional literature, or even a product prototype in a sales booth (see Trade Shows). For additional advice, see the informative publication, *How to Get the Most From Overseas Exhibitions,* published by the U.S. Department of Commerce's International Trade Administration.

TIP: Locating Prospects for Exporting

The following list gives you a few specific ideas for tapping potential leads.

1. *Commercial News USA:* A monthly export magazine of the U.S. and Foreign Commercial Service, it is circulated to a readership of roughly 200,000 business representatives, government officials, and buyers all over the world. For around $75 you can place a one-time listing; each targeted region is an additional $20. The listing describes your product or service, and includes a photo or illustration.
2. *Foreign publications,* such as *Japan Import News:* They often publish news releases, new product concepts, and photographs.
3. *International freight forwarders:* Many times they possess a network of contacts who may give some leads.
4. *Trade missions:* These are sponsored by various government agencies. Many states make a practice of sending government officials to foreign markets to promote certain industries in their own states.

Source: "Made in America Sells Abroad," *In Business* (September/October 1987), pp. 30–32.

To order, write to the Superintendent of Documents, U.S. Government Printing Office, Washington, D.C. 20402.

If you're still worried about finding leads or about the complexities of exporting, you could use an export management company (EMC), a private firm that acts as your own export department. It is an inexpensive way to start exporting. For a commission, fee, or retainer plus commission, these firms will sell your offerings abroad along with other allied but noncompetitive product lines. There are more than 2,000 EMCs in the United States. Most are small and usually specialize by product, foreign market, or both. Select one that understands your products, business, and foreign market targets and has well-established networks of foreign distributors.

Lloyd Hackman, president of Ribbon Technology Corporation and former winner of the U.S. Small Business Administration's Exporter of the Year award, suggests allowing a contractual period of around six months with an EMC. You can measure performance at the end of that time, such as number of contacts and actual sales. He believes that a year is too long a trial period.[5] Other export experts disagree. And some excellent EMCs may desire a one-year minimum trial period. Occasionally it takes six to twelve months before seeing some export sales. To prevent problems, carefully check the prospective EMC's references if you're negotiating a longer commitment.

Another issue to consider is the EMC's territorial coverage and if exclusive rights should be given to the EMC. You can give the EMC sole rights to sell your products in a particular country or region, but make sure that it will produce. Set some performance standards. Like kids in a candy store, EMCs' eyes are sometimes bigger than their stomachs. Evaluate whether they have the resources, dedication, and expertise to be given a large market.

Erik Wiklund, author of *International Marketing: Making Exports Pay Off*, believes that EMCs are useful in a low-cost, barebones exporting plan. He notes that they provide easy access to a number of lucrative foreign markets. First decide on the specific role you want the EMC to play and then look for the company or companies that best fit your needs. "Check references," cautions Wiklund. "Ask questions like: What countries are covered? How many lines carried? What major manufacturers represented? How long have you been in business? How many people are on the road?" Wiklund's sound advice is crucial in picking an EMC.[6]

For more information on EMCs, you might want to read some of these nominally priced publications:

U.S. Department of Commerce, *The EMC—Your Export Department* (Washington, D.C.: Government Printing Office).
The National Federation of Export Management Companies, New York, will give a list of EMCs for different regions.

The Directory of Leading U.S. Export Management Companies (Fairfield, Conn.: Bergano Book Company).

Two other exporting alternatives are remarketers (companies that purchase products and then package and mark them for their own specifications) and piggyback marketers (international firms do the actual selling and distributing because they want to sell a full range of products). But select these associates carefully because you lose control over your promotional efforts. Will they fairly price, promote, and service your products? *A Basic Guide to Exporting* gives additional information on these options, as well as other material on export trading companies, export merchants, and country-controlled buying agents.

Leigh A. Weiland, export consultant of the Tennessee Export Office, offers some basic advice for businesses new to exporting. "Do not be discouraged by the wealth of paperwork in exporting," she says. To save some headaches that small businesses could encounter, take advantage of others' exporting experiences by joining world trade clubs, associations, and exporting councils. "You can meet a good number of qualified people who are in exporting, including freight forwarders, international marketers, and government leaders."

Where to Find Financing

In financing your export sales, there are many avenues: the Export-Import Bank, Small Business Administration, Overseas Private Investment Corporation, Department of Agriculture (all in Washington, D.C.), state and local export programs, factoring houses, commercial banks, and some export trading or export management companies. There are ample programs to assist you with export financing, which may prevent a cash flow crunch.

Exporting is one area where there may be more free and low-cost assistance than any other area. Our government wants you to be successful, and it backs this up with a variety of resources at your disposal. Even if you're doing well in domestic markets, foreign business may offer additional growth or higher profit margins, counteract slow periods, or even give you personal satisfaction in your contribution to worldwide economic development.

For a checklist to control your decision points for exporting, a good source is *Essentials of Export Marketing* by Peter B. Fitzpatrick and Alan S. Zimmerman. This "AMA Management Briefing" has an export marketing checklist, a good starting point.[7]

Essentials of Export Marketing also contains a list of the most common mistakes made by exporters, as follows:

1. Failure to obtain qualified exporting counseling
2. Insufficient commitment by top management to overcome initial difficulties
3. Insufficient care in selecting overseas distributors
4. Chasing orders from around the world without a market analysis
5. Neglecting the export business when the U.S. market booms
6. Failure to treat international distributors on an equal basis with domestic counterparts
7. Assuming that a single marketing technique will be successful in all countries
8. Unwillingness to modify products to meet regulations
9. Failure to print message in locally understood languages
10. Failure to explore the use of an export management company
11. Failure to consider licensing or joint-venture agreements
12. Failure to provide servicing for the product

Further Resources

Business America—Worldwide Business Opportunities Section
International Trade Administration
U.S. Department of Commerce
Washington, D.C. 20230

Offers details about licensing, joint venture proposals, and opportunities to sell to foreign enterprises. Biweekly, $2.50 per issue; $57 per year. Send orders to the Government Printing Office, Washington, D.C. 20402.

Exhibits Schedule: Directory of Trade and Industrial Shows
Bill Communications
633 Third Avenue
New York, New York 10017

Schedule of trade, industrial, and public trade shows throughout the world. Information includes show name, sponsoring organization, address of contact person, number of booths, dates, and location. Published annually in January. $90 includes July update supplement.

Export Promotion Calendar
International Trade Administration
U.S. Department of Commerce
Washington, D.C. 20230

Lists Commerce Department–sponsored trade fairs, exhibitions, and other promotional events to market U.S. products overseas. List includes trade missions, technical sales seminars, and catalog exhibitions. Dates, locations, contact person, and other pertinent information. Published quarterly; free.

Importers and Exporters Trade Promotion Guide
World Wide Trade Service
Medina, Washington 98039

Lists more than 300 foreign trade organizations, foreign chambers of commerce, American chambers of commerce abroad offering trade services, and publishers of books and periodicals on world trade assistance. $5.

In addition, see the following, which are listed in Part III—
Further Resources:

- Department of Commerce of the United States—International Trade Administration
- *Export Licensing*
- *International Directory of Marketing Research Houses and Services*
- *International Directory of Published Market Research*

$

Free Lectures

If you learned that a book author was going to lead neighborhood youngsters on a "bug hunt," wouldn't you be curious to know what he was up to? Hugh Danks, who wrote *The Bug Book and Bug Bottle* (a children's book published by Workman Publishing Company, 1987), gave free slide shows and lectures for children in the cities he visited during his media tour. After the lecture, the children played games—like Bug Bingo—that tied into the book. Danks also took children on a bug hunt to find some of the creatures he had just talked about.

The Audubon Society of Portland, Oregon, hosted 170 children, more than sixty parents, four television stations, a major Portland newspaper, and radio commentators during one of Danks's bug hunts. The production was not only a hit; it was a sell-out. Of the eighty-five books the Audubon Society had in stock, only a few were left after the event.

The bug hunt and lecture "also helped sell a lot of other books in our bookstore," says Bob Wilson, business manager of the Audubon Society of Portland. "The bookstore is a good source of revenue for our organization. We like to attract programs like that to draw people to our facility."

If you have the time, giving free lectures is one way to increase recognition of your company or association. Although the publisher covered Danks's traveling expenses, the example can apply to anyone who wants to draw attention to his association or business. And organizations like the Audubon Society can use guest speakers as a revenue generator or a way to attract new members. Wilson, for instance, had seen a blurb in *American Bookseller* that Danks was going to be doing a tour to promote his bug book. He contacted Workman Publishing to see if Danks would be interested in stopping in Portland.

You don't have to travel far and wide to find a captive audience. Your own community is filled with opportunities to give free lectures. Women's groups, Rotary clubs, book clubs, garden clubs, social services groups, and adult education classes, among others, generally welcome guest speakers who have something interesting to say. Wilson calls it a "good way to combine a marketing approach with a good community-related program."

To make your lecture memorable, be sure it's pertinent to the group you're addressing. Don't just ramble on about your own company; that would be more of a sales pitch than a lecture. Talk about the history of your particular industry or noteworthy advancements in your industry and where it is headed in the future. Tailor the lecture to each audience. Make them feel as if they play an important role in what's going on in your industry.

To promote audience participation, you might follow Danks's example of making up games that tie into the lecture. Ask trivia questions about your industry or important people in its history. If you are a car dealer, for instance, offer some interesting trivia about Henry Ford. Or ask everyone to name the model of their first car—this usually brings back fond memories and establishes goodwill with the audience. If you're trying to downplay the negative image of car dealers, ask a couple of volunteers to do some role playing. This ought to give everyone a good laugh while providing you the opportunity to point out misconceptions about car dealers.

Take the opportunity at the end of the lecture to distribute discount coupons, company literature, or free samples. Follow up with a note to each individual, thanking them for the privilege of speaking to them.

You may not see an immediate result from your lecture, but if you have established a good rapport with your audience, their patronage or referrals are sure to follow.

$

Free Samples

One of the best ways to get people familiar with your product is to give them free samples—if you can afford it. People love freebies, and your generosity generates goodwill among prospective customers. Depending on your product, you can find freebie lovers at softball games, parades, church bazaars, community fundraising events, bingo parlors, local organization meetings—there are as many opportunities as your imagination can come up with.

Sophia Collier, president of American Natural Beverage Corporation, turned people on to her Soho soda by offering free tastings at convenience stores. It cost her no more than the price of a posterboard sign and a folding table. Check first with the store manager before you set up.

Nancy and Teressa Ellis, a mother-daughter team in Alexandria, Virginia, that publishes the *Washington Metropolitan Women's Yellow Pages,* found that distributing free copies of their directory at conferences, seminars, trade shows, and luncheons not only generated future sales but also gave them leads to potential advertisers. "When I see a conference advertised, I call the number in the ad," says Teressa Ellis. "I tell the person who answers exactly who I am, what I want to do and ask if distributing free copies is feasible. If so, I ask who I should talk to to work out the logistics."

Ellis says that conference and expo organizers frequently let people set up booths or tables to distribute hand-out material. Often exhibitors are required to pay a fee, but Ellis says the cost is well worth the exposure. Small conferences usually charge under $50 for a table; larger conferences may charge more than $100.

At the Mega Marketplace, a large expo in Washington, D.C., sponsored by the Small Business Administration, Commerce Department, and National Association of Women Business Owners to help women find contract opportunities with government agencies, Ellis distributed more than 2,000 copies of her publication. She paid $200 for a booth. "I sold five or six ads for the next issue, which more than paid for the booth and the books distributed," she says.

Ellis suggests making a colorful sign to advertise your booth at expos. "Do something to attract people to your table," she says. "I dress all in yellow, which matches the color of the book. It seems goofy, but it works."

Some smaller conferences may allow you to distribute your product only if you participate in the conference. Usually this means giving a speech about your industry or organization. (See Free Lectures.) Though giving a speech may not be what you had in mind, it's another way to get exposure and develop credibility with your target market. Being a speaker invites people to discuss their ideas with you after the conference. "We get good feedback on the directory when we speak," says Teressa Ellis, "and this helps us know what to do differently next year."

You can find local associations listed under "Associations" in the Yellow Pages. The National Trade and Professional Associations of America directory, which most libraries have, also is a good source for targeting a receptive audience for your product or service. Call or write association headquarters for schedules of conferences. If any are planned for your area, ask who to contact for information on distributing free samples.

In addition to distributing through conferences and expos, Nancy and Teressa Ellis give free copies to area doctors and dentists to put in their waiting rooms. Teressa says she's received many calls from people wanting to order copies because they had seen the ones they had placed in local chambers of commerce lobbies.

Giving out freebies worked well for the Ellis enterprise. After only one year of business, they increased ad sales 50 percent, and they generated a profit by their second year.

$

Gimmicks

The world's largest ice cream cone, a tweezer-proof vest, a chopped liver sculpture of Brooke Shields. Gimmicks—or "media events," according to public relations people—are designed to get publicity for your company. They're usually inexpensive, creative, and funny. They can increase customer traffic in your business or raise money for your organization. But gimmicks—if not well planned or executed—can bomb or, worse, embarrass your company or organization. Diane Shrago, senior vice-president of S&S Public Relations, Inc., well known for the gimmicks it has staged in the Chicago area, offers some guidelines to follow when creating the ultimate gimmick.

• Gimmicks are risky, says Shrago. They have to be extremely well planned from start to finish, or the desired effect could backfire. Gimmicks should also be used only occasionally. Sponsoring a gimmick every month, for instance, could diminish their effect.

• A gimmick should be outrageous but not offensive. Often there is a fine line between outrageous and offensive, and "you have to be very careful not to step over that," says Shrago. Get opinions from employees or friends about whether the gimmick may be offensive.

• A gimmick should be pertinent to your company or cause. You want people to associate the company with the gimmick when they talk about the event with friends.

• "The biggest is always the best," says Shrago. Nothing attracts the press better than touting a gimmick as the biggest in the world. Shoot for the *Guinness Book of World Records*, the encyclopedia of gimmicks and crazy stunts. S&S once built the world's largest ice cream cone in the world for a local ice cream parlor. It stood ten feet tall and was filled with more than fifty gallons of vanilla ice cream. It cost less than $1,000 to build; the cone itself cost only $200, says Shrago.

• Make sure the press knows who's sponsoring the gimmick. Sometimes the gimmick itself can attract so much attention that the sponsoring company or organization is overlooked by the press. When Ugly Duckling Rent-A-Car first sponsored the Great American Duck Race in Deming, New Mexico, it was virtually ignored by the media. The Tucson, Arizona–based franchise set up a booth to sell and give away promotional items, donating some of the proceeds to charity. But the press was more taken with the irony of the race's five-time winner Robert Duck (yes, that's his real name) and his champion fowls.

"You have to be very blunt with the press about mentioning the sponsor," says Shrago. But when the sponsor is credited, it's well worth the effort. "The *Wall Street Journal* did mention Ugly Duckling, and that alone was worth the cost of the promotion."

• Donate some proceeds or leftovers—in cases where a company has fifty gallons of ice cream from its world's largest ice cream cone that it needs to get rid of—to charity. Shrago's ice cream parlor client frequently donates ice cream to the local children's hospital or nursing homes. Donating to charity usually always attracts positive publicity, not to mention boosting company or member morale for doing a good deed.

• If your gimmick gets widespread, good publicity, be prepared for a huge influx of orders, calls, and customers. Not being prepared can kill your business, says Shrago. Several years ago, S&S came up with an idea for "fortune bagels"—the Jewish equivalent of fortune cookies—for a local delicatessen-bakery. The gimmick was such a success that the company nearly went bankrupt.

A Chicago TV reporter for an NBC affiliate had done a segment on the fortune bagels, and the story made its way to Linda Ellerbee, who anchored the show "Overnight." She opened up several bagels, which contained fortunes in English and Hebrew, on national television. Associated Press and United Press International wire services also picked up the story and sent it to newspapers across the country. Orders for the fortune bagels poured in, says Shrago, and the little bakery, though it tried valiantly to honor the orders, couldn't keep up. "It was an idea that should have been done by a much larger company—one that could have handled all the orders," she says. "Unfortunately, they weren't able to capitalize on their good publicity."

• The best gimmicks are timely. Shrago recalls a hit gimmick that was not only outrageous but timely. When S&S Public Relations was a start-up company, it represented a small restaurant in Chicago that was widely known for its chopped liver. The president of S&S, Steve Simon, arranged to have a local artist fashion a sculpture of Brooke Shields (because she was very popular at the time) out of chopped liver. He paid the artist $200 for his work. The chopped liver sculpture was pictured in *People* magazine and warranted one of *Esquire* magazine's "Dubious Achievement" awards.

• Look for photo opportunities. Local newspapers are always looking for good photo fillers, and gimmicks should always lend themselves to a good shot. One hot, lazy summer newsday, the same ice cream parlor that sponsored the world's largest ice cream cone created a double-cone ice cream treat and had twin four-year-olds mug and eat it for the camera. The photo and a mention of the ice cream parlor appeared in the *Chicago Tribune*.

If you can't get a newspaper photographer to attend the event, arrange for an independent photographer to take photos and send them to local papers. Provide a brief description of the event, including who or what is pictured in the photo, as well as your company or association's name and phone number.

• A gimmick should not be so wacky that your company loses its credibility. Know when your gimmicks have served their purpose and move on to other marketing techniques. Dal La Magna, who founded a Long Island–based personal grooming products company, loved his gimmicks but knew when to quit. Until La Magna started Tweezerman, Inc., there was nothing funny about stainless steel tweezers, or any other personal grooming product, for that matter. But La Magna knew he would have to do something out of the ordinary to get attention for his fledgling company. He first tried a normal route by taking samples of his tweezers to a grooming industry trade show, but exhibitors and attendees had no interest in his product. To get their attention, La Magna stuffed slabs of Styrofoam under his shirt, stuck tweezers all over his chest, and walked around introducing himself. Naturally, people couldn't resist checking out his tweezers. And the magnetic La Magna carried off the stunt tactfully. He started getting orders, and sales took off. La Magna also promoted his product by hauling around a six-foot pair of tweezers he fashioned out of wood. The curious were informed that the smaller version had a lifetime guarantee. Today Tweezerman grosses more than $1 million annually and offers a full line of grooming products carried by stores like Neiman-Marcus and Bloomingdale's. La Magna, however, no longer relies on gimmicks to get the word out about his product. "After you become successful, you have to get serious," he says. "You don't need to do crazy things to sell your product."

• Be prepared for the unexpected. There is nothing more serious than a gimmick that flops, especially if you invest a lot of money and time into it. One way to circumvent a flop is to have a solution for anything that could possibly go wrong. For example, one Valentine's Day, a Chicago ice cream and candy store had arranged to present the oldest woman in the city with a heart-shaped box of candies. S&S, the firm that coordinated the campaign, located a 103-year-old woman and sent out press releases with her name, age, and details about the presentation to local media. The woman died a day before the promotion. Though the firm had done its homework and presented the next oldest person, a man, with the box of candy, there was no way to avoid an awkward meeting with the press people who appeared the next day.

• Beware the consequences of a poorly planned gimmick. "A gimmick can result in negative publicity if not well thought out," says Shrago. She recalls that one start-up public relations agency thought it had come up with the ultimate attention grabber. The firm represented an exotic bird show that was coming to Chicago. Along with the typical press releases announcing the event, the firm sent live birds in small cages to the local media. Not only was the local humane society after the firm, says Shrago, but a television news program "showed what the firm had done, mentioned the firm's partners by name, and said that never in their lives had they ever seen anything done in such poor taste. It was in the papers. It was a total disaster."

• Always be honest with the press. Have facts and background material about the company or organization ready for the press when it asks for it. Never try to cover up for not being prepared. It can be a source of negative publicity or no publicity at all.

• A word of caution about sponsoring celebrity look-alike contests. If this is the way you choose to get publicity, make sure the celebrity you select and the prize you offer will draw contestants. S&S arranged a Superman look-alike contest for a new restaurant after the release of the movie *Superman*. There was a great turn-out of press people to cover the event—but no one entered the contest. The restaurant was clever enough to make lemonade out of lemons and served the press free dinners and drinks. The media were so impressed with the restaurant's sense of humor about the flop, as well as its appetizing fare, that several favorable articles were written about the restaurant.

• To get the press to attend the event, make press releases creative and use clever plays on words to pique the media's interest. Have fun with the release, but make sure to give all the facts about the event and then follow up with a phone call to remind reporters of it. "If you want the press to be there, you've got to call every one of them," says Shrago. "A lot of times they don't receive press releases, or releases get lost in the shuffle."

$

Home-Based Businesses

Home-based businesses—also known as the cottage industry—
are emerging as a viable alternative for some shoestring sellers.
A survey by the American Telephone & Telegraph Company estimated that 23 million people work at home nationwide. The
survey also showed that 13 percent of all households contain a
business, and more than half of these are full-time operations
that provide the major part of the household income. In addition, the results show it's more common to sell a service from
home than a physical product: 24 percent provided services; 16
percent sold products; 11 percent offered crafts or handwork;
and 10 percent sold bookkeeping services.[1]

The Department of Labor believes that half of the U.S. work
force may be working at home within the next ten to fifteen years
and that currently more than 13 million people—12 percent of
all U.S. workers—have home-based businesses or are corporate
home workers. The *Chicago Tribune* estimated that 10 million
Americans had cited their home address as their place of business on tax returns, a 50 percent increase over a decade ago.[2]

If you are a shoestring marketer, a home-based business is a
possibility for you. The market and local zoning laws for business may be your determining factors.

Overall, the usual benefits for a home-based business are lower start-up and fixed costs and overhead. There are usually fewer commuting expenses and less commuting time. You may realize some tax benefits if you have a home office. (Check with your accountant, though. The IRS has become extremely strict about business deductions for home-based businesses.) Perhaps the greatest benefit is the additional flexibility in your life-style.

There can be disadvantages, too, among them cabin fever, isolation from the traditional work world, cramped or inappropriate space, poor location, restrictive zoning laws, limited homeowners' liability insurance, more discipline needed to develop consistent work patterns, irate neighbors, and lack of personal home privacy.

Nevertheless, a variety of businesses are suitable for home operation. According to Ron Eastman, who sells sporting goods franchises out of his Minneapolis home, "Businesses that do not require that much space and staff, such as child care, tax and financial consulting, catering, lawn care, and home decorating, can easily be done in the home."[3]

Further Resources

For further information on starting and/or managing a home-based business, you could turn to some excellent sources:

National Association for the Cottage Industry
Chicago, Illinois

The 30,000-member association publishes a bimonthly newsletter, *Mind Your Own Business at Home,* and a quarterly publication, *Cottage Connection.*

National Home Business Report
Naperville, Illinois

A quarterly newsletter for people who work at home, edited by Barbara Brabec.

Women Working Home: The Home-Based Business Guide and Directory
WWH Press
Norwood, New Jersey

This excellent resource guide gives detailed information on marketing, financial, and legal aspects of working from the home. The coauthor, Marion Behe, is also founder of the Alliance of Homebased Businesswomen, Midland Park, New Jersey.

Home Businesses
U.S. Small Business Administration

This booklet is no. 2 in the Small Business Bibliography series. It contains a list of sources for some specific home-based businesses.

How to Make Your Home-Based Business Grow
New American Library
New York, New York

This book by Valerie Bohigian was published in 1986, $3.95.

$

Involvement in the Community

When Joan Bedell moved from southern California to a small, closely knit resort village of 6,000 near Lake Tahoe to set up her Pak Mail franchise (a packaging and mailing service), she knew that getting involved in the community was the only way to attract business. "To be successful here you do get involved in the community because it's so small. The highlight of activity here is probably a high school basketball game," says Bedell. "You have to be real careful with your image in a small town. You can't appear as if you're not going to be involved because people will take their business someplace else."

To start her service off on the right foot, Bedell asked the local high school band to play at her grand opening. "If you can imagine an entire marching band playing at a shopping center . . . it definitely got people's attention," Bedell jokes.

Bedell is just one example of how small companies mix civic involvement with business to boost their image in the community. It's only natural for people to prefer patronizing businesses that have an interest in the community over large, impersonal enterprises.

The community offers endless opportunities for a business to get involved, such as supporting a favorite charity or sports team or raising money for local school or church organizations. Whatever the deed, the business is helping raise the community's standard of living—and that is ultimately good for business.

Many restaurants and bars sponsor local softball teams, printing their company names on the team jerseys. These businesses are contributing to the team spirit of the community and getting some great advertising at the same time. If you're a bakery, why not donate cookies to a blood drive? You could serve them yourself out of boxes imprinted with your logo, or you could request that the volunteers place a sign at the recovery table saying your bakery donated the cookies.

Bedell asked the high school's band students to wrap gifts at her Pak Mail store during the Christmas season as a way to help them raise money for new uniforms. She charged customers $2.50 per package for gift wrapping, and the band received $1 for each package they wrapped. The fund raiser not only raised money for the band but increased customer traffic at Bedell's store.

Says Bedell: "It really did get the interest of the community. The parents were really pleased by that and I got a lot of favorable comments. It was a way of getting myself introduced, because no one knew what Pak Mail did." But Bedell didn't sponsor the fund raiser just to boost business—although that was a pleasant side effect. "I had seen a large article in the local newspaper about the band coming back after not having funds to play for five years, and they were using uniforms that were eight years old. They needed community support," she says."I played in the band years ago, and I have always been partial to the band, so I called to offer support."

Because the fund raiser was such a success, the French Club called Bedell to see if she would also help it raise money. Bedell says she plans to make supporting the school an ongoing project.

Barbara Fine, who runs the Map Store, Inc., in Washington, D.C., has also adopted a local school. To improve geography awareness among grade-school students, Fine regularly gives in-store lessons to students at the Capitol Hill Day School. Some of Fine's employees, who are geographers, explain how to use maps and globes and show the children how many different kinds of maps there are for different purposes. After each lesson, Fine gives the children bags stuffed with a miniature atlas, a map of the United States, and a balloon.

To celebrate geography awareness week, Fine asks the students to design their own maps of real or imaginary places. "They make some marvelous maps," says Fine, who puts the colorful creations in her store's window display. "One little girl named Kate did a map called Kate's Peninsula," recalls Fine. "We had several customers come in and want to buy the maps because they were so cute."

Fine not only wins young fans through her geography lessons; she attracts a new clientele as well. "All the kids come by at one point or another with their parents," says Fine. "Some parents even take pictures of their kids in front of their [homemade] maps in the window." And she says that customers really don't seem to mind having the children in the store. "They just walk around them and step over them." Most customers are amused and impressed by her dedication to community service.

While Bedell and Fine provide community service on a small scale, George Terzis's community service program has grown into an entire charity foundation. Terzis, founder of Candy Stripers Candy Company in Santa Ana, California, was inspired by his nieces' dedication to hospital volunteering—otherwise known as candy striping—and began donating scholarships out of his company's profits to other dedicated teen volunteers to further their educations in health-care fields.

To increase scholarship donations while increasing sales of his candies, Terzis developed a corporate scholarship program. When community-minded corporations buy a certain amount of Candy Stripers candy for their corporate incentive and gift-giving programs, Terzis gives them a scholarship to present to teen volunteers at the hospitals of their choice. The corporations benefit from the good publicity they receive for presenting scholarships, and teens across the country get a head start on their tuition funds. In addition to the scholarship, volunteers receive plaques and gold pendants imprinted with Candy Stripers Candy Company's logo.

"It's just a beautiful program," says Chris Terzis, George's son and the CEO of Candy Stripers. Since the scholarship program's inception in 1984, it has grown into an entire foundation for hospital volunteerism. Candy Stripers Volunteer Scholarship Foundation has signed singer-actress Shirley Jones as its official spokesperson, and is adding nursing home volunteerism to its cause.

Whatever your business or service, a cause or organization in your community is waiting for your attention. Your involvement does not have to take time away from managing the business. One restaurant, for instance, gave special cards to a local charity to distribute to members and people they were soliciting for contributions. If a cardholder presented his card at the restaurant, 10 percent of the meal tab would be donated to the charity.

Go to community leaders, hospitals, charity organizations, high schools, day care, churches, sports centers. Whatever you want to become involved in, whatever you believe in, and whatever service you think will make the most impact on the community and your business, go directly to that particular organization and ask how your store can help.

Joan Bedell, for example, joined two community improvement committees of her local chamber of commerce and asked her county commissioner to appoint her to several community advisory boards. "I think that's one way to really meet the people who would use my services."

$

Joint Distribution

Joint distribution, piggyback marketing, strategic marketing alliance: they all mean the same thing: pooling marketing efforts of two or more companies whose products or services complement each other to get a bigger bang and distribution reach for the buck. For our purposes we'll call it joint distribution, because, frankly, we needed a chapter that began with the letter "J."

A small business or association can benefit greatly from an alliance with a larger business by having access to its advertising efforts, mailing lists, distribution channels, suppliers, creative staff, and a host of other firmly established marketing elements. The objective of any alliance is to steer each other's customers into each other's businesses.

The payoffs are many. Greater visibility and brand awareness via a doubled audience, better image (a big company may help a small company overcome its mom-and-pop image), new ideas for ways to increase sales, and the ability for a company to appear bigger than it really is by becoming a part of national campaigns that normally would have been cost prohibitive are just a few strategic alliance benefits.

But along with these payoffs comes responsibility. Increased visibility and brand awareness, for instance, mean increased demand for the product or service. Be prepared to fulfill that demand.

The quality of your alliance with another company is as important as the quantity of the market it delivers. All companies convey an image to the marketplace, and, whether intentional or unintentional, your alliance will transfer your partner's image to your company and product, says Chet Swenson, president of Marketing and Financial Management, Inc., the firm that organized cooperative programs for Reebok/Lincoln-Mercury/Bally Fitness Corporation and General Nutrition Centers/fitness walking clubs.

Disneyland, for example, is family oriented, and its alliance with Sears has been very successful. Such an endorsement can be a powerful marketing tool for a company—especially one with a bare-bones budget. On the other hand, when a company teams up with another firm, it carries all its image baggage. Choose your joint distribution partner wisely, investigating its historical reputation. Mobil Oil, for instance, frequently airs its political views in the mass media. A company not sharing Mobil's views would not want to form a strategic alliance with it. Doing your homework up front will help avoid any embarrassments.

An example of a small business that developed a successful strategic alliance is Health Communications, Inc., in Washington, D.C. It piggybacked on several large businesses to introduce TIPS (Training for Intervention Procedures by Servers of Alcohol). This is a nationwide skills training program designed to educate employees in effective ways to prevent alcohol abuse in any setting where alcoholic beverages are sold, such as hotels, restaurants, bars, amusement parks, and sports arenas. For a fee (paid by either companies or the employees themselves), TIPS participants take courses on alcoholism prevention; they are tested and certified to safely serve alcohol. TIPS also offers a course for people who want to be TIPS trainers—also for a fee.

Health Communications was born out of a nonprofit organization founded by Dr. Morris Chafetz, an authority on alcohol abuse and director of the National Institute on Alcohol Abuse and Alcoholism. Nonprofit programs traditionally do not have much—if any—marketing funding. Likewise with Chafetz's start-up Health Communications, Inc. However, Chafetz did have contacts at Anheuser-Busch and Miller Brewing Company from his studies of alcohol. He also had contacts at major insurance companies across the country.

Capitalizing on these contacts, he arranged for a network of Anheuser-Busch and Miller distributors—as an extra service to their customers—to train tavern owners and employees to spot and prevent alcohol abuse in their establishments. Chafetz also persuaded a number of insurance companies to provide incentives for establishments to have their employees TIPS certified by offering discounts of 10 to 25 percent on liquor liability insurance.

A strategic alliance has to be mutually beneficial to both partners. The beer distributors, for instance, were providing a service—which offered the chance of discounted liquor liability insurance—to clients that they could not otherwise provide due to lack of independence, expertise, and credibility. Health Communications benefited from the enormous channel of distribution that would have taken years to form on its own. The alliance literally launched a business that now no longer relies so heavily on its beer distributor network. Health Communications trains up to 5,000 people a month who want to become certified alcohol servers or trainers.

Where do you find a good joint distribution or strategic alliance partner? The best place to start is within your own family of suppliers and vendors. Study other successful alliances and see how you can plug their strategies into forming your own alliance. You may even find an overlooked networking opportunity within another alliance that your company can fill. Look within your own community for alliances with schools, local churches, civic organizations, and related but noncompeting businesses that you can share marketing dollars with. And don't forget about your competitors. Occasionally they may be receptive to cooperative advertising campaigns.

Further Resources

Standard Rate and Data Service—Co-op Source Directory

Standard Rate and Data Service, Inc.
MacMillan
3004 Glenview Road
Wilmette, Illinois 60091

Lists more than 3,700 cooperative advertising programs offered by manufacturers across the country. Information includes manufacturer name, address, phone number, contact person, products, participation percentage, and other specifications. Biannual, $124 for one issue or $149.40 for both.

$

Kudos (Tickler File)

This entry is devoted to quick and innovative tickler ideas that you could start using in your business immediately. We offer kudos to the creative shoestring marketers mentioned for their entrepreneurial spirit and drive.

Free Market Research

"So many companies miss tremendous opportunities to get free market research," says Phyllis Z. Miller, a marketing consultant in Los Angeles. One way you can obtain valuable customer input is by asking your customers for suggestions. It does not take any time away from your busy schedule, and it's as easy as putting blank cards by the cash register. Place a sign by the cards asking customers what products they would like to see in the store that the store doesn't already carry. "People love to give you their opinions," says Miller. "Let them fill out the cards, including their names and addresses while you're ringing up their sale." This technique tells you not only what your customers want but who they are.

Follow-Up

Now that you know who your customers are, let them know their patronage is appreciated. "This encourages repeat business and recommendations," says Miller. Send customers a postcard thanking them for their business or give them, as preferred customers, advance notice of a sale. One retail store in Maryland requires all salespeople to write at least three thank-you postcards to customers each month.

If you've purchased some inventory that a customer has suggested, let him know that it's in stock. "People want to feel special, and a follow-up validates their initial purchase and makes them feel appreciated," says Miller. "It's easier to sell them again than new customers who don't know about you."

Judy Greason of the Bay Window Boutique, Rye, New York, sends birthday cards to her customers. She gets their addresses from checks and from a guest book in the front of the store. Greason asks them to include their birthdates with their names and addresses. Greason and her employees address the cards by hand and sign it, "From Judy and the girls at the Bay Window." She says customers really appreciate the personal touch. "Some customers will make a special trip to the store just to thank us. And some say ours was the only card they received."

Say Thank You

Another free marketing technique often overlooked, says Phyllis Miller, is thanking a customer after a purchase. "I watched a salesman take money for an entire computer system and not say thank you or escort the customer graciously to the door," she says. If you want to encourage repeat business, reassure the customer that he or she has made a good choice by shopping at your store and that you appreciate it. "It doesn't cost you a penny, and it can increase sales dramatically since so few marketers do this," says Miller.

One way Greason thanks customers is by mailing festive surprise coupons with a seal that hides a 15 to 50 percent discount on merchandise. Customers are invited to bring the coupon to the store, where a salesperson will remove the seal to reveal the amount of the discount. Greason buys her surprise discount coupons from Business Boosters, a company in Mesa, Arizona, that creates promotions by mail.

How's Your Advertising Doing?

Are you getting the most for your ad dollars? Unfortunately most small-business people—who can afford to advertise—don't. "A business recently showed me a new ad to be run in the *Los Angeles Times*," says Phyllis Miller. "I asked, 'But how do you know whether this ad entices more people into your store than the old one?' They admitted they didn't know."

How do you find out which ads are pulling in the most customers? When serving customers or answering an inquiry over the phone, simply ask, "How did you hear about us?" Consider dumping the ads that customers do not mention.

Educate the Customer

You've got to tell them, tell them what you told them, and then tell them again. "Know what makes your business unique from the customer's viewpoint, not yours, and make sure the customer appreciates that uniqueness," says Miller. Don't assume that because you're offering a lifetime warranty that potential customers will know that every other company offers only a one-year guarantee on the same product, she says. "You must educate your customers to appreciate the value you offer them."

Pool Association Members' Talents to Raise Money

Every Christmas season, members of the Washington Area Printmakers Association put together a beautiful, eclectic collection of their silkscreen prints, linocuts, intaglios, and etchings for a calendar. Each month features a new, original print that can be easily detached from the calendar for framing. All works are signed and numbered by the member artists. The calendars, which sell for about $75, are usually sold out within two months of publication. Advertising is mostly word of mouth in addition to brief paragraphs in local newspapers.

Projects such as this are a way to use members' talents to raise money for an organization, as well as gain recognition or publicity in the community.

Use Your Neighbors

When business gets slow at Judy Greason's women's apparel and gift shop, she sends her employees to the salon next door. No, they're not getting make-overs; they're modeling the Bay Window's latest fashions for the salon patrons. "The customers of the salon love it, and the salon owners love it because we're entertaining their customers," says Greason. "It's amazing how much business we get from that."

A midwestern video store draws business from salon patrons next door too. The video store's marketing manager persuaded the salon to buy a VCR and several monitors so its patrons could watch video movies while they're getting glamorous. Each monitor is imprinted with the video store's name and logo. The video store lends the salon free videos each day. Salon customers appreciate the service; the salon owners get free videos; and the video store gets a steady stream of customers as they leave the salon.

Make Your Advertising Pay for Itself

When a midwestern video store wanted to distribute a coupon book to the surrounding community, it went to other businesses for funding. Local businesses paid the video store an advertising fee for inclusion of their coupons. The video store used the advertising funds to cover production costs and produce a snappy coupon book imprinted with its logo that would conveniently hang on customers' doorknobs at home or work. Consumers were easily reminded to take their coupon book with them on errands; participating stores received inexpensive advertising; and the video store received free advertising. Other businesses have done the same thing with calendars and other items used frequently by consumers.

Make Your Store's Packaging an Event

Instead of buying plain, white paper bags for her store, Judy Greason uses a florist's cellophane corsage bags. For small purchases, Greason stuffs a clear bag with pink tissue paper, ties it with pink and silver ribbon (the colors of Greason's store and signage), and puts a silver logo sticker on the finished product. The bags cost only two cents each but make a big impression on customers. For larger purchases, she uses hot-pink gift boxes imprinted with her silver logo sticker. "Some people say, 'You should see how many pink boxes I have under my Christmas tree,'" she says. "The fact that you can't wrap them (because they're too pretty) means you can't hide the logo, either. People walk out swinging them as they leave the store."

Customer Service With a Twist

Don't be afraid to ask customers to help with the business, says Judy Greason. When she began compiling a mailing list, she found it was a time-consuming task without the aid of a computer. Luckily, a special customer came to the rescue: "I'm fortunate enough to have a customer who just retired, and she loves her computer. She computerized all our mailing, and every time I need names for direct mail, she'll put them on self-stick labels."

Don't Forget Your Name

The following slogan appears on the inside paper part of a wire hanger: "We [*heart*] our customers. Your Garment Care Center."

This expression shows how a small dry cleaning/laundry business appreciates its customers.

However, there's one costly mistake: The owner should have included the firm's name because there are more than ten similar businesses in the area. (One of the nearby competitors has "One-hour Martinizing Certifies the Most in Dry Cleaning" on the paper covering a wire hanger.)

Moral: When you're trying to communicate with the marketplace, be sure the name of your establishment is prominently displayed. It makes good selling sense, and the extra cost is usually modest.

Stuff It

Donna Seitzer, owner of a yarn shop in St. Peter, Minnesota, recommends slipping advertising stuffers into customers' bags at point of purchase or mailing them with monthly statements. The stuffers may be coupons, consumer tips, newsletters, upcoming sales notices, promotional flyers, or a questionnaire about the shoppers' experiences. The last stuffer—in survey form—might give you some good selling ideas. "A completed and returned questionnaire could be good for a small discount on the next purchase," says Seitzer.[1]

Smart Suggestions

One of the biggest selling mistakes is poor suggestion selling. When a customer does make a purchasing decision, you have a wonderful opportunity to ask if he would like a related product or service to go with the purchased good:

- "Would you like a matching tie to go with the suit?" (Classic example)
- "We are well known for our homemade desserts. Would you like to try one?" (Small restaurant)
- "Would you like a low-cost homeowner's contract to protect your heating system?" (Small heating and cooling contractor)

With good employee training, you may substantially improve sales through suggestion selling. Classic Car Wash Company in middle Tennessee has carefully emphasized this selling technique. Every employee is taught to stress the extras that can be purchased at little additional consumer cost (but nice added profits to the car wash): "Sir, we have a special on our total works car wash program," says an enthusiastic employee who first greets the customers.

Emphasize suggestion selling to your customers while avoiding high-pressure tactics. It's sound low-cost marketing.

Art for Business's Sake

A founder of a small, quaint, country inn restaurant took a historic building and refurbished it. She currently serves excellent homecooked food from famous recipes of the Southeast.

To create a lovely, historic southern atmosphere, she carefully selected from aspiring artists original oil paintings that blended in nicely with the wallpaper of various rooms. She borrowed these beautiful paintings free because the artists wanted the much-needed publicity and exposure. More important, the pictures created an elegant and beautiful image and decor that complemented the type of meals served.

A Van, Doughnuts, and Ten Pounds

Sharon Bendickson, founder of a successful small home and office cleaning business in Milwaukee, says that one of her wisest and most inexpensive marketing approaches was putting a big sign on a van she purchased for her business. "I would park in very high-traffic areas—especially in front of banks or a Mister Doughnut shop—to give passersby an opportunity to see my van," she recalls. "At the doughnut shop, I would sit and drink lots of coffee and eat doughnuts. Eventually people would ask about my services." This visibility gave her excellent leads to numerous sales presentations, which resulted in a number of new accounts when business was slow. Bendickson also met other small-business owners at the doughnut shop and ended up chatting with them about how to improve their own operations.

This marketing ploy was great for building a successful stream of steady customers. While exposing the van to a high-traffic area was fantastic for business, it created another problem: Bendickson "gained ten pounds from eating all those doughnuts."

As a side note, Bendickson sold her business to relocate with her husband in another town. But the advice she gave customers at the doughnut shop about starting their own businesses spawned another company for her. She enjoyed the informal counseling sessions so much that she is now an instructor and counselor for entrepreneurs for the state of Wisconsin.

A Gourmet Image

A small midwestern retail shop located in a well-to-do neighborhood desired a high-class image and began carrying expensive and exclusive brand-name items. To project an upscale image, the owner serves gourmet coffees and teas in a sitting room. The hot beverages also give shoppers time to reflect on some major purchasing decisions. This added service is fairly inexpensive. The clientele—mostly couples without children—are neat and orderly and rarely spill, so clean-up costs are nominal.

Because many of the retailer's items have a very high profit margin, the added expense for coffee and tea and the nonselling area is modest in comparison to the traffic it generates.

Quiet Room

Many rock-group promoters find that attendance increases when a quiet room is provided for the parents or grandparents of teen rock fans. This quiet room may have books and easy-listening background music typically enjoyed by the older set. Parents also tend to feel more confident that their children are safe since they are in the same building.

Often customers—especially teens—are unable to purchase or consume a product without the help, such as transportation, of another group. If your business fits this scenario, be sure to satisfy the influencers who decide if your target market can consume your product or attend your event.

Class Act

Jay Lauer, of Event Coordinators, Inc. in Milwaukee, Wisconsin, had a problem getting the attention of busy executives. Most managers are bombarded with promotional flyers, brochures, and sales letters from vendors of products or services. Because there is so much competitive clutter and frequent business mailings, promotional direct mail materials are often discarded quickly or easily misplaced.

To overcome the attention problem, Event Coordinators rented a tuxedo, purchased fifty special packaging tubes, and hired a college student to make deliveries. The student called on fifty highly selective prospects and personally delivered the tube containing the company's promotional literature and a personal letter.

The delivery person told the secretary or receptionist that the contents were only for the executive on the address and that he had specific instructions to deliver the contents personally. This method is quite dignified and gives a professional image. According to Event Coordinator's president, the technique was so novel that most people allowed the delivery person past the door.

The total fixed costs were estimated to be a little over $200, and the part-time delivery person earned $25 for any sale that was made.

Reading Material

A few retailers find it helpful to include some magazines and a comfortable area in their stores for pleasure reading. For instance, a small, independent specialty women's apparel store provides a reading area stocked with business and sports magazines. The spouses or male friends of the shoppers spend their time reading instead of waiting impatiently. The cost is nominal.

Retailers that offer this service say that shoppers—especially women—are pleased with the concept. Instead of merely glancing quickly through the store, the shoppers have more time to browse. And with more time to shop, they frequently increase the amount they originally intended to purchase.

Free Résumés

A small northeastern corporate professional employment agency gave a lifetime guarantee of providing a free résumé service to its clients—and previous clients. While this may seem like an expensive and time-consuming service, the agency generates a constant stream of viable candidates to place. The agency's principals say that producing a résumé is a minor expense compared with the thousands of dollars that may result if they make an executive placement. As clients gain status and experience, the types of jobs they seek offer higher compensation, resulting in higher fees for the agency.

The service also helps attract first-time clients who like the idea of getting some assistance on future résumés. By offering this service, the agency not only gains goodwill but finds it less expensive than buying advertising space.

Hold, Please

Don't put your phone customers on hold with a radio station that could be advertising your competition. A case in point: Don Weinrauch's wife was placing an order for meat from a local butcher when he had to put her on hold. While waiting for the butcher, she heard a commercial that advertised outstanding meat selections from a major supermarket. This small butcher shop was giving free air time to a major competitor. Telephone customers on hold are a captive audience when they have something to listen to on the other end. What happened to the woman waiting for the butcher? She decided to buy a roast from the supermarket instead.

Shoestring marketers cannot afford this type of gaffe. Even a simple and seemingly minor incident like this can have a negative impact on sales while helping the competition.

$

Leasing

Like many young, single people starting out in the work force, many small-business marketers cannot afford to buy their own home—that is, a worksite facility. Because the cost of land and building are too expensive for their shallow pockets, they must rent or lease for a while. In fact, it's frequently more prudent to invest money in the business and operations than the overhead, especially when starting out. Your own limited resources may be better spent on marketing and developing the business. As your business grows and is successful, it may be wise to invest in fixed assets.

The Small Business Administration (SBA) publishes an excellent guide, *Locating or Relocating Your Business*, which gives some excellent points for making a leasing or buying decision:

1. Are your requirements going to change rapidly over the next few years? If they are, you should probably consider leasing.

2. Do you find yourself in a very short supply of capital? Can you use your available money better if it's not tied up in a build-

ing? What return can you expect from your funds if they are invested elsewhere? If your capital is tight, leasing may be preferable. (Lack of capital is one of the most important reasons for leasing.)

3. Can you secure a favorable lease from the owner of the building with an option to purchase? Because of tax considerations, a property owner may prefer to lease the property rather than sell it. In such a case, he is likely to make the lease price more attractive than the selling price. You should explore this possibility.

4. Your accountant can advise you how leasing or purchasing might affect your financial picture. If you can buy property at a favorable price and the purchase does not cause a shortage in your working capital, purchasing may be indicated.

5. Consider resale. Is the building one that will be readily resold? If so, to purchase may be wise. On the other hand, leasing may be better if there is something about the building (for example, little or no adjacent land for parking or plant addition) that would limit resale of the property.

6. Some states and cities have revenue bonding programs, tax forgiveness, and other assistance. Check your state or local economic development group to determine what help is available.

If you do decide to sign a lease, be sure to read the contract carefully. Even though it will cost a few dollars, have an attorney explain the proposed lease agreement to you. It may even be necessary to negotiate some clauses, make counterproposals, or include your own escape clause. There are some vital issues to consider:

- Should you include an excessive vacancy clause?
- What happens if surrounding stores from the same landlord are unoccupied for too long?
- Can you break the contract if the desirability of the shopping area is rapidly deteriorating?

Before signing a lease, see if the rent, as a percentage of fore-casted or actual sales, is in line with your own industry figures. You can contact the appropriate trade associations or look at fi-nancial publications (such as the Robert Morris publications on financial data for certain industries).

To save some costs, you may be able to pay rent as a percent-age of net sales or profit. This method may then allow you more money for promotion. However, many landlords may dislike this percentage approach and do not share your entrepreneurial spirit. But you may find a landlord who is flexible. Perhaps you could find a site where the landlord needs help in fixing the building up. With "sweat" labor, you may significantly reduce the rent.

The specific lease arrangement depends on comparing the cost of rent with your feelings for potential sales. Be somewhat con-servative on forecasted sales; otherwise your uncontrolled enthu-siasm (along with the landlord's optimistic feelings about the property) could create a poor leasing agreement.

$

Location

You probably have heard the trite but famous real estate advice about buying a home: To experience homeowner appreciation, the three keys are: location, location, location. And probably you've also heard this adage: It's better to buy the cheapest home in an excellent neighborhood than the most expensive home in a fair or poor neighborhood.

Like serious home buyers, shoestring marketers must be extremely careful about their business locations. A location that offers inexpensive rental fees may still be quite costly in other aspects. For example, it could be too far from suppliers and customers or have inadequate traffic flow. On the other hand, a costly location may take too big a bite out of the revenue your business produces.

Therefore you must consider the costs versus benefits of a certain location site. "For our particular business, location has been the key to increasing sales and profits," says Marvin Adkins, founder of a grocery store, mobile-home park, and laundromat within the same cluster site in Knoxville, Tennessee. He believes a proper location can partly offset some entrepreneurial disadvantages of price, promotion, or product assortments. "Since our cluster of businesses are located on a heavily traveled road and we're several miles from the nearest competitor, we have found it unnecessary to advertise," says Adkins. "An irony here is that I used to teach two college courses in advertising." But, he adds, without the best location, he would have had to spend additional money on other marketing strategies.

Donald Hauck owned three small department stores in Minnesota, but the third store was in a poor location, and the losses from it caused him to lose all three stores. Hauck had a retailer friend who told him not to be afraid of the rent. Hauck's friend also told him that the rent would take care of itself if the location were right. Hauck selected a building primarily on the basis of price, however; a banker offered to lend him $125,000 to lease, remodel, and stock a 7,000 square foot building where Montgomery Ward had formerly been located—and the price sounded right to Hauck. This location was at one end of the business district and maybe about forty feet too far north of vital traffic flow, according to Hauck's friend. And it didn't work out. But like a typical entrepreneur, Hauck picked himself up. He opened a bridal shop, and it's right across the street from a major shopping center and has a big, lighted sign. He says the location and the sign are what draw people to his business. "I'll never again make the mistake of being forty feet too far north."[1]

It's difficult to give specific rules on selecting the very best site. Your decision depends on your market targets, traffic count and flow, competition, suppliers, location-related expenses, available financial resources, rental or building and land costs, and the type of business you are operating. For example, high-tech businesses are often located near universities, research centers, or government agencies. And to be near the political heartbeat and lobbying centers, many associations reside in Washington, D.C.

For some frugal marketers, a "quality of life" quotient outweighs traditional factors, such as cheap labor. James F. Smith, director of the Bureau of Business Research at the University of Texas, suggests that marketers decide where they would like to reside and then determine what kind of business would permit them to live there. In fact, advanced technology has allowed some businesses to be out in the sticks, points out David Burgum, president of Great Plains Software, Inc., Fargo, North Dakota. Express mail service and good telecommunications, for example, have given some businesses greater flexibility.[2]

Sometimes an old house, a factory, a barn, a hangar, a supermarket, a storefront, or even a chicken coop may suffice, says Darby McQuade, founder of a pottery business in Santa Fe, New Mexico. "You don't need to put up a fancy front. Just a place that catches the spirit of what you're doing. That's enough." Cheap doesn't always mean ugly. In the Northeast, it is often cheaper for a business to begin in a lovely, renovated mill or factory than an expensive modern industrial park. In short, it's not how much is spent on building or location but how well the money is spent.[3]

When making location or relocation decisions, use Worksheet 6 as a starting point and evaluate your own business options. The checklist identifies thirty critical factors that can offer you some insight when evaluating sites.

For further help, call your local chamber of commerce. In cities of 125,000 or more in population, the chamber may have its own division to assist you with some free real estate information. Also contact a reputable and professional real estate or business broker for advice. Sometimes they have specialists who are knowledgeable about choosing a specific business location.

Finally, you can get free information from city, county, regional, or state government agencies. They frequently collect relevant data, such as traffic count statistics, for making decisions on location.

Further Resources

For more information, see the American Economic Development Council and the National Business Incubation Association listed in Part III—Further Resources.

WORKSHEET 6

Making Location Decisions

	Favorable	Unfavorable	Not Sure
Proximity to your customers	____	____	____
Current and future traffic flow and access routes	____	____	____
Pedestrian traffic count	____	____	____
Automobile traffic count	____	____	____
Quantity and quality of competition	____	____	____
Complementary nature of adjacent businesses	____	____	____
Availability of raw materials	____	____	____
Closeness to suppliers	____	____	____
Housing availability for employees and managers	____	____	____
Quantity and quality of work force	____	____	____
Current and future labor rates	____	____	____
Environmental factors (schools, culture)	____	____	____
Adequacy of utilities (electric, water supply)	____	____	____
Zoning regulations	____	____	____
Quality of local public services (police, fire)	____	____	____

(Continued)

WORKSHEET 6 (*continued*)

	Favor- able	Unfavor- able	Not Sure
Parking facilities	——	——	——
Potential transportation costs	——	——	——
Cost of a site	——	——	——
Energy costs	——	——	——
Taxation burden	——	——	——
Vulnerability of site to unfriendly competition	——	——	——
General appearance of area	——	——	——
Topography of the site	——	——	——
Cooperation of landlord	——	——	——
Local financing arrangements	——	——	——
Local business climate	——	——	——
Direction of area expansion	——	——	——
Provisions for future expansion	——	——	——
Distance from your home	——	——	——
Does site meet your own "quality of life" expectations?	——	——	——

$

Mail Order Catalogs

Can you imagine picking out your car or home from a mail order catalog? It may happen in the not-so-distant future. Shopping at home via mail order catalogs has grown tremendously. Consumers seem to have less and less time to spend shopping, and they appreciate the convenience of a quality mail order service, especially if it has a toll-free number for additional information and quick ordering.

Selling your products or services by mail can help you expand into new markets quickly and can help you cut overhead if you don't need to operate a retail outlet also. Many companies have been launched on the success of mail order catalogs operated out of entrepreneurs' homes.

Starting a catalog is not a simple task. There are many dos and don'ts, and everyone seems to have an opinion on the right and wrong way to produce a mail order catalog. However, there are endless sources of information about starting a catalog business—as a spin-off of a retail business or as the sole channel of distribution. Libraries and book stores have a variety of how-to books on the subject. There are also trade associations that provide assistance to members and nonmembers alike, although nonmembers are usually required to pay a nominal fee for certain services and publications.

Because there is so much information about starting a mail order catalog, we are distilling only the most helpful and creative tips to get you started in the right direction.

Before you do anything, determine what you would like the mail order catalog to achieve. For example, is your goal to reach new markets or increase orders from old ones? After you've decided on your objective, identify your audience. If you don't know who you're sending the catalog to, you're taking a shot in the dark. What is your market's life-style? What can your products do for these people to make their lives easier or more productive?

Another important factor to consider is to make sure that your product can be easily transported through the mail. Would it break easily in shipping? Consider postage costs. If the product is heavy, it will be expensive to mail. Potential customers are more inclined to buy the product from a retail store than pay the extra money required to ship a heavy product. Additionally, a product that is complicated to put together or requires parts that are difficult to obtain may not be a popular mail order item. Ask yourself these questions before embarking on a mail order campaign.

The next step is determining whether there is demand for your products. Consider placing a classified ad in target publications to see if there is interest in your catalog. If you get some inquiries, start a small-scale mailing campaign. Send out a one-page flyer featuring a few items; it is far less expensive to produce 1,000 8½-inch by 11-inch flyers than an entire catalog. If you have a retail store, put the flyer in customers' shopping bags and include it in other mailings, such as credit card invoices. Make sure you have suppliers who can provide you with greater quantities of product on the spot if demand is unexpectedly large. Make sure also that you have adequate shipping supplies for mailing. These are all fundamental considerations but are often overlooked.

You may decide that you would rather be included in someone else's mail order catalog than undertake producing one of your own. If this is the case, call the catalog company directly. For a list of catalogs on the market, contact the Direct Marketing Association (DMA) publications division. For about $100 it will send you *The Directory of Mail Order Catalogs*. Your public or university library may have it.

If the results of your questioning and experimentation indicate that a mail order catalog would be a profitable way to market your product, an important first step is to develop a strong mailing list. Like company newsletters, you should have a mailing list before you develop the mail order publication. Use your current mailing list or buy one from a list broker listed in the Yellow Pages. The Standard Rate and Data Service (SRDS) publishes compilations of lists broken down by product or specific target audience. You can find an SRDS *Direct Mail List Manual* in public libraries or contact SRDS in Skokie, Illinois, at 312-256-6067.

It is also critical to draw up a written marketing plan with product description, market, marketing research, objectives, lists, fulfillment, back-end marketing, budget, and projections. A mail order catalog is a business, after all, and you should treat it like a separate extension of your enterprise.

Start collecting other catalogs you find effective and eye-catching to get an idea of what you would like yours to look like. Determine a way to make your catalog stand out from the many others stuffed into customers' mailboxes. Will you do it with interesting graphics or catchy copy? Will you use special incentives and discount offers, guaranteed customer service, or fast delivery? Whatever you decide, be prepared to live up to your claims. Be prepared also for returns and requests for refunds.

Give your catalog a theme much like the theme or philosophy your own company projects to its customers. Having a single theme helps potential customers identify the catalog with your business.

Next, create a catalog layout and copy. You can hire a professional service or do it yourself with special computer software. For a nominal fee, the DMA will send you a list of companies that sell software packages specifically developed for direct marketers. Contact the association's publications department. If software programs are not available or not tailored to your needs, the DMA will make referrals to consultants who can work with you on this.

Writing Copy That Sells

To write copy that generates sales leads, the DMA suggests following these simple guidelines:

1. Make sure that the information is useful and full of facts.
2. Let readers in on inside information that helps them do something better, quicker, less costly, or solve a problem.
3. Promise a benefit in the headline or first paragraph and immediately enlarge upon your most important benefit.
4. Tell readers specifically what they will get.
5. Back your statements with proof, experts' endorsements, and customer testimonials. But don't oversell; readers may get suspicious. The copy can be more flamboyant when announcing a sale than it should be in a serious fund-raising effort.
6. Keep phrases and paragraphs short. Underline important ideas or phrases. Stress your big selling point several times. Keep your copy flowing smoothly.
7. Reiterate prominent benefits in your closing offer. Encite action with a prestamped response card or by listing a toll-free telephone number on every page. (If you do this, however, you must have someone at the phone during the hours that you've advertised. The person answering the phone should also have telemarketing training.)

Designing a Layout That Sells

To create an appealing layout, follow these ten basic rules of layout established by Thomas Register and found in the Thomas Register of American Manufacturers and the Thomas Register Catalog File:

1. Avoid fancy typefaces. Stick to simple, legible type.
2. Use readable type for your body copy (at least a 9-point type size).
3. Use subheads to break up copy and assist readers who merely scan your copy.
4. Use a number of small tables rather than a few, all-inclusive ones.
5. Avoid technical, highly complicated graphs unless you are sure your readers need and understand the information.
6. Use well-prepared photographs and illustrations. They communicate better and give a quality image.
7. Use continuing design or running headlines to help a reader know whén a product description is carrying over onto several pages.
8. Change your design motif when a new section is introduced.
9. Don't construct your layout page by page. Design in spreads (two open pages side by side). This is how your reader sees them.
10. Use color functionally to describe how products work, to highlight features, or to provide organization.

An additional note: the layout and graphics should be different in presenting a big-ticket item as opposed to a low-cost item.

Additional Tickler Ideas

• Take advantage of your 800 number if you have one. Include it on every page and encourage customers to use it not only to place orders but for additional information on orders already placed.

• Include helpful information, like short how-to articles by company experts on making the most of your product. If you are selling office equipment, for instance, an office manager may be lured in by an article on how to increase worker productivity. You might subtly show how your products can lead to the favored result.

• Provide information on shipping, such as "most orders shipped within 48 hours." If an order is not delivered within the advertised time period, refund postage and handling.

• Use a different color other than the headline to highlight "New" or "Sale" in a headline.

• Print "Priority Handling—Rush This Order" on reply envelopes.

• For customers who have not placed an order after two catalogs, send a note with your next catalog asking how you can provide better service. Enclose a reply card with feedback questions. Make it clear that if the card is not returned or an order is not placed, you can assume only that they want to be taken off the mailing list.

• Leave spaces on the order forms for people to write in names and addresses of other potential customers.

• Send "preferred" customers (they can actually be customers who consistently place orders or you can tell everyone he or she is a preferred customer) a card in an envelope with a $5 gift certificate and a letter from the president.

• Offer multiples of lower ticket items, like "a set of three for $15," to increase order size.

• Send additional order forms for additional parts or complementary products to a customer's order with the order shipment.

• Include teasers, like "lift this flap and find your special discount offer inside!" to involve the reader.

• Insert in orders two extra order forms for friends or for reorders.

• Print this special offer on order forms: "Nobody home during the day? We'll ship to your work address."

• Send a personal cover letter with your catalog. Even if it is a form letter, it has a more personal appeal than the catalog alone.

• Offer an extra incentive, like 10 percent off the price, to customers who enclose full payment with the order or order two or more or one of each color.

Once you get heavily into the mail order business, you will want to keep it very organized. Investing in special bookkeeping software is wise.

Like any other marketing strategy, don't expect one or two catalogs to produce instant results. Many readers will save the catalog and order from it when a need arises.

As a side note, once you have a mailing list of 3,000 names or more, you might consider leasing your list to a mailing list broker. This is a little extra money maker, and you still retain the right to mail to your list.

Self-Help Publications

William A. Cohen, *Building a Mail Order Business* (New York: John Wiley and Sons, 1985).

Katie Muldoon, *Catalog Marketing: The Complete Guide to Profitability in the Catalog Business* (New York: AMACOM, 1988).

Julian Simon, *How to Start and Operate a Mail Order Business,* 4th ed. (New York: McGraw-Hill, 1987).

Further Resources

• ***Direct Marketing Association Great Catalogue Guide***
Direct Marketing Association
6 East 43d Street
New York, New York 10017

Lists 740 mail order catalog companies.

In addition, see the following, which are listed in Part III— Further Resources:

- *Direct Marketing Marketplace*
- *Directory of Mailing List Houses*
- Mail Advertising Service Association International
- *Marketing Communications—Directory of Special Agencies Issue*
- National Mail Order Association
- *Standard Rate and Data Service—Direct Mail List Rates and Data*

$

Manufacturers' Reps

Many businesses cannot afford their own sales force. The overhead, salaries, incentives, training costs, fringe benefits, and expenses for keeping them on the road are prohibitive. They must instead resort to an outside sales force, called manufacturers' representatives, agents, or independent salespeople.

About 50 percent of U.S. firms use some outside agents. For small businesses and associations, this percentage is a lot higher. And it appears that the use of reps is steadily increasing in all types of industries. If you are like many other shoestring marketers who must carefully watch costs, cash flow, and overhead, you should seriously consider the merits of using or expanding the role of sales agents.

Bert Casper, vice-president of marketing for Remmele Engineering, Inc., St. Paul, has developed a comprehensive network of manufacturers' representatives throughout the United States. He says that reps provide the least expensive sales coverage available to a small company that is interested in marketing over a big area. They are paid a commission only when they make a sale, and you share the cost of maintaining a good sales organization with the rep's other principals. Casper believes that it's almost impossible for small businesses (machine shops are his industry) to finance a good, nationwide direct sales force working exclusively for one shop. Within its industry, his firm is well known for a successful outside sales organization.[1]

Your organization doesn't have to be in the machinery industry to use reps. Says James Gibbons, president of the Manufacturers' Agents National Association: "Remember that an agent only gets paid if he makes a sale." Anthony S. Vespoli, a former direct salesperson, sales manager of over 200 rep firms, and now an independent rep in his own electronics business in Ashtabula, Ohio, notes that established reps know the best companies for handing over leads for proper follow-up. "Through painstaking effort, reps can also identify the prime customers (and the most credit-worthy), so a company doesn't have to sort the wheat from the chaff at its own expense."[2]

Whether your small organization is in a manufacturing or a service field, profit or nonprofit, or in the entertainment, publishing, wholesaling, or retailing field, an outside sales force could offer you a viable and low-cost way of building revenues. There are reps who represent products or services from A to Z. We even know of some small businesses and nonprofit organizations where 100 percent of their revenues are generated from the outside sales force.

The following list summarizes the advantages and disadvantages of using reps:[3]

Advantages	*Disadvantages*
Reduces fixed costs and administrative demands	Divided loyalty among different principals
Costs more predictable, no expenses	Carries many items
Overcomes cash flow problems	May sell competing goods
Gives immediate market access and penetration	Harder to train, monitor, motivate, and control

Shares advertising and promotional costs	In-depth product knowledge may be lacking
Provides experienced sales force	Customer may not be sure if deal should be made with the reps or the principals
Offers wide variety of markets	
May increase frequency of calls per customer	Potential communication problem with another layer of people
Lowers cost of training	Could be mere order takers
Offers industry market intelligence	

In studying these pros and cons, you can see that reps provide excellent market potential at low cost. On your shoestring budget, you don't pay unless a sale is made, and the reps' commissions are factored into your selling price. On the negative side, reps must be motivated to push your products. You must work hard to convince them that it's in their best interest to sell your line of goods diligently.

Jack Miller, president of Automation Tool Company in Cookeville, Tennessee, uses reps for penetrating markets throughout the southern and midwestern territories. Based on his experience, he offers a number of good tips. First, it's a mistake to sign up a rep and expect this person to carry the ball. You have to work closely—especially the first year—with reps. He says, "With reps, you must recognize going in that they are just people and you have to maintain their enthusiasm." To maintain excitement, you need good communication, and most of the communication is from owner to rep, says Miller. Many reps take the path of least resistance and sell for products that are the easiest to move. However, Miller warns: "It's wrong to say that reps are the only way to go. If you choose to go with reps, don't expect a rep to carry the ball on his own because he will fail. He will absolutely fail."

If you want more information or are thinking of starting an

outside sales force or just want to make your current one more productive, contact the Manufacturers' Agents National Association (MANA), located in Laguna Hills, California. The MANA has more than 9,000 manufacturers' agents and manufacturers who currently hold membership. Besides publishing an excellent magazine, *Agency Sales*, which gives handy suggestions for principals and sales agents, MANA provides a superb support system for successfully using an outside sales force. Among its services are the following:

- Directory of members for networking
- Information exchange about prospective agents or principals
- Discreet counseling services for members with sensitive problems
- Special reports, research bulletins, newsletters, studies, and seminars on subjects of vital and timely interest
- A complete contract kit that covers virtually every aspect of contract law for agents and manufacturers. (Some of our own consulting clients' lawyers have used this kit to customize a legal agreement. It's excellent.)

The association also publishes a code of ethics for its members. This code of conduct enables everyone to feel more at ease with this marketing partnership. Finally, through its directory and/or classified ad section in *Agency Sales*, MANA serves as a good conduit for locating professional-level agents or principals.

Word of mouth is another effective way to locate good reps. Your customers, vendors, and business associates are quite useful. If you are going into new territories, ask potential customers about the good reps who are calling on them. Perhaps you are already impressed with some reps who call on you. Are they available and qualified to carry your line? If not, can they recommend good agents who do carry your product mix and sell to your market target?

Bert Casper warns principals to be careful in screening and selecting reps. Hire them as carefully as you would your own employees. He advises seeking reps with educational backgrounds that will enable them to understand your business and services. He emphasizes finding sales agents who are already established in their territories and cover an appropriate amount of territory.[4] We would add to Casper's qualifying list for selecting agents: the rep's current customer base, financial strength, experience, years in operation, turnover of sales staff, self-motivation, and personal chemistry with you and your own staff.

Jack Miller makes an interesting point. He believes that "sales agents are most effective the further they are geographically from where you are." They can then reach territories that may be difficult for small businesses to penetrate because of geographical constraints. Sales reps located near your business will often expect you to help call on prospects and frequently make the sales, says Miller. He thinks that too often his firm does the work *for* the reps instead of *through* the reps. Thus, Automation Tool decided to sell direct to clients located within the immediate area.

Do not be afraid if you're attracted to some sales agents who are also carrying your competitors' lines. They are able to do this since there is no exclusivity clause in their contracts. From time to time, you'll find sales agents who are quite strong in a certain market area. They have great loyalty among customers and are known for having a complete line of goods to sell. If you really want to succeed in this market, you might use these popular agents. On your limited marketing budget, this decision is often easier, less costly, and more profitable than either locating or developing new agents or employing an in-house sales force.

If this relationship is to be effective, communicate with your agents by having in-house visits, training sessions, frequent correspondence, product and promotional literature, backup technical assistance if needed, and cooperative promotional efforts. Also, be available if your agents have questions or need a little extra help to close that big deal.

You can motivate your outside sales reps by making sure that your commissions are normal or even above the norm for the industry in question. The annual *Survey of Selling Costs* (published in *Sales & Marketing Management* magazine) provides the average range of percentages for many industries:

Selected Industries	% of Commission Paid		
	High	Average	Low
Advertising products and services	24.23	16.17	8.11
Arts and crafts	11.13	8.33	5.54
Building materials and supplies	10.68	7.65	4.62
Electrical/consumer	6.70	5.64	4.58
Electronic/communications, audiovisual and professional products	10.38	8.46	6.54
Furniture and furnishings	11.86	8.75	5.65
Industrial supplies	13.80	10.29	6.78
Lumber industry	6.38	5.05	3.73
Photographic supplies	13.85	10.46	7.07
Retail consumer products and services	11.88	8.48	5.08
Robotics	12.39	10.27	8.16
Textile/apparel trade	8.37	7.12	5.87
Toys, gifts and novelties	12.82	9.33	5.85

Special contests, awards, sweepstakes, incentives, and the like will help to motivate reps to concentrate on *your* products. More important, develop a reputation for excellent product quality, service, fair prices, and promptness. Admittedly these attributes sound like hollow platitudes. Yet a good reputation will help your reps sell your merchandise and/or services. When it's simpler for them to sell and they have a higher ratio of sales to calls, they become more confident and push your goods.

You may have heard that an agent-principal alliance is only a short-term proposition. When the small business or markets become bigger, a divorce will probably occur. Yet this relationship is stable, according to MANA's latest survey ("Agents and Manufacturers Tell Why They Stick Together," *Agency Sales*, July 1987, pp. 11–15). The average number of years of the responding sales agents was sixteen; for principals, it was ten years.

According to MANA, if you use an advertising agency or

management consultants, you'll have a much shorter business relationship. In its survey summary, the association notes that despite a few businesses that jump from agency to agency, this is not the true picture that emerges from the average agency-principal dealings. It's knowing the people whom you work with, respecting their efforts, and doing whatever you can to build the relationship—as well as building sales. In the *Agency Sales* article, Charles Jacobs, owner of a Largo, Florida, agency, echoes this point: "When each partner really feels that he or she is on the other's team, there is a feeling of mutual respect."

Smart selling is the lifeline of your business. As a shrewd marketer with shallow pockets, see if you can exploit the business opportunities of using an outside sales force. If your business or organization is already using agents, can you strengthen this relationship?

Further Resources

Manufacturers' Representatives Educational Research Foundation
P.O. Box 247
809 South Batavia Avenue
Geneva, Illinois 60134

In addition, see the Manufacturers' Agents National Association, listed in Part III—Further Resources.

$

Marketing Research: Act Now

As a shoestring marketer, you often face a paradox: Your small business or organization cannot afford a major marketing mistake that drains your precious financial resources. You need important demographic information about your target market to prevent a catastrophic decision. But numerous in-depth marketing research studies can be quite expensive, especially if you take a Fortune 500 approach of trying a variety of expensive marketing research studies.

Although you may lack the vast resources for extensive marketing research, there are inexpensive sources and low-cost procedures that you can use. In the marketing research entries, we offer some helpful economic tips and anecdotes germane to marketing research. These entries are not arranged alphabetically but by the steps you may follow in doing low-cost marketing.

$

Marketing Research: Internal Secondary Data

For many decisions, you may have available information within your business, called internal secondary data. Sometimes we all ignore some excellent low-cost information that is already internally available. First, you must be aware of them. Then you need to reorganize your process and forms for gathering information.

Earlier we mentioned the importance of some internal secondary data when doing a marketing audit. For marketing research, some valuable sources are sales invoices, salespersons' reports and expense accounts, customer credit applications, inventory cards, warranty cards, electronic cash register receipts, customer correspondence, and past records of previous customers or members or donors of an association.

With proper planning and design, you can develop good forms that will provide a wealth of marketing information. These forms may easily identify the following:

- Customers' names and locations
- Credit versus cash customers
- Revenues versus direct costs of certain products sold
- Quantity of each item and price per unit

- Average dollar amount per order
- Where, when, why, what, and how customers purchase your products
- Household consumers (e.g., by age, sex, profession, income)
- Industrial customer classifications (e.g., health care, lumber, textile, and so on)
- Geographic locations by zip code
- Terms of sale and discounts
- Timing of purchase (day and time)
- Special terms

We find that many marketers must learn to cultivate and exploit the data that are readily available within the organization. Frequently small businesses and associations do not need to search beyond the organization; enough internal data may exist for making marketing decisions and carrying out effective strategies for certain types of problems. These data can be obtained with less effort, time, and money than obtaining external secondary data or doing primary research, such as a survey or marketing experiment. In addition, this internal information is usually more relevant to your marketing questions because they deal with prevailing issues within your own business. It particularly amplifies the successes and failures of certain marketing strategies.

In sum, the shrewd application of internal information sources is one of the major first steps to low-cost—and effective—marketing research. A sophisticated computerized management information system is not always a prerequisite. It's a matter of learning how to record, tabulate, and analyze the marketing-related experiences of your business.

$

Marketing Research: External Published Sources

Throughout this book, we mention good, inexpensive publications for obtaining useful information. External secondary sources—otherwise known as published surveys, studies, dissertations, articles, and so on—are another excellent low-cost way to do some marketing research.

With a limited budget, we suggest a few of the following popular sources:

1. *Sales & Marketing Management* publishes four special yearly issues: (1) "Survey of Buying Power," (2) "Survey of Buying Power II," (3) "Survey of Selling Costs," and (4) "Survey of Industrial Purchasing Power." These four sources could help you forecast sales, control promotional expenses, spot market targets, plan promotional campaigns, and analyze your marketing program. The four issues provide data on population, retail sales by selected industries, factory shipments, income by states, counties, cities, and Standard Metropolitan Statistical Areas. You could, for example, find out how many aluminum foundries are in Cook County, Illinois, by reading "Survey of Industrial Buying Power."

2. The *Survey of Current Business,* the *Business Conditions Digest,* and the *U.S. Industrial Outlook* (three federal government publications) present a good background of recent trends and future projections for more than 200 industries.

3. Census data, published by the U.S. Bureau of the Census, Department of Commerce, are available for retail trade, service industries, manufacturers, and housing. The latest *Census Catalog and Guide* is a good beginning for locating census data. It provides prices and sources for printed reports and microfiche and outlines files that are available for computer use. The census data might be used for planning sales territories, deciding on small-business location, determining market potential, examining competitive conditions, or measuring your performance.

4. If you want to do more business with the federal government, be sure to look at *The U.S. Government Purchasing and Sales Directory, U.S. Government Manual,* and *Doing Business with the Federal Government.* The *Commerce Business Daily* offers a complete listing of products and services wanted by the federal government—products and services that you may be selling. To save subscription costs, see if a nearby college library is a designated government depository library—that is, receives free copies of selected federal publications.

5. Predicasts, Inc., in Cleveland, Ohio, publishes *Predicasts Basebook* annually. This provides statistical information on past and future performances of various industries and individual products. Its quarterly *Predicasts Forecasts* contains 50,000 short- and long-range projections for products, markets, industries, and the economy. The company also publishes a weekly newsletter, *Marketing Update,* with the latest news and research findings on sales, marketing, communication, public relations, and other essential topics in marketing.

6. The *Dun & Bradstreet Million Dollar Directory* is a comprehensive listing of business firms. For individual businesses, it gives sales revenues, number of employees, four-digit Standard Industrial Classification numbers indicating lines of businesses, and names and addresses of top executives. The information may

be helpful for prospecting, credit analysis, or a competitive profile. Most public or college libraries should have this directory.

7. There are countless numbers of business abstracts, directories, encyclopedias, and indexes that provide lists of available data sources by subject matter, topic area, and the like. Also, many libraries and commercial firms offer computerized searches for locating potential sources of secondary data. A professional reference librarian at a public or university library can help you scan through the maze of secondary data searches.

8. FIND/SUP, a New York–based information and research firm, offers information services that can be electronically delivered directly to the marketer's terminal. If you don't have on-line computer capabilities, they'll send you a computer printout. The service gives reports on selected industries, companies, and demand for certain product categories. The cost of these reports may vary from about $100 to $2,000. Depending on the size of your small business, these reports may be low or high in cost.

9. Your own trade association can be a valuable source of secondary data. Good ones publish background data about members, marketing data, consumer trends, common problems and issues, operating costs data, and most important, recommendations for developing a successful, ongoing marketing campaign.

10. Clipping services that you can subscribe to review articles from newspapers and business magazines about your customers or competitors. Be sure the service covers the area where your customers or competitors operate. Usually the cost is a set monthly fee for the first business and a few dollars a month for each additional business studied, with an extra charge of so many cents per clipping.

11. Trade journals are an inexpensive source of information. Most trade magazines regularly publish reader surveys and market data on current issues. Many publishers also offer special reports and tips for selling and marketing within your industry.

As you can see, there is a variety and wealth of external secondary data. Although it's a challenge to locate and find the type of data you may need, it's one of the most economical methods of market research. Successful shoestring marketers know where and how to tap already available data.

If you're new to secondary data collection, the process will seem slow and confusing at first. But once you learn the ropes, you'll be surprised at the type of information that is readily accessible. In our own business consulting and research, we're frequently amazed at how external secondary sources have answered some tough marketing questions.

To help you with this seemingly overwhelming search, you could use professional librarians, a moonlighting MBA student, syndicated commercial data base services, trade association executives, or helpful government officials with local, state, or federal agencies. Regional offices of the Small Business Administration are excellent sources of free information on every facet of business (call your local courthouse or state capital to locate your regional SBA office). Many of these sources are either free or an inexpensive alternative to a costly in-depth survey. Often the challenge is *not* finding external secondary data but deciding on which of sundry data will best solve your particular marketing problems.

$

Marketing Research: Panels and Advisory Boards

Many small businesses, nonprofit organizations, and associations have created groups of people who serve as their sounding boards on a regular and steady basis. You can do the same. Your sounding board group can define ways to improve your marketing strategies and help you spot trends. Your accountant, attorney, banker, clergy, or anyone else whose opinion you value could sit on your advisory panel.

If you are in a private business, you may have to offer some incentive to get cooperation; some people need a strong reason to be on a consumer panel or advisory board. But for associations and nonprofit organizations, it is usually easier to attract an advisory board of volunteers who are committed to the purpose of not-for-profit organizations.

In either case, a group of individuals may offer some good brainstorming tips while preventing a significant marketing blunder. This additional type of marketing research could be extremely effective.

$

Marketing Research: Focus Groups

Group interviews are often less expensive to conduct than individual ones. You can conduct one- to three-hour interviews by having a group of individuals collectively express their attitudes, opinions, and emotions about your business, product, or industry. This group interview method usually saves precious time because each respondent need not be interviewed separately.

The most common type of group qualitative marketing research is the focus group interview. It started from psychiatrists' work in group psychotherapy. Focus group interviewing is basically an unstructured group interview of a few people—usually eight to twelve—that is led by a group leader. Freedom of expression and free-flowing ideas on some relevant topics are strongly encouraged.

Nearly every major company uses focus groups because they give extra insight into emotional responses, which is often unavailable from statistical and quantitative studies. "It lets customers express their feeling about your product," says Jay Qualman, director of advertising of the Buick Division of General Motors. "You can go into depth of why they feel the way they feel."[1]

Because you know your business the best, it should be feasible to learn effective ways for listening to the market. The key is to take an objective and commonsense approach. You must first appreciate what focus group interviewing may accomplish. Respondents provide many original and fresh brainstorming ideas that you may have ignored. They also give you a wide range of marketing ideas that could be explored or fine-tuned later. Open and frank discussion may uncover problem areas that must be addressed. Finally, an informal and relaxed atmosphere allows a bandwagon effect, which gives you more ideas than one-on-one interviews.

You don't have to be a Fortune 500 company or a psychotherapist to use this tool. You can conduct interviews wherever you find consumers—in your own place of business or on a street corner, for instance. Take along a clipboard to write down notes. Stop passersby and politely ask if they would answer a few questions. Be honest about who you are, what you're doing, and how the group or individual's opinion can help your business. Focus groups give you the goals and expectations of your consumers for your business and products.

Conducting group interviews at the site of your business can be particularly effective—if you have the space and privacy. By being on-site, the group members may more likely think of something that pertains to the surroundings of your business. On-site sessions can jog their memories on likes or dislikes.

If you feel uncomfortable in a group or too inexperienced to lead the focus group sessions, you can hire a professional marketing consultant with prior focus group experience. But this could become an expensive process. As an alternative, consider hiring school counselors or other professionals who can relate well with people in a group. You can then make your own interpretations about the information discussed in the group sessions. (We realize that this last tip is unpopular with our professional peers in marketing research. But many businesses cannot afford their expertise. Why completely forgo valuable focus group discussions because you can't hire a professional?)

You'll find that focus interviews can help you increase sales in many ways. New ideas for products, services, and revenue-producing business ventures can surface—not to mention suggestions for strengthening your marketing approach. Group members often have ideas on strategies in such areas as market expansion, selling, advertising, pricing, distribution, and dealing effectively with customers.

A small, independently owned Louisiana pipe tobacco shop experienced great success with focus group sessions. The owner picked all types of customers to attend the sessions. During the sessions, he gave them a few free samples of old and new tobacco. He encouraged candid comments about different brands and discussed the operations of his business. On the basis of the consumers' helpful comments, he made critical buying decisions for tobacco brands and also expanded in some nontobacco product lines. This latter decision helped build sales while counteracting antismoking campaigns. To encourage cooperation and participation, the sessions included postsession wine and cheese parties for the "preferred" customers. This gave the participants an added incentive to come. The costs for the owner were modest compared with the excellent marketing advice he received from the best consultants of all—his market target.

You don't have to go outside your business to find a good focus group. Focus group sessions for your own staff can also be effective, especially for associations or large nonprofit organizations with have limited resources. The Division of Continuing Education at Indiana University at South Bend had stagnant enrollments; the demand for its courses and seminars had not achieved a growth pattern commensurate with product quality. Norma Singleton, marketing manager, realized the continuing education programs' image was not clearly defined and segmented from the personal interest and leisure programs traditionally associated with community continuing education. Some type of strategy was needed to turn things around.

One staff member suggested looking at the problem from a private industry point of view, coming up with marketing strategy to promote continuing education courses. The small group process (with a focus group mission) was used to develop creative solutions to problem solving, and as a result a marketing strategy was developed. The outcome was highly positive. Not only did the program successfully build enrollments, it received the Michiana Marketing Excellence Award from the Michiana Chapter (southeast Michigan and northern Indiana) of the American Marketing Association. So don't overlook your own employees and in-house professional staff for group brainstorming sessions on ways for building revenues.

How do you know if a focus group meets its objectives? In a good session, participants will talk to each other instead of merely answering a moderator's questions from a topic guide, says Richard A. Zeller, CEO of his own research firm in Toledo. He also advises the moderator to keep the discussion on certain topics while avoiding preconceived notions about how the discussion should proceed.[2]

Robert Inglis, president of Techanalysis, Inc., a Canadian market research and consulting firm, says, "You must learn to listen critically and analytically. To get the most out of a focus group, you must learn to listen for what is not said, as well as for what is said." Inglis recommends that the moderator take notes during the sessions, jot down first impressions, and tape the sessions for later review and analysis. He emphasizes that focus group discussions need not be conducted in a special focus group facility with a one-way glass mirror for observation. He has successfully conducted sessions in hotel meeting rooms, hotel suites, church basements, and living rooms.[3]

In sum, keep an open mind about the sessions. You may uncover some things that might surprise or even disappoint you. As a shoestringer, this marketing research technique enables you to spot problems and issues that may have otherwise gone unnoticed. For your convenience, we conclude with some helpful dos and don'ts to enhance your own focus group sessions.

Do	*Don't*
Create a relaxed atmosphere	Allow one or two people to dominate discussion
Look for subtle signs and behavior	Make quantitative and statistical generalizations about your

Do	*Don't*
Carefully screen the participants. They should have some prior experience or knowledge of questions being considered	total market. This is not "nose counting" research
Jearch for the best size of the group, usually six to twelve members per session (on size, you'll learn fast from your own experiences)	Limit group conversation or pass up an opportunity for multiple social interactions
	Ask leading questions and try to pull certain answers from participants
Welcome free-flowing comments	Become emotionally involved as a moderator with the group discussion
Prepare a guide of general ideas you want to cover in the session	Ignore the tone of the respondents' voices and their nonverbal behavior (such as eye contact and facial expressions)
Check the facilities and equipment—you want a comfortable experience for the respondents	Keep the respondents for an unreasonable time or inconvenience them
Prepare realistic materials, samples, prototypes, or situations to gauge practical reactions	Forget to thank them for their cooperation
Make this an upbeat, friendly, and positive experience for the group members. You certainly don't want to alienate your customers	

$

Marketing Research: Fieldwork

After looking at internal and external secondary data, you may still have to collect primary or original information for a specific task. This means you may need to go out into the field to answer questions or solve problems.

There are some things you can do that won't bust your budget. Too often we think that marketing research always requires big bucks; an elaborate, complex, and scientific methodology; an automatic survey; quantitative and statistical expertise; and a graduate degree in marketing research. Consider instead some of the following strategies.

1. Question your friends, relatives, and close business associates about your business. Seek their ideas and encourage them to be objective in their opinions. Ask them to be a devil's advocate. They should give you the pros and cons of specific marketing issues.

Because your relatives and acquaintances may lack marketing expertise about your small business, venture idea, organization, or association, you must weigh and balance their comments. Yet they have two major advantages: (1) they are genuinely interested in your well-being, and (2) they know your strengths, weaknesses, expectations, and capabilities. If you get negative feedback, reevaluate your marketing ideas in the light of this free, friendly advice.

2. For gathering information in your marketplace, use government officials, volunteer executives, or business students. The last group may be seeking projects in the real world for course credit. You could contact the Small Business Administration, Service Corps of Retired Executives (SCORE), or a marketing research class at a local college. Perhaps college students will do a study—for example, a survey—at a nominal cost. Frequently, they want the practical experience and will charge nothing.

3. Personally interview key people—association presidents, buyers, suppliers—in your industry or in the industries or markets you are selling to. Certain people have a keen feeling about the various opportunities for increasing your revenues. Although this is not always a good representation of the entire market, it's a cheap survey technique.

Some industry people and leaders often have access to vital marketing information. If they don't, they know where to look for answers or, at the very least, tell you if that type of information is even available.

4. Traveling sales reps who call on you are excellent sources of market information. They know which companies and communities are expanding or are just good prospects, says Jack Miller, president of Automation Tool, Cookeville, Tennessee. "You get a lot of referrals and cooperation from traveling sales reps because they are trying to sell a product to you."

As an excellent low-cost research source, learn how to deal effectively with the people who call on you. Salespeople are in the field and usually encounter the latest trends and economic conditions. They are usually the first ones who find out what's happening—good or bad. It costs you very little to probe business conditions in their territories. As long as you're polite and patient, you'll find them quite helpful. Of course, avoid putting them in an awkward position by asking sensitive questions about your competitors.

5. Scan public domain documents and legal notices in your community. These data will keep you current about the local economy while giving you opportunities for prospecting, expanding your business, or starting new ventures.

Marty Flatt, owner of a small interior design service near Nashville, Tennessee, has done some frugal fieldwork by studying public domain documents. At the beginning of each month, he carefully examines the required building permits in the local county courthouse. This information gives him a picture of the economy. It also identifies business contacts, registered builders, and prospective residential and commercial real estate owners. He then sends sales letters to these prospects.

6. The *Official Gazette of the United States Patent and Trademark Office* prints reports on patented material, with data cross-indexed to the businesses filing them. You'll get a good overview of inventions and innovations. You may find these data attractive if you are in the high-tech field.

Although not all patents are brought to the market, depending on your line of business you may get some potential contacts. A review of the patent dockets may also tell you something about the competition.

7. Attend trade shows and conferences in your industry. This is an excellent—and inexpensive—way to observe your customers, suppliers, independent reps, and competitors. Ask questions and brainstorm with exhibitors. Sometimes a wealth of marketing information is given away—even by a loose-tongued competitor.

8. Scan want ads to see who is hiring and expanding. Many industrial suppliers and small vendors have found this useful in developing a prospect list. This may sound simplistic, but some entrepreneurs have made eventual sales to businesses that advertised in the "help wanted" sections of newspapers or trade publications.

9. Reverse engineering is another effective way to study your competitors' products and compare their strengths and weaknesses with your own products or services.

Ford Motor Company became well known for buying its competitors' products and tearing them down. It would slowly (1) dismantle the merchandise; (2) reassemble the entire product; (3) estimate the costs of putting the product back together; (4) establish break-even and profit projections; and (5) then compare this whole endeavor with its own products. Ford learned more about its competition, how to improve its own products, and how to promote its improved products to the customers.

As a low-cost marketer, you too can practice "reverse engineering." It's ethical and legal—as long as you don't violate any patent rights.

10. Ask for help from your large suppliers and vendors. Many of them do marketing studies on the industries and markets they are serving. On an informal basis, their sales force will often share with you some major conclusions of these studies. If not offered, ask them if they are even aware of any studies.

As a service to their customers, large vendors and suppliers also will provide some of the data in published form. First, see if any of your own suppliers have published documents and ask if you can obtain a copy. If the documents are unavailable for distribution, indirect questions may allow you to make some intelligent guesses about the contents.

11. If you're part of a franchise or license system, determine what type of marketing assistance—other than what is provided by the parent company—will enhance your individual operation. By being an active franchisee or licensee, you can learn about the dos and don'ts for building your business. Certain information, such as formal marketing research studies and experiences of other franchisees, will give you a good feel on what will work in your own marketing program. We find that the most successful franchisees-licensees are the ones who are active within their own franchising or licensing system.

12. As an advertiser, you'll have various media (for example, newspaper, radio, or magazine) sales reps calling on you. Since you're buying some advertising for your business, these reps are eager to give you information about their publications or sta-

tions. For example, they may have readership or listening surveys or data on the changing market characteristics and demographics of a particular geographic region.

Before buying media space or time, ask the salespeople why their medium is the best. Do they have any information or studies to support their argument? Do they have any secondary or unbiased information from such sources as the Audit Bureau of Circulations about their medium? More important, does their medium reach the people you're targeting? Is the advertising cost reasonable compared with other types of media?

Don't be bashful about asking these questions. You must have data to make informed and intelligent decisions on where and how to spend your hard-earned promotional budget.

13. In almost every community, there are professionals who are well connected and knowledgeable about what's happening in the local community. They have a good grasp of what products or services are needed or not needed in the area. Depending on the town, the people in the know will vary. Usually these individuals are lawyers, accountants, banking executives, publishers of local newspapers, radio or TV executives, realtors, and builders. People associated with such institutions as the chamber of commerce, country clubs, and Rotary and other professional, community, and civic organizations have a good grasp of economic community conditions and the resulting business opportunities.

Remember, the boundaries and geographic markets for many small businesses are the local communities. Thus, it's vital to develop a network of good contacts on "Main Street." This network is good for fieldwork research, as well as increasing your sales.

14. Teach your employees to be good listeners and ask probing questions of customers or prospects. Employees should learn to ask customers routinely: Is everything satisfactory? Do you need or want anything else? How did you find out about the business? Did anyone refer or recommend our business to you? Is there anything that can be done to be of better service?

Good employee training on asking probing questions has nominal out-of-pocket costs to you, yet it is an extremely effective way of improving sales. Your employees must appreciate the benefits of constantly gathering more information that will strengthen your selling and marketing efforts.

You can formalize customer feedback by using a suggestion box, wish list, order request forms, register forms, sign-up sheets for a mailing list of special sales, or a customer comment card. These economical techniques can give you some good information for building sales. They also make your customers feel special because you care and welcome their feedback.

15. Many shoestring marketers for years used the "eyeball" method—better known as observation studies. Today, with advanced electronic, automated, and mechanical technology, observation marketing studies may be done by machine—or a patient human. Depending on your time and type of small business, you could adopt such ideas as these:

- In those states where counties are shown on the license plates of cars, surveying the cars in your parking area to see where your customers live.
- Counting the number of people or cars passing a particular site (sometimes this information is already available from your state's department of transportation).
- Observing traffic flow and patterns within your business (popular in retailing).
- Counting the number of responses from a special offer from a particular commercial (for example, about 75 percent of your respondents will usually call within a twenty-four-hour period of hearing your radio or television ad if a toll-free number is given).
- Using an electronic or mechanical device, such as an audimeter or mechanical counter, to total the number of people who are watching a television show or passing by an intersection.
- Taking a walking tour of your marketplace. If you sell to businesses, try to visit some of them to get a feel for their method of operations. If you serve the household market, locate the typical residential area of your market. Observe the type of homes, cars, and atmosphere of the area.

The eyeball method of research may give you some clues and insight on ways to increase sales.

16. Try to measure the response of your promotional or marketing efforts. To test certain advertising decisions, you could use redeemable coupons in newspaper, magazine, or direct mail ads. You may try a free gift, sample, or hidden message in an ad to see how many people recall or follow through on your ad. You could code your mailing address, for example—Department BL and SL for *Better Living* versus *Southern Living* magazine classified ads, respectively. The response rate may tell you which magazine is a better draw for your business. You may criss-cross two different ads by running the ads in two different magazines. For one period, you test one ad in one magazine and the other ad in the other magazine. During the second period, you switch the ads for the two magazines. You can then compare the results to see which ad copy is pulling better.

You can directly ask your customers for the reasons why they buy from you. Their responses will tell you which aspects of your marketing are the best. The key is to look for ways to measure the results of your marketing tasks. As a frugal marketer, you cannot afford wasteful or careless marketing.

17. Test market your products, services, innovations, or small pilot business wherever you may find your typical customer (e.g., at flea markets). Consumers actually try what you want to sell. Although this method may not be a full-blown test marketing study, consumers can give feedback about your offerings. They may spot some weaknesses or ways to improve your product. Because they are the users, their insight and suggestions are often dramatic. Although the samples or testing cost some money, the marketing information will often outweigh the expenditures.

18. Survey your customers and noncustomers. It's beyond this section to explain all of the intricacies of doing surveys. However, here are a few salient tips for minimizing survey costs:
- Carefully define who you want to survey to avoid wasted responses.

- Identify your survey objectives. Know what you want to study with specific information goals.
- Try a minisurvey first to see if a major survey is even needed.
- See if you can collect data through phone interviews or mailed questionnaires. Personal interviews are expensive and not always necessary.
- Ask only relevant survey questions. Avoid interesting questions that have no impact on your future decisions.
- Whenever possible, see about using a convenience sample where people are the easiest to reach. A complex statistical random sample usually costs more money.
- To share the costs, periodically consider doing a joint survey with other businesses.
- Precode your questions on the questionnaire to eliminate high tabulation costs.
- Determine if your surveys can be consolidated to save start-up costs.
- Consider some type of incentive to encourage people to participate in a survey (especially important in mailed questionnaires) to increase the rate of returns.
- Assure anonymity and confidentiality of the respondents.
- Most important, do a postsurvey analysis to learn from your mistakes and successes.

Formal surveys are difficult and sometimes require some formal education, training, and experiences in surveying. Yet this challenge shouldn't stop you from trying to ask questions of people or organizations in your market target—even if your surveys contain only a few open-ended questions. The feedback may result in better serving your customers and more sales.

$

Marketing Research: A Final Word

We sometimes find that some small businesses and associations are afraid of and confused about marketing research, and so they ignore the benefits of doing any type of information gathering.

Marketing research is a tool, not a substitute for decision making. If you don't try to collect any information—secondary or primary—you're at a major disadvantage in a highly competitive marketplace.

This entry contains but a sampling of the variety of marketing research techniques. We focused specifically on how you can do some research on a limited budget. It's a critical beginning to good marketing. As your budget grows, you may need more sophisticated—and expensive—information.

Don't delay in trying to know more about your own business, industry, trends, competitors, and customers or prospects. In marketing, there are countless trade-off decisions on ways to invest your limited dollars. Marketing research is the artery to smart selling—especially for shoestring marketers.

TIP: Hiring Professional Marketing Research Help

As a shoestring marketer, we believe you should concentrate on the do-it-yourself type of marketing research. It will save you money while keeping you abreast about secondary data sources and your market targets. We are, therefore, biased toward doing your own marketing research.

We do understand, however, that you may feel it's too difficult and tedious to do certain projects by yourself. Furthermore, the risks of doing it by yourself may far outweigh the costs of hiring consultants. When this situation does apply, consider these tips:

1. Ask for an explanatory letter or brief written proposal that outlines your situation as seen by the prospective consultants.
2. Get the research consultant involved with your company, and give all necessary background information.
3. Challenge the researchers to find inexpensive and creative ways to do the work without hurting the results or usefulness of the project.
4. Ask for specific research objectives, research methods and logic for doing the work, maximum cost, and a time frame for completing the marketing research tasks.
5. Ask consultants to project how the results of the proposed study might be used to plan and implement specific selling and marketing strategies.
6. Develop criteria for deciding which consultants to hire. For example, you may look at:
   —The backgrounds and experiences of researchers
   —Any previous work within your industry or similar type of business
   —Length of time in business
   —Experiences in solving your type of problems or needs
   —Reputation, references, and their codes of ethics
   —Their plans for analyzing and presenting the data
   —An estimated completion date
   —Fees

Further Resources

For more information, see the following, which are listed in Part III—Further Resources:

- *Bradford's Directory of Marketing Research Agencies and Management Consultants in the United States and the World*
- *International Directory of Marketing Research Houses and Services*
- *International Directory of Market Research Organizations*
- *International Directory of Published Market Research*
- *Market Access Reports*
- Marketing Research Association

$

Names and Logos

Do you realize that you are bombarded with about 550 ad messages a day, but you probably remember only twelve of them? And the U.S. Patent Office adds 25,000 new trademarks to its registers every year. Imagine your product in a sea of brand names on store shelves. Is your product's name strong enough to surface in consumers' memories?

"Choosing a brand name that rises above the clutter and is favorably associated with its business is crucial—especially for a small company," says Laurence Ackerman, founder of Identica, Inc., a corporate identity and marketing firm in New York. "The first strategy is to obtain leverage otherwise unavailable based on financial resources. A good corporate identity can give a small company that leverage against larger companies."

The key to creating an effective name for a product, service, or business is to choose one that immediately conveys your unique capabilities as an organization. Apple Computer is an ideal example. It chose a name that signaled the most important aspect of Apple the product: its easy application rather than its state-of-the-art technology. Says Ackerman, "Apple is all about being user friendly and being simple and fun and very human in its capabilities. Apple says, 'We're fun, we're friendly, you know us, you eat us every day.'" In addition to being user friendly, the name has another dimension: knowledge. The apple—the same fruit that fell from a tree and clunked Isaac Newton on the head—is the symbol of knowledge and education.

Although at first glance the name "Apple" seems trite, with some thought—intentional or subconscious—the name evokes many connotations and associations, all of which represent the company's philosophy. This was the company's strategy in choosing its name. "The name Apple for what was then a very small company has become a compelling hallmark of capability," says Ackerman.

The best brand and company names, he says, are those that capture their target markets' imagination. "Capture my imagination and I'll never forget who you are," he says. But according to Ackerman, small businesses tend to adopt a name that is product oriented or the name of the product itself: "It's logical. Say you're going to develop a new software piece. You call yourself Software, Inc. Generic names are very typical of small company names." Small-business owners say, "'Well, here's what we're making, so let's tell people what we're making.' But that is not what moves markets, and that is the most common problem with small companies," continues Ackerman. "They look at their company as the product and their product as the company."

In general, says Ackerman, small-business owners need to take the process of name development seriously. "They're so preoccupied with product costs, revenues and profit margin, they say, 'Names? don't bother me with names, I have to worry about my revenue stream; I have to worry about my cash flow,'" he mimics. "The implication is that the whole business of identity is not looked upon as a mainstream activity," and that's the biggest misconception small companies need to overcome.

Names have a great impact on how prospective customers perceive businesses. Time and money spent on a quality name development and corporate identity program are well spent in the long run, says Ackerman: "You're going to have to give it [the company or product] a name. You might as well do it right."

Zeroing in on a particular image or philosophy with your

name can make it memorable, but there are also dangers in selecting too specific a name. If you're like most other business
owners or marketing managers, you eventually plan to diversify
the business. A small business that starts out with the owner's
name or the name of its one and only product may find itself
limited in the future when it wants to diversify into other business ventures. If this happens, it may be necessary to change the
company's name but only after careful research—preferably by
a naming or corporate identity consultant. Because you could be
throwing away thousands of dollars of accumulated advertising
and promotional efforts spent to build name recognition, you
want to be certain that your new name is worth the money and
hassle of consumer readjustment. After some research, you may
find that all your old name needs is to be revitalized—perhaps
by shortening it or giving it a fresh visual treatment of a new logo
or colors.

Also important to keep in mind when creating a name is the
possibility of someday marketing your company's products or
services abroad. Many large companies with big marketing
bucks have created name flops by neglecting to check foreign
pronunciations and slang. Chevrolet's "Nova," for example,
means "no go" in Spanish, and Colgate means "hang yourself"
when given a Spanish pronunciation. Even Coca-Cola made a
blunder when it tried to market its famous soft drink in China.
The company wanted to keep its English pronunciation but discovered—after bottling and distributing the drink—that the
Chinese translation meant "bite the wax tadpole."

Choosing a name is a highly personal and creative activity, according to the Salinon Corporation, a name development firm in
Dallas. If you plan to forgo consultants to develop the name
yourself, Salinon suggests some elements you will need to create
a successful image. The following guidelines and checklists are
excerpts from *The Naming Guide: How to Choose a Winning Name
for Your Company, Service or Product,* developed and published
by Salinon:

- Time—enough to do the job
- A good set of reference books and sources for name ideas

- Broad knowledge of your company, service, or product and a clear understanding of where it's going
- An ability to see what you're naming from the prospective customer's point of view. For the naming process you need more than an engineer's understanding of the product and the manager's grasp of your company's strengths. You have to distance yourself from what you're naming to find out how your customers perceive it—what they want from it and what it can do to fill their needs.
- Creativity and an ear for the right combination

If you meet these requirements, you may be ready for Salinon's "Do-It-Yourself Naming Checklist," a simple step-by-step guide to creating a winning name that you may find useful in your own endeavors:

1. Describe what you are naming: key features and characteristics, competitive advantages, and anything else that sets your product or company apart from the competition.

2. Summarize what you would like the name to accomplish. Should it describe an important product feature? Convey a particular image or connotation?

3. Define the types of people you want your name to appeal to.

4. List the names you like and dislike. Try to name at least a dozen in each category. What are the commonalities among the names you like? Are there certain roots or phrases that you find especially attractive? What about name length, sounds, images, and letters?

5. Write down your competitors' names. Leaf through trade journals or directories to make sure you get as many as possible. One good source for product and service names is the *Trademark Register of the United States*. It lists more than 600,000 names currently on file with the U.S. Patent and Trademark Office. Names are categorized by class to make the search easier. Most

large public or university libraries will have a copy, or you can purchase one for about $250 from:

Trademark Register
300 Washington Square
1050 Connecticut Avenue, N.W.
Washington, D.C. 20036

Consider which names you like and dislike and decide how your name could stand out from these.

6. Check the names you've narrowed down for possible off-color meanings. A good source is the *International Dictionary of Obscenities* by Christina Kunitskaya-Peterson (Oakland, Calif.: Scythian Books, 1981).

7. Conduct a trademark search on state and national level. Trademark and patent attorneys are worth the money at this point; you may value an expert's opinion about the registerability of your name, and you can save yourself hours of legal headaches, not to mention production time wasted on a name that's already taken. If you'd rather do this on your own, there are a number of services that maintain federal and state trademark data bases. Contact your state department of commerce for sources. Register your name at once when you decide on one and it has been checked.

8. Test your name before adopting it. Does a focus group like it and think it is a good name for your company, product, or service? Or does it remind them of something else? What images or connotations do they associate with it? Are they desirable associations? Can the group pronounce and spell the name correctly and easily? You should try to create a name that is easy to pronounce and looks good in print. No name will be memorable if consumers can't pronounce it. Above all, find out if the focus group can remember it or whether they confuse it with any other existing names.[1]

If you plan to create a new logo design to fit your new product or company name, you may find it helpful to follow the same guidelines as name generation. The process is fairly similar, depending on your objectives. Consult with freelance designers and artists for innovative ideas. As with a name, a logo should instantly epitomize what your business is all about. "I've developed a nice logo and I use it frequently," says Judy Greason, who owns the Bay Window Boutique in Rye, New York. "Our customers can relate to a picture. They don't have to read our name. They see our picture on our boxes and on our mailings."

Further Resources

For more information, see *Brand Names: Who Owns What*, listed in Part III—Further Resources.

$

Newsletters

"What is the best method of shaking and slicing my coal stove?"
"What is the right way to cook milkweed?" "What kinds of wood
should I burn so that I don't get any creosote?" These are just a
sampling of the burning questions answered in *Vermont Castings
Owners' News*. No, it's not some off-the-wall underground newspaper, though it does have an avid readership of thousands. It's
a tabloid-style newsletter sent to current and former customers
by Vermont Castings, a cast-iron, wood- and coal-burning stove
manufacturer in Vermont. Other typical features include articles
about life in Vermont, tips on how to improve stove performance,
recipes, profiles of distributors, notices asking current readers to
pass on a response coupon to past customers who are not receiving their newsletters, and change of address forms—all the elements of a successful newsletter marketing program.

Vermont Castings has established a personality for itself
through its homespun publication—a critical goal of any newsletter. "People like to deal with companies that have a personality. They don't like to deal with faceless, souless entities that they
can't relate to or understand," says John Klug, president of CCG
Newsletters, Inc., a Denver-based newsletter production com-

pany that produces publications for companies like Sears, Citibank, and Signet Bank. "If a trade association or any group can somehow create a personality, the impression of warmth or humanity, it is going to be more successful than an [enterprise] with a sterile identity." A newsletter lends an air of credibility to start-up businesses in particular. Potential clients and the media see a newsletter as an indication of a substantial client base.

Another reason newsletters have proved to be such an effective, low-cost marketing tool, says Klug, "is that business people especially are busy and don't tend to read books. They read few newspapers and need a very convenient way to get their information. Pamphlets, newsletters, or something they can fold up and put into a breast pocket and read on train, plane, or at a convenient time is the way business people especially like to access information."

The first step to starting a newsletter, he says, is to make up a list of people you want to send it to. This could include present and past customers, prospective customers, suppliers, prominent people in the community, and the media. The point is to keep important people informed of what your company or organization is doing.

"The list in any direct promotional program is the single most critical variable, and the most important determinant of the success or failure of your program," says Klug. You can start by building a list of current customers. When a customer makes a purchase, ask him to write down his address for future mailings. At Radio Shack, for instance, you might buy only a ten-cent part but the cashier will ask for your name, address, and phone number.

You can build a list of prospective customers by compiling names from a local phone book. If you want to appeal to people who live in a certain neighborhood or you're looking for certain businesses that could use your service, flip through the Yellow and White Pages for ones that fit the bill. This task is a bit time-consuming, but it is a money saver.

If you don't have time to flip through the phone book and you have specific criteria you want your mailing list to meet, contact a mailing list broker. Listed in the Yellow Pages under "Mailing

List Brokers," these firms will either sell or lease a customized mailing list for two cents a name on up. Some list brokers charge by the 1,000 names; $50 is the average cost per 1,000. But be specific about your needs and the type of customers you are seeking. Some brokers will try to sell you an outdated list that doesn't fit your criteria at all. Be sure to ask brokers many questions about their lists to determine which one best suits your needs. Many small-business people claim that Dun & Bradstreet and American Express mailing lists are effective.

Once you have an audience in mind, start gathering interesting pieces of information to put in your newsletter. You can assign this job to one or several people on staff, perhaps asking some employees or distributors to write articles pertaining to their areas of expertise. You might include a small photograph of the writer by the article. Readers like to put faces with names— especially if the employee is someone they deal with over the phone. This tactic personalizes your business.

If you don't have the staff or the time to write articles for the newsletter, hire a freelance writer. Their fees are usually negotiable. You can find them listed in the telephone book or through a freelance or independent writers' association in your community, which may also be listed in the phone book.

The person who writes your newsletter's articles must be familiar with your customers. Tailoring articles to appeal to their needs is crucial, says Klug. The following are his ingredients for a successful newsletter:

1. It should be newsy and like a personal letter, with a friendly and conversational style. Include readers' letters or comments. "Our clients often confuse that," says Klug. "They want us to do a newsletter, but in effect they want us to do an ad and fold it three times and call it a newsletter. That's not the way a newsletter works." You might include fictional short stories or, like Vermont Castings, features on interesting attractions around the region where the company is headquartered.

2. It has to contain information that helps readers with some problem or appeals to a particular interest. The newsletter has to

show readers a better way of doing things—a way to save money or time. "If you try too many sales pitches and self-serving information it [the newsletter] comes across as no more than an advertising flyer in a newsletter's clothes," says Klug. "The readership is going to be turned off and it's not going to be successful. We recommend to our clients that no more than 50 percent of the content should be self-serving or product promotional kinds of information." The bulk of the newsletter should be helpful tips.

3. Include profiles of successful customers. Write about customers whom other customers can easily identify with. You want customers to be inspired to say, "If he can do it, I can too." Encourage readers to write in about their comments and experiences. Occasionally illustrate how your product or service played a role in making that customer successful. But keep the sales pitch subtle. Again, the information has to be useful to readers and immediately applicable to making their lives easier.

4. The newsletter editor and writer have to put themselves into the shoes of the readers and write from the readers' perspective. It's a classic copy technique but so often forgotten.

5. "There's an old axiom in the newsletter business that says 'The worse the better,'" says Klug. The slicker and fancier and more professional you make your newsletter, the less it's going to be read. "People are turned off by advertisements, which tend to be slick, glossy, four-color and professional with beautiful typefaces." The slicker and more beautiful a newsletter gets, the more it starts to look like advertising and not a helpful newsletter. "Don't worry if your newsletter looks a little like homecooking," says Klug. "It should look like homecooking. There's nothing wrong with a smudged fingerprint on the newsletter." It's all a part of conveying a personal message. On the other hand, the newsletter should not look so messy that the reader is afraid to touch it.

Klug does not recommend hiring a consultant to produce a newsletter unless you have excess money and absolutely no time to spare. Newsletter production companies (several should be listed in your phone book) can handle a newsletter project from the first step to mailing them out.

If you have the time and are short on cash, on the other hand, there are several books that offer tips on how to write a company newsletter with examples of layout design. Even quicker are desktop publishing computer programs. You can walk into most universities or quick printing franchises and rent time on a Macintosh computer with desktop publishing software and instructions for about $15 an hour. If you have any trouble with the equipment, employees in the store or at the university can show you how to use it. You can type up your articles and design a layout with graphic illustration in less than two or three hours, says Klug. "A lot of quick print stores have gone to putting in these Macintosh computers with desktop publishing software because they feed their printing presses," he says. "When you get done making your newsletter, you simply go to the man behind the counter and say, 'Print 500 of these.'"

Printing costs vary according to the number of newsletters you want to produce, the type of paper you want to print it on—heavy-stock paper is usually more expensive—and how many colors of ink you want to use. Your local printer will advise you about these elements. And if you use a desktop publishing program, there is no need to hire a typesetter; the publishing program takes care of this, eliminating another costly expense. Keep in mind the homecooking strategy of newsletter production. The more you do yourself, the more personality it will have.

Now it's time to address your newsletters. You're probably getting writer's cramp just thinking about it, but your computer will take care of this too. There are extremely inexpensive and simple mailing list software programs you can buy for any personal computer that will sort your mailing list by zip code or last name or any other way you want to sort it. And your printer will spew out the mailing labels for you. You can walk into any computer software store and tell a salesperson that you want a mailing list software package. For less than $50, says Klug, you can buy an excellent mailing list software package that will sort the list and print the labels.

To save money on envelopes, fold your newsletter three times lengthwise and staple to form a self-mailer. Slap on mailing labels, and take the newsletters to the post office. If you have more than 500 newsletters you can mail third-class bulk, which is nearly ten cents cheaper per item than mailing it first class. Generally you will not need to mail your newsletter first class unless it includes some timely information that needs to reach customers within two or three days. If you have certain minimum density—number of pieces going to certain zip code—you can get your cost down a few more pennies than third class. You will need to buy a special permit from the post office—about $40 a year—to receive bulk mail rates.

How often should newsletters be mailed? Consistency is the key. Readers should look forward to receiving the newsletter at a certain time of the month or year. Naturally, the more often you send a newsletter, the more impact you will make. But you should send newsletters only when you have enough news to print. "If you send billing statements, a newsletter is an ideal and relatively low-cost way to enhance your promotional effort by simply enclosing it in the statement," says Klug. This technique offers consistency, and the newsletter is likely to be opened and read. Most credit card issuers are moving toward sending out a quarterly newsletter with their statements.

How do you know whether your newsletter is making an impact on customers? Fortunately, the effectiveness of newsletters can be more easily measured than radio or television advertising. Klug recommends including a clip-out coupon, a reply card requesting more information, a change of address form, or a request to be taken off your mailing list to elicit reader response. "This creates two-way communication," says Klug. "You don't just mail out 1,000 newsletters about your shoestore, for instance, and just wait until something happens. If you do that you're really not doing anything different than taking out an ad in your local newspaper." Always try to make your newsletter accountable by including some way to respond.

One way to track reader interest is to include your phone number—preferably a toll-free 800 number—at the end of your newsletter and encourage readers to call. If you have four extensions or rollover lines, assign your last rollover line exclusively to newsletter calls and print only that phone number in your publication. If you get a call that comes in directly on that line, you will know that call came as a response to your newsletter. Be sure that the person answering the phone keeps track of these calls. Compare the cost of producing the newsletter to the results you got from phone calls, response cards, and increased store traffic because of a specific sale publicized only in your newsletter.

Further Resources

How to Write a Company Newsletter
TIB Publications
2922 North State Road 7
Margate, Florida 33063
(305) 782-4553

In addition, see the *Typesetting Services Directory,* which is listed in Part III—Further Resources.

$

Open-House Parties

Can you imagine planning a coffee and doughnut party for about 200 customers and 3,000 fans of your company show up? That's what happened several years ago to Duncan Syme, founder of Vermont Castings, Inc., a cast-iron, wood- and coal-burning stove manufacturer in Randolph, Vermont. The second year the company expanded the event to include live music, square dancing, games, clowns, a plant tour, and product demonstrations. Vermont Castings invited the community to set up food tents and to turn their homes into temporary bed and breakfasts to house traveling customers. That year, more than 10,000 patrons—many of whom lived in the community—attended what would become an annual, weekend-long "Owner's Outing."

The community's involvement helped defray costs to Vermont Castings while also generating revenue for community organizations. The event raised somewhere around $300,000 for the area surrounding Randolph. With a party that big, Vermont Castings still spent thousands of dollars and a lot of planning time to make the event possible. But it also sold a lot of stoves as a result of word-of-mouth marketing and repeat business.

Why did Vermont Castings go to so much trouble to show

customers that they are appreciated? "We've found that it's good
business to be concerned with your customers after they've made
a purchase," says Steven Morris, manager of domestic marketing. From an idea that started as a brainstorm at the breakfast
table, Vermont Castings has grown into a multimillion-dollar
business. Although the company has outgrown its small-business
status, it still treats customers as though they are family. Letters
continuously pour in from stove owners who write how happy
they are with their purchase, the Owner's Outing, and their lifetime subscription to the company newsletter, *Vermont Castings
Owners' News*. (See Newsletters.)

"A high percentage of sales come from word-of-mouth referrals from happy owners," says Morris. "Maybe there's no way to
track it, but we know that the people at our outing are going to
help us sell some stoves by speaking highly of Vermont Castings
to other people who are interested in buying a product like ours."
(See Word of Mouth.)

Customer appreciation parties do not have to be as elaborate
or as costly as Vermont Castings' to be as effective. Joan Bedell,
who owns a Pak Mail franchise in a small town near Lake Tahoe,
Nevada, simply provides hot cider and cookies or doughnuts
once a week for her customers. Some make it a point to mail
packages on cider day. "People really look forward to it," says
Bedell.

Roger Ford, director of the Entrepreneurial Center at James
Madison University, used customer parties as a marketing tool
when he owned a retail liquor store in upstate New York. Ford
and his wife occasionally threw theme parties for customers to
sample wine, cheese, and special liquor brands. "While building
a lot of goodwill, we were able to gauge customers' interests and
preferences," says Ford. "Our costs were minimal since vendors
were anxious for prospects to try various products and give feedback." Ford took advantage of the many free samples offered by
vendors.

Customer appreciation parties can be as simple as offering
punch and cookies on Friday afternoon or dressing up in cos-
tumes for Halloween and giving out product samples and candy.
Parties can be as simple or as elegant as your product or service

requires. If you're looking for a big turnout, put a notice in a local newspaper or community calendar. Or, like Vermont Castings, advertise the event in your company newsletter.

Keep in mind that the event has to be worth customers' time to come to your business. Offer them something they can benefit from. Ask customers and newcomers to sign a guest book, including their addresses. The guest book can serve as an updated mailing list for future direct mailings.

One caveat: If you advertise your event, be prepared for more customers than you expect. Like Vermont Castings, your business may be swarming with customers when you were planning on only a few.

$

Packaging

"What really made Soho [soda] succeed was when we changed our packaging in 1982," says Sophia Collier, founder of American Natural Beverage Corporation. "When you're selling a product, your label is a little, tiny billboard."

Packaging for the company with a very limited advertising and marketing budget is not a luxury but an insurance policy, says Flavio M. Gomez, a principal in the San Francisco–based marketing and design consulting firm Sidjakov Berman Gomez & Partners. A label has a heavyweight responsibility on the store shelves. It has to attract consumers' attention away from similar products with big brand names that are backed by millions of dollars of advertising. An effective package design, in a way, can be your insurance policy for success.

Collier realized this when she set out to change Soho soda's packaging. She and her partner, Connie Best, had designed the original soda label—not because they fancied themselves excellent designers but because they had no money to hire a professional. The label they designed presented a health-food-type image. It was colorful, Collier realized, but not distinctive or eyecatching. "We realized that in consumer products, you're in a war for shelf space—you have to perform quickly on the retailer's shelf or you're going to be discontinued."

So Collier went to the library to study up on package design and production. Pouring through reference books, she gained an idea of what type of design she thought would make her label stand out. Once she had an idea that she wanted her label to be "art deco-ish—something evocative of New York," she looked through more reference books for names of designers who specialized in this style.

It was in one of these design books that Collier discovered the work of Doug Johnson, known for his art deco graphics. She went to him with her project idea, and at first he seemed interested. But when she told him that she had no money to pay him, "he said—in a nice way—you don't have any money . . . forget it," Collier recalls. But she kept going back. She presented him with the idea of designing the label on a royalty basis. Collier says it was that idea that helped win him over. "He liked the idea of earning money when he wasn't working," she says. "For every label that sold, we would give him 1/10."

Before going to consultants with a package design project, Collier offers this advice:

> Learn all you can about printing, so you know exactly how things are going to look when they're done. Learn about your medium. A lot of times your low-cost promotions are going to be printed, so learn all about printing and how to get special effects with low prices. Learn how to use two-color to get special effects and how to use special papers to get packaging that is unusual. Talk it over with a printer. Get lots of books on the subject and read. Call up trade associations and read their magazines. Get totally involved in it. It doesn't have to cost much, and people will remember your packaging when it's distinctive.

How to Select a Designer

"Selecting the right designer is extremely important—not only is your corporate image at stake, but a substantial amount of your time and money will be involved," says Flavio M. Gomez. His firm, which specializes in package design, corporate identity, and retail planning programs, has created designs for Frito-Lay, Levi Strauss, Quaker Oats, and Carnation.

Design firms range in size from large design organizations to one-person studios. Your choice, says Gomez, will depend on the scope of the project, your budget, and the compatibility between you and the designer. "To find the right design consultant, you might need to look outside of your area if your business is in a small city," says Gomez. "Go where the talent is, even if it means travel expenses." You could also call companies within your industry and contact corporations whose logos and designs you admire. "If you have always admired the IBM logo or identity, or thought the design of the Sunmaid raisin package was noteworthy, call the company and find out who created that particular design," he says. As a rule, if you are interested in a corporate logo or identity program, ask to speak to the corporate communications director. For a package design or other type of design project, the marketing director or brand manager should be able to answer your questions.

Look through the most recent design annuals (yearly issues of graphic design publications, which display the best in design from designers across the country). *Communication Arts*, *Print*, and *Graphis* are useful. Contact design organizations such as the American Institute of Graphic Design, New York, or the Package Design Council or the Art Directors Club in New York, Los Angeles, and San Francisco. They can steer you in the right direction. Try contacting the alumni office of a major art school, such as the Art Center College of Design in Pasadena, California, for ideas.

If you have an advertising agency or know someone at an agency, ask for pointers on choosing a design firm. Ad agencies are usually an excellent resource.

Gomez offers ten steps for choosing the right designer and ensuring a successful project:

1. Before meeting with a designer, finalize your communication objectives and marketing strategy. Be sure you know your

target audience for the project and have a clear idea of your expectations for the design. Midstream changes in objectives can be expensive and can lead to missed project deadlines.

2. Check each designer's track record and references in your field of business. Most designers will provide you with a list of clients and former clients for you to talk to. Make sure the designer fully understands your industry and the concerns of your business within your industry's climate.

3. Once you have narrowed your choices, obtain a complete budget estimate and a step-by-step project methodology, including a timetable. An experienced design company can accurately estimate all costs and timing before the work begins if given adequate project specifications. A designer unable to satisfy these basic requirements doesn't deserve your business.

4. In most cases, don't try to negotiate costs. If you have set your sights on one particular firm but it exceeds your budget, consider scaling down the creative executions and reducing the number of design phases. For example, the initial concept development phase of a package design project can be limited to one product flavor. For a corporate logo or identity program, the initial design phase can be restricted to the display of the logo only in primary applications rather than all its proposed forms of usage.

5. Choose a designer you feel comfortable with. Personal chemistry is very important. Respect and trust are keys to your project's success.

6. At the outset of the project, involve your advertising agency—if you have one—in the design process. It can provide valuable help in creating a successful design and help to ensure that the design can be easily applied to any advertising. Keep in mind that it's a team effort; your advertising agency should be an integral part of your marketing team.

7. At the start, give the designer all pertinent project data, such as size and structural specifications, any written copy you want included, and positioning requirements. Time—and money—can be lost if key information arrives late.

8. Reconfirm dates and stay on top of the design firm's progress. Request any changes in budget or deadlines in writing for documentation.

9. Open an ongoing communications channel between your designer and your printing suppliers to avoid pitfalls that can trigger project delays at the most inopportune times. Effective communication is essential.

10. Help build a strong and lasting client-designer working relationship. Make sure the designer's invoices are paid in a reasonable time. It helps to build longevity and loyalty into the relationship. All designers enjoy repeat business best of all, and if you use their services again, they are already familiar with your business and your objectives.

Further Resources

One helpful source for finding solutions to your packaging problems is the Packaging Institute International. This association publishes a quarterly newsletter, *PACK INFO*, which details the latest packaging innovations, *Who's Who in Packaging*, profiling industry leaders, and a glossary of packaging terms. For more information, write to the association at:

20 Summer St.
Stamford, Connecticut 06901

Another source is the *Design Firm Directory for Graphic and Industrial Design*. Published by Wefler & Associates, it lists firms by city and includes each company's staff size and range of services. For more information, write to the publisher at:

P.O. Box 1591
Evanston, Illinois 60204

The *Packaging—Reference Issue and Encyclopedia* lists 3,500 manufacturers of containers, machinery, and supplies used in packaging. The directory also includes contract packagers, consultants, associations, and service organizations. Write to:

Cahners Publishing Company
1350 East Touhy Avenue
Des Plaines, Illinois 60018

In addition, see the Package Design Council International and
the Packaging Institute International listed in Part III—Further
Resources.

$

Point of Purchase

How many people sit down at their office desks or kitchen tables before running an errand to write a detailed list of what they need? Apparently very few, according to the Point-Of-Purchase Advertising Institute, Inc. (POPAI). In a 1987 study it discovered that 69 percent of shoppers don't use a shopping list and that two of every three purchases are decided while the shopper is in the store. Most of today's two-income families and busy singles don't have time to spend clipping coupons, the institute says. A whopping 75 percent of consumers in the survey said they ignore newspaper ads before shopping.

So how does a small consumer-product company reach consumers if they are not paying attention to newspaper ads or other media? Right where they shop, with point-of-purchase (P-O-P) advertising.

P-O-P advertising comes in many forms. We've all seen them: elaborate, colorful corrugated cardboard towers filled with paper towels or cat food that grab your attention as you nearly run into them with your shopping cart. Or they might be wire or plastic bins—"dumps" in P-O-P jargon—that hold piles of hardware or other loose items with a sign usually introducing a new, improved product with a special low price.

According to many marketing experts, consumer product manufacturers are increasingly turning to P-O-P displays to boost sales. "Media today is terribly expensive," says Walter Nathan, founder of RTC Industries, a leading P-O-P display manufacturer based in Chicago. "For the same dollar you can get a wide-ranging point-of-purchase campaign on a local, regional, or national level and have the P-O-P piece remind consumers for three months to a year that here is something they need to buy. You don't get that with a one- or two-time exposure of an ad."

P-O-P displays can be beneficial to retailers as well. "Studies show that when consumers perceive a store to be well merchandised, fun and exciting that sales increase an average of 15 to 20 percent," says John M. Kawula, president of POPAI.

Some retailers have strict regulations about what types of P-O-P displays they will set up in their stores. Some will accept only signs or special shelf organizers. Others are more receptive to freestanding displays. Before embarking on a P-O-P campaign, first talk with the retailers who stock your product to find out which types of displays they are most likely to accept. Retailers generally do not charge extra for setting up P-O-P displays, but this is something to bring up when discussing displays with them.

Freestanding displays seem to offer the best promotional exposure for hot, new items, says Nathan: "Products get much more exposure when they are off the shelf rather than on the shelf. It's been our experience that there's a tremendous increase of any product that's sold outside the shelf, because it hits the consumer right in the stomach when he walks down the aisle versus having to choose from among thousands of items that are lined up on the shelf."

According to Nathan, many studies indicate increases in sales ranging from 15 to 60 percent when products are displayed off the shelf. Some stores will not permit off-the-shelf displays, however.

Produce Partners, Inc., a small Chicago-based company that sells a line of powdered mixes made with fresh fruits and vegetables, has used P-O-P displays from its first day of operation. Sold through major grocery store chains throughout the country, Produce Partners' products compete with thousands of other items for consumers' attention. If the packets of mix were stacked on shelves, says Alan Lakin, general manager, they could be easily overlooked. But "when we get a big ad and big [free-standing] display we move five to ten times the product than you do conventionally," he says. "Almost all of our dollars are spent in-store trying to get up mass displays."

For advice on which P-O-P display best suits your needs, Nathan advises going right to a P-O-P manufacturer or supplier. The best place to find them is through the industry's trade magazines, particularly *Creative*. Nathan calls it "the most popular magazine in which the P-O-P industry advertises." Suppliers also advertise their services in *Advertising Age* and other magazines catering to the marketing trade.

P-O-P suppliers will counsel you on the most effective display and design for your budget. "Cost depends on the size of the display, its degree of sophistication, quantity ordered, and permanency of the unit," says Nathan. "But generally corrugated [paper signs or displays] would be in the high one-digit or low two-digits price range per item"—anywhere from eight to twenty dollars.

A P-O-P piece can be anything from an inexpensive, colorful sign placed in a store window or hanging from the ceiling to a mechanical metal Santa Claus that waves you to a display of eggnog at Christmas time. A P-O-P piece can be composed of paper, plastic, sheet metal, wood, or wire, and it applies to all types of goods and services. They can be as creative as a designer's imagination and your budget will allow. In recent years, electronics have become significant additions to the P-O-P industry.

"Point-of-purchase pieces encompass advertising that is located in, on, or adjacent to the area where the advertised product or service is available for purchase," says Nathan. A few examples are displays, signs, counter units, video kiosks, mobiles, shelf talkers, and floorstands. "P-O-P provides impact, grabs the consumer's attention at the point of sale, and reinforces previous advertising messages," he says.

Produce Partners provides some funding for grocery stores to advertise special sales on produce in local newspapers. "If Giant Food runs a big ad on potatoes, for instance, it includes an ad for our cream of potato soup—buy one get one free," says Lakin. The grocer then places a freestanding tiered display of soup mix next to the potato bin. Lakin believes "that's a better way to go. If [the grocer] sells a lot of potatoes, we're going to sell a lot of potato soup."

Nathan says the best P-O-P display meets the following criteria:

1. It has to meet the budget and parameters submitted by client, as well as the retailer who will use it.
2. It has to be easily set up. Displays are generally set up by store personnel. If they are too complicated to construct or require too many tools, they don't get set up.
3. The display has to attract buyers. A P-O-P unit is generally used to highlight special promotions or discounts, which typically attract more consumers.
4. The graphics on the signage should not steal the color from the package. "Let the package do the talking—more so than the P-O-P unit itself," says Nathan. The P-O-P should carry copy that indicates what's going on, but it should not overpower the product's packaging, especially if the package is well designed. For products with poorly designed packages, the P-O-P should do the work.
5. Retailers are provided an incentive to use your display. Most store managers are receptive to setting up displays that they can later use. This is called a "dealer loader," which means that the P-O-P piece should be a useful object that a store manager can take home, such as a dump bin that can be used later as a laundry basket. On the other hand, the display should not be so attractive that the manager is tempted to take it home before using it in the store.

One way Sophia Collier, of American Natural Beverage Company, encourages retailers to use her P-O-P displays is by offering prizes. Periodically she advertises contests among retailers for those who make the best use of her displays. One recent contest prize was a dream vacation worth $5,000 for the retailer who set up the biggest display of Soho soda and kept it up the longest amount of time.

Further Resources

Creative—Guide to P-O-P and Promotion Issue
Magazines/Creative, Inc
37 West 39th Street
New York, New York 10018

Lists more than 400 manufacturers and producers of point-of-purchase displays, signs, exhibits, and other promotional material.

Directory of Professional Color Labs Offering Visual Marketing Services
Eastman Kodak Company
Rochester, New York 14650

Listing of about forty color film labs that offer services related to exhibit, display, and other promotional photography, including enlargements, lighting, mounting, installation, design, and graphics services. Free.

Point-Of-Purchase Advertising Institute, Inc.
60 North Van Brunt Street
Englewood, New Jersey 07631

In addition, see the National Association of Display Industries listed in Part III—Further Resources.

$

Pricing Decisions

Pricing is more of an art than a science. "It is usually assumed that marketers use scientific methods to determine the price of their products. Nothing could be further from the truth," says David Oglivy in *Oglivy on Advertising*. "In almost every case, the process of decision is one of guesswork."[1]

We can't recommend the exact prices for your offerings. But we can highlight some important things to think about. If it's any consolation, even big-bucks marketers have frequently agonized over the same decisions.

Avoid making the common mistake of figuring your prices only on costs. Some marketers falsely believe that the best prices are those above cost, including some set (formula percentage) amount for profit markup. Cost-plus pricing ignores the other forces that will influence your prices:

- Competitors
- Consumer preferences and attitudes
- Profit margins and goals
- Market targets' sensitivity to prices (elasticity)
- Financial strength (e.g., cash flow strength)

- Strategies for how you position your offerings (e.g., prestige)
- Niche in your market targets, products, technology, or location

Ask yourself these questions: Are you pricing your products and services too low or too high compared to the competition? Are your products and services of high enough quality to command premium prices? Will a price increase hurt your unit sales? If so, will the decrease in dollar sales be greater than the additional revenue from the higher prices? By lowering prices, are you buying market share but not consumer loyalty? Will consumers shift to the next lower price seller?

As you can see, these sample questions are hard to answer. Perhaps this is why so many have said that pricing requires some management guesswork. As a shoestring marketer, you can improve your pricing decisions by following some critical dos and don'ts.

Do	*Don't*
Perform pricing experiments to observe changes in sales	Assume that your prices are correct and thus forgotten
Tap sources of pricing information (e.g., surveys, focus groups, and trade association data)	Keep price constant when busines situations in the market may have an impact
Watch your competitors' price patterns	Have too many price points (levels), which confuse buyers
Check with your suppliers, wholesalers, or retailers for pricing suggestions	Ignore the impact of your prices on other marketing variables
Identify relevant costs and determine the prices needed to	Forget related pricing decisions on credit, rebates, discounts, and bonus offers

break even or achieve certain profit objectives

Encourage head-on price competition with larger and deep-pocketed companies

Define your market targets—what is their tolerance for different price levels?

Try to compete merely on price. Since this is very hard for shoestring marketers, look for other possible competitive benefits

Vary price enough for different product items and market targets

Revise prices to reflect changing market conditions

Study the relationship of prices and postsale services you offer

Use your customers as a sounding board on your pricing strategies

Develop some niche—market, product, technology, service, location—to give more freedom on pricing decisions

See if there is a positive correlation between higher prices and consumer perceptions of higher quality

Another aid to you in analyzing whether or not you are currently pricing your products or services at the optimum level is the self-test provided in Worksheet 7.

We have not gone into great length on pricing strategies for a specific reason: There are countless number of chapters on pricing in many marketing books. Many of these books' suggestions are germane to marketers who may have deep or shallow pockets. (Books are sometimes priced according to the number of pages

WORKSHEET 7

Self-Test: Do I Have a Pricing Problem?

	Yes	No	Not Appli-cable
1. Do I have too many pricing points that confuse buyers?	_____	_____	_____
2. Do I know my break-even points?	_____	_____	_____
3. Is my cost data inadequate by different products or other categories?	_____	_____	_____
4. Do I get many customer complaints that my prices are higher than the competition?	_____	_____	_____
5. Do I have too many markdowns?	_____	_____	_____
6. Do I often have a problem with too much inventory?	_____	_____	_____
7. Do my customers *always* want to negotiate lower prices?	_____	_____	_____
8. Is my company unable to win its fair share of bidding contracts?	_____	_____	_____
9. Have I not matched different pricing strategies with different market targets?	_____	_____	_____
10. Do I really have no specific pricing objectives?	_____	_____	_____
11. Do I compete on price alone?	_____	_____	_____

	Yes	No	Not Appli- cable
12. Do I constantly engage in price cuts?	___	___	___
13. Does our cost of goods seem higher than that of our competi- tion?	___	___	___
14. Am I unable to pinpoint costs/profit contributions for certain business units?	___	___	___
15. Are my write-offs above the in- dustry average because of slow- moving merchandise?	___	___	___
16. Is my company unaware of how sensitive our customers are to prices?	___	___	___
17. Does my company have a constant cash flow problem?	___	___	___
18. Does my company have high bad debt expenses?	___	___	___
19. Is my company unable to take ad- vantage of the discounts from ven- dors?	___	___	___
20. Does my company not review its pricing strategies as often as it should?	___	___	___

If you answered "yes" to ten or more of these questions, you may need to rethink your pricing decisions.

in a book; thus, we're trying to lower the cost to you of this one.)

One parting thought: Today the popular word on pricing is toward offering good-quality products at higher prices. (See Quality.) Oglivy may have summarized the current mood: "Time after time our marketers force me to give them an inferior product at a lower price. I was able to tell him that there are now unmistakable signs of a trend in favor of superior products at premium prices. The consumer is not a moron."[2] Remember to monitor your prices frequently. Your competition can change this faster than any other marketing activity.

$

Pricing: Loss Leaders

"Have I got a deal for you." We've all heard that line, usually from a salesperson who wants to sell a product at a supposed discount price. You look over the product, and it looks like a steal. You get excited over finding such a bargain.

This technique is called a *loss leader*—selling products or services below cost—and it has served some shoestring marketers by increasing sales and/or profits. Loss leaders are used as a promotional tool because they generate excitement. Shoppers love to find bargains or "good deals." And many sellers are able to build traffic flow in their businesses with these deals.

As a frugal marketer, you may find the strategy of loss leaders quite useful. In addition to generating traffic or creating interest in your business, loss leaders could turn over slow inventory, improve short-term cash flow problems, take business away from competition, create a consistent image of having competitive prices, sell other products, and help penetrate new products.

If you're using loss leaders or thinking about it, you should ask yourself the following questions:

1. How is your product positioned in the marketplace? Is it a high-ticket item that does not lend itself to discount pricing?

2. How receptive is your market target toward loss leaders? Are your targeted customers more concerned with quality than price? Will you confuse them if you're positioning your business as a high-class establishment with outstanding products?

3. Do your loss leaders bring in added traffic? Do they attract the right group of customers? Do the patrons actually buy, or are they merely lookers who create traffic congestion problems?

4. What type of products are best to sell below cost? Usually well-known, national brands make the best loss leaders. However, these items may give you the highest profit margins when not on sale. Should you use them as loss leaders?

5. When consumers buy loss leaders, do they buy other products that will more than cover the costs of using loss leaders? A few retailers have found that some customers would buy only the products below cost and nothing else. In this case, the strategy can become quite expensive since the other product lines are ignored.

6. Are you already operating at full capacity? Do you have all of your employees quite busy and thinly stretched? In this situation, your loss leaders are counterproductive. You may not want to expand, grow, or refinance your business to handle the extra business.

7. How will prospects perceive your business if you use loss leaders? In certain businesses, a loss leader may seem silly to prospects. Professional services make little use of loss leaders. Customers are not even aware of the providers' costs. More important, customers equate quality with a fair but constant price. Compared with discounters and supermarkets, there are few loss leaders among doctors, dentists, engineers, consultants, and other professions, where it's difficult to measure quality and costs and do price comparisons.

8. When and how often should you use loss leaders? Timing and frequency are critical in coordinating such concerns as selling seasons, cash flow, promotional events, introducing new product lines, and cannibalizing sales of other products. If you

offer loss leaders too frequently, consumers may lose interest and become blasé about your business.

9. Will your loss leaders initiate a price war among competitors? Frugal marketers want to avoid a price war. If your competitors—especially if they have strong cash reserves and a healthy balance sheet—continually match your loss leaders, you could start a no-win situation. You must anticipate and watch the possible reaction of your competitors, especially those with deep pockets. On the other hand, the effective use of loss leaders can help you with a temporary cash crunch or with a slow selling season that needs some rejuvenation.

In summary, loss leaders are a popular pricing option for many shoestring marketers. Don't use them as your sole strategy in the pricing area, but they can help your selling efforts. Like other marketing strategies, you must constantly watch your loss leaders to see if they accomplish your defined objectives. For instance, did they increase sales of other products? traffic flow? cash flow? turnover of slow inventory? exposure in new markets? Did they create a greater awareness of your business?

We recommend loss leaders if you recognize the caveats that are identified in this entry.

$

Prospecting for Gold

Prospecting for new business is hard work. It takes time and creativity to obtain good leads. Entrepreneurs and salespeople are sometimes unenthusiastic about prospecting because they must navigate into uncharted waters.

Yet it's an important marketing task for frugal marketers. No matter how hard you try to please current customers, you will lose some to attrition, competition, or bad economic conditions. New business is an essential goal even just for maintaining certain sales levels. It's also necessary for growth and expansion.

Some shoestring marketers get in trouble when they're unaware that their customer base is slowly aging. The firm's future is really bleak without *new* accounts. We've especially seen this occur in fast-growing rural markets where new businesses are opening to serve an influx of companies and households. The old, passive sellers who have relied on their existing customers have no solid future building blocks with which to increase sales.

Prospecting is a continuous process. You or your sales force should have specific times set aside—daily or weekly—for the purpose of finding and selling new prospects. It must not be an afterthought; otherwise, you may find yourself putting it off for later.

Here are some valuable tips and suggestions for low-cost ways to prospect:

1. Prospecting should be a total commitment by everyone within your organization. Your employees should be trained, encouraged, and rewarded for generating good customer leads.

Computer Specialists, Inc., a $5 million computer service company in Monroeville, Pennsylvania, believes that nonsales employees can also spot potential customers. Employees receive bonuses of up to $1,000 for any prospect that becomes an account. In one year, the program produced seventy-five leads, which resulted in nine new accounts. "We can't afford fifty salespeople scouting around for new business," says president Warren Rodgers. "Everybody who works here is a salesperson." Your employees can also help with prospecting if the right system is created.[1]

2. Your customers' trade associations are a good source for leads. Some associations are somewhat flexible on taking members or will at least allow vendors or suppliers to obtain an associate membership status if full-time membership is discouraged.

Stu McKay, a marketing consultant in St. Charles, Illinois, joined associations in the heavy-duty trucking industry. Because he got to know the officers of the association and did good work, the officers often referred his name to members who needed help. He eventually developed a data base of industry information that brought in additional revenues.

At a nominal cost, you may be able to join associations that are popular with your market targets. If so, be active by joining committees and volunteering some of your services. In the long run, you could reap the benefits of many promising leads.

Many associations produce newsletters and other publications and are often looking for information, tips, or ideas relevant to the whole group. Talk with the publications' writers to make yourself available as an expert source in the field they're covering. Check with them periodically to see if you can help them with a story or if you can write one. The more your company is mentioned in the publication, the more credibility you will build with its readers. You'll find that viable prospects will be calling *you*. Now that's low-cost marketing.

3. Join your own trade associations. They can give you advice about trends, prospecting, and some data on the latest targets to consider. In addition, many associations publish directories, which list their members and the products they sell. The cost is usually reasonable since it's a service to the members. More important, these directories are sometimes distributed to people who may want to buy from some of the association members.

As freelance writers and consultants, we have received lucrative assignments from companies who found us from our own associations' directories.

4. Current customers are an excellent source for getting leads. As part of the postselling process and servicing your accounts, you should habitually ask buyers if there is anyone else who may need your products. Can they even offer three or four specific names? In a few cases, some customers will go with you to make the necessary introductions. This situation is possible when you and the customer have a good, long-term relationship.

Remember, smart selling includes two simple rules: (1) ask for the order and (2) ask for other leads from a satisfied customer. It's dynamite when a happy consumer gives an endorsement to other people. These leads become viable prospects.

Smart sellers are not bashful about asking for leads. Moreover, you can do it in a professional manner without being overbearing. For example, when Charles Schwab & Company sends information to its brokerage accounts, it includes a self-addressed stamped postcard that welcomes a list of referrals who may also like to receive some informative financial planning literature. These names become excellent prospects.

5. Trade shows are a good source for prospect names. (See Trade Shows.)

6. You can buy lists of names from list brokers (usually advertised in *Direct Marketing* magazine, and in any Yellow Pages directory). These lists are detailed and are broken down by key market characteristics. (See Zeroing In on Your Markets.)

7. At the public library and in government offices, you can find some good directories that list a variety of organizations. *National Trade and Professional Associations of the United States* (Washington, D.C.: Columbia Books), which is published annually, is an excellent source. Sometimes the directories are not expensive for the number of sales leads you may generate. For an excellent summary of various directories, see the *Directory of Directories* (Detroit: Gale Research Co.), also published annually.

One of the most popular low-cost directories is your own state's directory of manufacturers. If you are interested in the manufacturing markets, contact your state government about buying the directory for the state you live in (some are either published by the state government or by private firms).

8. Noncompeting sales reps are quite knowledgeable. They know who is expanding and need certain goods. If you're fair and polite to these sales reps, they're willing to exchange some useful information.

9. Foreign markets are sometimes ignored by frugal sellers. To get started on generating international leads, contact the International Trade Administration (ITA) of the Department of Commerce. It offers many valuable services, such as organizing trade promotion events and monitoring foreign government practices and sales opportunities. The ITA's office of business liaison is a good contact point. (See Exporting.)

10. Because the federal government is the largest buyer of goods and services, many low-cost marketers have found government sales to be very lucrative. For military contracts, you can begin with the Small and Disadvantaged Business Utilization Officer at your nearest military base. The Department of Defense also publishes a helpful book, *Selling to the Military*. For nonmilitary government prospects, you can use the *U.S. Purchasing*

and Sales Directory from the Superintendent of Documents of the U.S. Government Printing Office, Washington, D.C. 20402.

In addition, *Commerce Business Daily* identifies specific agencies that are looking for certain types of goods and services. Finally, you can visit a counselor at one of the twelve business service centers of the General Services Administration.

11. Businesspeople and professionals within your local community are valuable for providing information concerning new businesses, expansions, and consumer household expenditures. Successful sellers know how to network and be active in local, social, community, and civic organizations and events.

12. To keep costs down, telemarketing is becoming a popular strategy for prospecting. (See Telemarketing.)

13. The creation of special events or offers can draw new leads to your business. For example, you could use:
— Free seminars (e.g., "tax planning" talk from a small CPA firm
— Special sales with a registered drawing
— Premiums, contests, and sweepstakes whereby people can also register
— Free publications that you advertise in the classifieds, which are effective tools for getting prospects to contact you
— Rebates and coupons with a space for buyers' addresses
— Free entertainment programs in which you can formally tabulate the attendees
— Package inserts from promotional flyers that seek a response
— Charity events that have a common thread and interest to your business

14. The old standby of cold canvassing is still another way to get leads. To save precious time and resources, try to identify your potential market segments. Also, get qualifying background information about different groups. You need some predetermined criteria to use before investing your time in making actual calls. If no prescreening is done, cold canvassing becomes an expensive proposition.

Prospecting for new business can result in fool's gold or the real thing for low-cost marketers. To get the real thing you must follow a systematic plan: (1) decide on who you want to reach with a sound criterion of qualifying the names (e.g., by household income or size of firm); (2) determine how you can best contact them; (3) manage your time for going after this potential business; (4) organize the prospecting process; and (5) be persistent and consistent about prospecting.

Don't be discouraged with potential rejections or a strange, new environment. If you do, your business will become stagnant from attrition of your current customers. Marketers with shallow pockets must sell, sell, sell—especially to new accounts.

$

Publicity

Publicity. Good or bad, it generally makes a strong and lasting impression on your audience. The best thing about publicity is that there are a million ways to get it. They range from zany gimmicks (see Gimmicks) to satellite TV interviews. Deciding which is best for you depends on your personality and the personality of your company. If you are shy, you wouldn't want to be interviewed on live TV. On the other hand, if you have a flamboyant personality, you could get more mileage for your cause on radio or TV than merely writing a letter to the editor of your local paper.

Here are a few ideas that have worked well for others. Their costs range from virtually pennies to thousands of dollars.

Encouraging Employees to Write Articles

Ron and Katherine Harper, founders and owners of Harper Corporation of America, Charlotte, North Carolina, encourage their technical employees to publicize the company. Harper Corporation is an umbrella organization of a string of companies that range from manufacturing printing cylinders and an industrial hand cleaner to installing heating and air conditioning systems. The businesses have a combined annual revenue of $20 million and employ 115 people.

For every article that employees write for technical and trade journals in the companies' fields, the Harpers pay $500. "Articles are usually three to six pages long and go to customers we want to reach," says Ron Harper. In ad terms, he says, a four-page article is the equivalent of $12,000 worth of full-page, color ads, or $8,000 of full-page black-and-white ads (including production costs).

"An article that is published by a technical person has more credibility because it's not advertising, and the average reader assumes it has been pretty well edited for commercialism," Harper points out. "And you never know how much you solidify a relationship with an existing customer." Although the articles create sales leads, they are most effective at boosting the company's image. As Harper says, "The company gets credit as being an involved, concerned citizen of the industry, which is capable of attracting good technical people."

Harper employees have been published fifteen times over the past several years. To encourage more employees to write articles, the Harpers publicly recognize the ones who have had recent articles published and send the articles to people in the organization that the Harpers feel are also capable of writing an article for publication. The Harpers see that every article is edited before it is sent to the trade publications to provide it a better chance of being published. "Trade magazines are always looking for good technical articles," says Ron.

Pitching Story Ideas to Writers

Pat O'Brien's business, Chicago-based Golf Adventures Unlimited, got its first growth spurt from magazine publicity. When O'Brien founded Golf Adventures five years ago, he tried placing ads in trade magazines, but he discovered they didn't convey the excitement of his company's services: arranging exotic golf tours around the world. "I found that if nobody knew you, you had to create some identity first and then take advantage of it later with ads," says O'Brien. "I had to find a marketing identity that would set the company apart from others in the field."

On an all-night flight from Hong Kong to Italy, a groggy O'Brien came up with the idea for a tour that would take golfers to the northernmost, southernmost, easternmost, westernmost, highest, and lowest courses in the world. When he returned to Chicago, he spent several months working out arrangements for getting the tour off the ground.

O'Brien knew the only way he could get people to sign up for such an unusual tour was to get publicity. He contacted the editors of two golf magazines and pitched a story idea about his tour. "They're always looking for filler copy, and I tried to give them something of journalistic value that they thought was neat." After several months of regular correspondence with the magazines, articles about O'Brien's company and its unusual tours appeared in both publications.

"I got twelve pages in *Golf Digest*," says O'Brien. "If you think of it in ad terms—a one-page color costing more than $25,000—I got more than $350,000 of advertising." But, he says, "I wasn't particularly concerned that the trip got a lot of response. I wanted to get our name out so people would call about our normal trips."

O'Brien also contacted a *Wall Street Journal* reporter. Initially he called to respond to a story the reporter had written, but in the course of conversation, O'Brien told the reporter about his unusual business. A month later a profile on his company appeared as a front-page feature.

Sending Press Releases and Clippings

Once O'Brien had been mentioned in a couple of articles, he reproduced the clippings and sent them to publications he thought would be interested in his story. Sending one-page press releases (they can be written by yourself or a freelance writer—located in the Yellow Pages under "Writers" or "Editorial Services") about your latest product, service, or television appearance also helps pique writers' interest.

Once you have been featured in articles or have appeared on television "you get into a media jet stream," O'Brien says. "You continue to bounce from magazine interview to television appearance to newspaper interview."

To date O'Brien has appeared on NBC's "Today Show," ABC's "Good Morning America," and a local CBS news program, and he has been featured in a *Chicago Tribune* column—which was syndicated in the *Los Angeles Times*, *The New York Times*, and *Greenwich* (Connecticut) *Times*, among others, as well as being mentioned in regional newspaper and magazine articles.

But living in the limelight is not that easy, says O'Brien. "It only works as long as you have a string of ideas to keep it going. You've got to be creative and come up with ideas that make people sit up and take notice."

His advice: "You can't be afraid to press your story to the media in your town, even if it seems off-beat. You have to have a little gall, obviously. Sometimes it takes a little P. T. Barnum to get noticed. But if you follow your intuition and feel there's something that justifies the story, then follow it. Get the media to work with you." (See the sidebar Tip: "Establishing a Good Rapport With Writers.")

Promoting Your Product or Cause in a TV or Radio Interview

You don't have to wait for a television reporter to contact you for an interview about your company's exciting new product or your association's dynamic survey findings. You can drop a ready-made taped interview right into their laps.

Electronic publicity firms are becoming a popular and glamorous promotional tool with services that range from producing TV and radio feature segments (most often used as fillers on TV news programs) to arranging live satellite tours (the firm arranges for media reporters around the country to interview a particular

TIP: How to Make Your Television or Radio Interviews More Memorable

TELEVISION

1. Always have props. "No television host wants to interview a talking head," says Nancy Trent, president of New York–based public relations firm Trent & Associates. Give a product demonstration; hold up pictures; be imaginative. Trent's firm represents Sandicast, Inc., a company in San Diego that produces handcasted animal sculptures. "The funniest visual is Sandi Brue [the firm's owner] introducing the host's dog to the figurine dog that she has modeled after the real dog," says Trent. "When a Shar-pei meets a Shar-pei model, it flips. You're letting the TV audience in on something that's fun."

2. Do something to the host. If you represent a make-up company, make up the host.

3. If your company does not lend itself to interesting visuals, be armed with interesting facts, statistics, and anecdotes about your business or industry. Trent also represents a trade publication for the beverage industry. During interviews, her client talks about humorous names of strange drinks and gives recipes.

4. Get the audience to participate. Ask questions; give quizzes. "If someone is just blabbing, it doesn't matter how interesting the information is, after a while the audience loses interest," says Trent. Give people something to mail away for or contests they can enter.

5. Don't wear clothing that has a complicated design. Such clothes distract the audience and make your message less memorable.

6. Think of three important points you want to cover during the course of the interview and keep going back to them so that the audience will remember them easily. But don't reiterate them so often that you start to sound like a broken record.

RADIO

1. Use descriptive words to help the audience get a picture of what you're talking about.
2. Take a list of the points you want to cover and anecdotes you want to tell.
3. Don't wear clangy jewelry that may knock against the microphone.
4. Be animated. Don't speak in a monotone voice.
5. Like television interviews, you can give the audience a quiz or offer them something to mail away for.

To avoid being nervous during the interview, practice what you want to talk about. Have friends pretend they're the host and ask you questions. Keep your answers short. Television interviews typically last around two minutes; radio interviews can last up to ten minutes. The time will fly by more quickly than you anticipate. Talk quickly but not so fast that the audience can't understand you. "Imagine you're on the first and only date with this great person and audience. Be as entertaining as you possibly can be," says Trent.

---

client). These firms also produce video product demonstrations for department store displays.

"This service is especially important to small-business people or organizations," says Stacy Hunt, executive vice-president of On-The-Scene Productions, an electronic publicity firm in Los Angeles. "They don't have time to go on a six-week jaunt to get the word out about their service or product, spending valuable time away from their businesses." Hunt points out that touring the country to introduce a new product or increase association membership is expensive: "You can count on spending about $1,000 a day, including transportation, lodging and meals, when you're on tour." But by using an electronic publicity firm to get the word out, "you don't have to leave your home base. In a matter of hours you can talk about your product or service on the air, then leave and go to lunch," she says.

TIP: Establishing a Good Rapport With Writers

"Getting publicity is a great way to get visibility for you or your product," says American Natural Beverage founder Sophia Collier. "One of the first things that got us some visibility was when *New York* magazine put Soho in its 'Best Bets' [column]." But to get publicity, she says, you have to be willing to promote yourself: "Don't be afraid to contact journalists about what you're doing. Journalists are always looking for neat stuff to write about."

The following tips will help get your foot in the door when contacting journalists about your product, service, or association:

- Study copies of magazines, newspapers, newsletters, and trade publications that you would like to do a story on your company or association. For each publication, analyze its audience, the types of subjects it covers, the writing style, and whether it covers local, regional, or national stories. For instance, you wouldn't want to plug a story on your coat hanger manufacturing firm to a magazine that writes about the service industry. Read several issues of each publication. Knowing the publication will impress the writer and make him or her more willing to work with you.
- Find out which writer (in many magazines, the title "editor" often means writer) covers the stories pertinent to your business or association. Go right to the source. If you are a tax consultant, contact the magazine or newspaper reporter who covers taxes. This will help you get around the runaround.
- Ask the publication's receptionist when the writers are on deadline. Most writers are impatient with (and sometimes rude to) people who call to plug a product when they have an editor breathing down their necks.
- Outline what you want to say to the writer before you call. Be articulate and brief. Writers are usually on the phone or

out covering a story all day. They usually don't have time to chat at length. If you feel uncomfortable making a cold call, send a brief letter first with a press release. Enclose a product sample and photographs and then follow up with a phone call.

- Introduce yourself with your first call and ask the writer if he or she could meet you for lunch or arrange a quick meeting at his or her office. A face-to-face meeting—if you can get it—makes you more memorable to the writer. Take this opportunity to give a quick product demonstration or supply the writer with interesting company literature. Pitch a story idea, but make sure it fits into the publication's content.

- Don't be intimidated if the writer says the story idea has already been covered, or that it just doesn't fit in right now. Think of another angle. Call back periodically to see if the writer plans to cover the story for an upcoming issue. Be polite and persistent unless the writer says he absolutely will not do the story. Try another writer on staff who might be interested.

- If a writer says he or she is going to do a story on your product or cause, don't be disappointed if you don't see it in print for several months. Magazines work several months to a year in advance; newspaper feature items often get bumped to another day, week, or month. Keep tabs on the story's status. Sometimes a little reminder is often all a writer needs to prod the production editor into putting your story into the next issue.

- After you receive publicity, write a thank-you note to the writer. This helps establish an ongoing rapport. Keep in touch with the media as your business, service, or organization grows. They can open doors to future interviews.

Satellite interviews can be conducted from nearly any location in one day. On-The-Scene, for instance, scouts a client's area to locate satellite uplinks. The client appears at a studio or other satellite uplink location, gets some brief media coaching, and is

interviewed at ten-minute intervals by a local journalist in the
target markets the client wants to reach.

On-The-Scene also produces taped news features—called
video news releases—which are like the stories you see and hear
on radio and TV news programs and talk shows. The client
works with the production crew to put together a two-and-a-half-
minute newsworthy feature.

An in-house placement staff calls stations in the client's target
markets to see if they would be interested in airing the feature
news piece. The staff then sends the segment (including twenty
extra minutes of interview footage in case the local reporter
wants to put together a longer piece or use a different angle) to
the interested stations.

"The most important part of what we do," says Sally Jewett,
On-The-Scene president, "is our post-campaign analysis. After
we send out the cassettes the placement staff calls them back on
the phone to see if they used the cassette." If a station didn't air
the video news release, the placement staff works with the local
producer to come up with another angle that he may find more
interesting. They also look for a local angle to incorporate into
the piece whenever possible.

The cost of a satellite interview or taped news feature segment
is not inexpensive. On-The-Scene charges $8,500 for a two-hour
satellite interview that reaches ten to twelve cities and $13,500
for a four-hour interview that reaches twenty-four cities. A one-
day shooting for a video press release–taped news feature segment—where no travel is required—costs $14,000. That price
includes sending up to 150 cassettes to stations around the country. But Jewett says the fees are commensurate with the effectiveness of their work. Hunt, a former award-winning radio
personality, and Jewett, a former producer-director of "Entertainment Tonight," have up to a 75 percent success rate of video
segments airing: Jewett knows what it takes for something to get
on the air:

It has to be a valid news piece. On the other hand, we recognize our responsibility to effectively get the client's message across. Generally when people are doing this for the
first time their reaction is to want to make a two-and-a-half-

minute commercial, and that we cannot do. It won't air. We sit down with them and work out what the angle is going to be. Through discussion we walk away with something that feels like an interesting news piece.

At press time, On-The-Scene was working with the Fund for a Feminist Majority, a fledgling Los Angeles–based nonprofit organization that encourages women to run for public office. Eleanor Smeal formed the organization after she left the National Organization for Women. "She was aware that one of the missing elements to getting attention for the women's movement is that they didn't use the media as effectively as they could have," says Jewett. On-The-Scene was working up a media plan where they will tape rallies around the country and Smeal's speeches for TV and radio station use, as well as motivational videotapes for women's organizations.

For information about electronic publicity firms in your area, look under the "Video Production Services" listing in your Yellow Pages directory.

Further Resources

Writer's Market
Writer's Digest Books
F & W Publications
9933 Alliance Road
Cincinnati, Ohio 45242

Magazine Marketplace (MMP)
R. R. Bowker
245 West 17th Street
New York, New York 10011

Bacon's Publicity Checker
Bacon's Publishing Company
332 South Michigan Avenue
Chicago, Illinois 60604

The National Research Bureau
310 South Michigan
Suite 1150
Chicago, Illinois 60604

Publishes newspaper, magazine, TV and radio, feature writer
and photographer, and internal publications directories.

$

Public Relations

Sponsoring charitable and community activities, giving free lectures or seminars, staging media events, getting articles published in a trade publications: all of these fall into the category of public relations. It is a way to establish goodwill between your organization and your target market.

If you're creative, you can come up with endless public relations opportunities. It can be as simple as sponsoring a local softball team and printing your company's name or logo on their jerseys. Or if you want to make a big impression, you can create a community-wide event—like a job fair or a community olympics.

Depending on how much time or money you have, using public relations is one of the most effective ways to market your business. For the medium-sized business with a healthy marketing budget but neither the time nor personnel to put it to work, hiring a public relations agency can often yield desirable results.

You must plan your objectives and choose your agency carefully. A big investment is at stake if you hire an agency that does not produce the results you want. And there's no guarantee that public relations will work 100 percent of the time.

If hiring a public relations firm to develop a marketing program and generate publicity is the way you want to go, first do some self-evaluation, advises Scott Kronick, a New York–based public relations executive whose expertise is in meeting the special needs of small businesses. Before actually hiring a PR firm, Kronick counsels small-business owners and marketing managers to answer the following questions: What are the specific communications needs of your business or organization? Do you want greater awareness for a product or service nationally or in a targeted market? Who is your target consumer? What is your company's objective? A typical objective, he says, is increasing sales or creating a better public image.

Many public relations agencies specialize in general awareness and reputation building, while others offer direct sales support. Still others will assist in compiling marketing information. Most PR firms can do all or a combination of these services, but the more the client wants, the more the work will cost, cautions Kronick.

How to Select a PR Firm That Is Right for You

"If your market covers the country, or is international in scope, you should look for a firm that has worked in that capacity," says Kronick. A firm knowledgeable about your business and its size should generally know what tactics, events, media, and measures are most effective for accomplishing your objectives. Here are some tips:

1. Get references. Many companies hire public relations firms on referrals from other satisfied clients, says Kronick. If you do seek references from business acquaintances or friends, "be sure the agency can address your needs and does not represent clients that could create a conflict of interest," such as a competitor. Most public relations firms generally will not represent two competing clients, and it is usually stated in the contract.

2. Check *O'Dwyer's Directory of Public Relations Firms*, which is found in most libraries. It lists most existing public relations

firms, noting their rank, specialties, number of employees, and clients. The directory also breaks down the agencies by regions. Businesses or organizations looking to hire PR firms for national, international, or specific markets can find most reputable firms in this directory.

3. Call journalists. Contact approachable journalists at local or national (depending on your market scope) newspapers, magazines, radio, or television stations and ask their opinions. Ask who does the best job and who they would recommend for a company like yours. Be sure to call four or five from each area to eliminate favoritism. If one name is mentioned favorably a few times, look into the firm. If several names come up, a number of them should be pursued. Most PR agencies you contact will respond with presentations and/or proposals.

4. If you're really working on a shoestring, try to find a freelance public relations professional by advertising in a newspaper's classified section. Many professionals who are employed by larger public relations firms also freelance on the side. By hiring a freelancer, you can cut the cost of a company's overhead and other expenses that would normally be passed on to the client. But be aware that a one-person shop can lack the many resources that a firm can offer. "Hiring freelancers can be very cost efficient if they really know what they're doing," says Kronick. Just as with an agency, you should ask a freelancer for references.

Once you have contacted one or several firms, the next step is to arrange meetings to select the agency that can help achieve your objectives. Set a deadline for all proposals to be in your hands for review. Before receiving final presentations or proposals, the business owner should provide the agency or agencies with as much background information about the company as possible. "Well before the proposal deadline you should plan to discuss your company and its needs with the agency contact for at least an hour," says Kronick.

Also talk with the agencies' clients to get a feel for the type of service you may be getting. How long has the client worked with the agency? (Note: During the first three months of a contract, the agency will be learning your business. Initial public relations results usually come after the agency has worked with your company for approximately three months, says Kronick.)

Are the agency people pleasant to work with? It is most important that you choose an agency you feel comfortable working with. Is the agency receptive to your calls? Is it responsive to your requests?

How is the communication network? From the date you hire the agency, you should have a clear idea of what will be taking place weekly or monthly, says Kronick, and you and the agency should fully understand these action plans.

Does the agency do a follow-up presentation on the effectiveness of its campaign? A follow-up could include clipping reports—a compilation of published articles—or consumer/media awareness surveys of your organization or product. The report should communicate clearly the effectiveness of the program, tactics, project, or activity.

What to Look for in a Proposal and/or Presentation

1. *Objectives.* Has the agency successfully identified your needs and objectives?
2. *Understanding.* Has the agency worked in your area of business (or activity if you are an association) or in a related area? Are the agency representatives knowledgeable about your type of business and how to solve its needs? Are they up to date on current industry trends?
3. *Organization.* Does the agency present a well-organized and easily understood plan? Do you know exactly what the agency will be doing to accomplish your desired objective? Are agency representatives receptive to questions?
4. *Creativity.* Are the agency's ideas creative? When you evaluate several agencies, typically one or two will present creative plans that stand out well above those of competing

companies. Are the ideas unique to your particular company, or are they standard for most of the agency's clients? Are they realistic and affordable?

5. *Expectations.* Not everything pursued always develops; however, just because you have a small budget should not mean the PR firm can't get results for you. Ask if you can negotiate the billing procedure, as Sophia Collier did, for instance. Because she had no money with which to hire a famous package designer, she arranged to pay him a royalty based on product sales. (See Packaging.) Sometimes smaller public relations firms will accept stock in a client's company as a form of payment. During the start-up phase, many companies cannot afford PR, but it may be critical to their success. They offer stock to the agency and later buy it back when they have greater cash flow.

6. *Realistic approach.* The agency should not be overly ambitious with what it can accomplish. Like the wildly successful fortune bagel gimmick (see Gimmicks), a public relations firm should not create more demand for your product or service than you can handle. An overly successful campaign can even hurt the business.

7. *Demonstrated success.* You're hiring the agency for its knowledge in your area of business or activity, knowledge of the media, and its success rate of assisting companies and organizations in communicating their messages. Each presentation or proposal should cover demonstrated success. This includes brochures, press releases, generated stories on television, radio, newspapers and magazines, direct mailings, special events, market research, and direct mail campaigns. The agency should show you its portfolio of media articles aimed at your target market or one similar, as well as records of special events that have reached the people in your market. Ask what the agency charged for particular projects that you see in the portfolio and how your price range may compare. Ask the agency to leave its portfolio behind for a few days for you to review. This gives you time to read the articles to see what kinds of messages the agency gets across for its clients.

Fees and Charges

Billing procedures by most agencies incorporate the set fee (that is, retainer, staff time, project, hourly, or clip) plus "out-of-pocket" expenses. A business hiring a new agency should ask what is included in these. Out-of-pocket charges generally should not exceed 15 percent of the retainer, hourly charge, or story clip fee, or an understood amount for a project. "This 15 percent is usually accurate unless the agency has cleared further expenses with the client," says Kronick. Out-of-pocket expenses often include telephone, postage, administrative services, supplies, photocopying, travel, and business meals. Be sure to ask for an itemized list of out-of-pocket expenses if they exceed the 15 percent level.

After working with an agency, some business owners or managers pick up some public relations savvy and take the work in-house. Working with a PR agency on a project may be a way for you to learn a few tricks of the trade.

Further Resources

Public Relations Society of America
33 Irving Place
Third Floor
New York, New York 10003

Its *Public Relations Journal* frequently highlights case histories of effective PR campaigns—often for small organizations.

The National Retail Merchants Association publishes *Ad/Pro* magazine, which reports on how retailers worldwide advertise, promote, and publicize sales, events, openings, and many other public relations activities. For more information, write to:

NRMA
100 West 31st Street
New York, New York 10001

Getting Your Message Out
Michael Klepper Associates
805 Third Avenue, 8th Floor
New York, New York 10022

For more information, see also *O'Dwyer's Directory of Public Relations Firms*, which is listed in Part III—Further Resources.

$
___

Quality

Today's business outcry is to push for high-quality products or services. Stiff global competition and problems with international trade have put renewed emphasis on quality. The popular press has publicized this interest with articles on the plight of the automotive, steel, electronic, and appliance industries.

Frugal marketers are often unable to compete with big-budget marketers in such areas as pricing, distribution, or huge promotional programs. They cannot afford a price war, buy in bulk, or have widespread distribution outlets. As a result, the goal of high product or service quality becomes a worthy and powerful option for businesses with limited budgets. Those who are successful seem to have a strong desire to offer products and/or services that meet the highest possible quality standards.

Before we get too far, you should probably know what we mean by this abstract term "quality." We use it in an all-inclusive way to encompass such positive things as reliability, durability, precision, longevity, ease of operation and repair, compatibility, safety, and style.

"Quality is not evangelism, suggestion boxes, or sloganism—

it's a way of life," says Armand Feigenbaum, founder of his own consulting company in Pittsfield, Massachusetts.[1] The pursuit of high standards is not a periodic and intermittent task but a steady, far-reaching process.

Your own constant concern and attention to high quality standards is a worthy endeavor. Good quality could have a positive effect on lowering costs while increasing your sales, profits, market share, or level of customer loyalty. Many small businesses and associations have found that the better product, additional services, or extra attention is a strong antidote to the aggressive deep-pocket marketers.

Good quality should not be short term. Previous studies show that constant high standards make good long-term economic sense. Consider these interesting facts:

- As many as one quarter of American factory workers don't produce anything. They simply fix other workers' mistakes.[2]
- Poor quality costs manufacturers about 23 percent of sales and is even more expensive to service firms.[3]
- Over a twenty-year period, companies that provide quality products and services have ranked in the top of their industries in at least four out of six financial criteria (e.g., asset growth and return on sales). See the best-selling book by Thomas Peters and Robert Waterman, *In Search of Excellence.*[4]
- In general, businesses selling high-quality products or services are more profitable than those that sell goods of lower quality, according to a major study, "Profit Impact of Marketing Strategies (PIMS)," done by the Marketing Science Institute.
- A classic article in the *Harvard Business Review* makes some startling conclusions: The value of lower prices is often short-lived since competition will quickly match them. Thus, lowering prices may have little relationship to increasing market share. Also, advertising has only a minor impact on market share changes.[5]

These facts, some highly controversial, illustrate the possible argument for selling the notion of good-quality merchandise. If you agree, you must decide on realistic ways to achieve this philosophy.

Members of the American Society for Quality Control (ASQC), an association interested in quality control and management methods, send out a "quality check card"—a customer feedback card—with each shipment to allow the association to understand better its customers' expectations. It takes guesswork out of improving the ASQC's services.[6]

From a marketing perspective, good quality standards should be defined from the customers' viewpoint. We must not assume that customers lack the capabilities or information to measure quality. Some of the busiest doctors, dentists, or counselors are those with popular bedside manners—even if they're not the most competent. Therefore, to succeed, competence must be in the eyes of the beholder—the consumers.

Customers will define quality in broad terms. They look at such factors as postsale services, warranties, guarantees, location, convenience, packaging, and return privileges. Your offerings will be carefully compared with the competition. This is why you must let your customers state their own preferences and feelings about your level of quality.

To gauge customer interests, you can use surveys, customer comment cards, observations, focus group sessions, and the like. You should also rely on your own sales force or outside reps, suppliers, and business partners who are in constant contact with your markets.

Suppliers must match your own expectations for quality. Jack Shoemaker, editor-in-chief of Northpoint Press in Berkeley, California, believes in searching for good-quality printers: "The biggest problem with most printing companies is that quality control has become a thing of the past. "Companies have decided it's cheaper to wait for a complaint and reprint a book rather than to watch over quality."[7]

Your employees need to be concerned and committed to high-quality standards too. When you're involved with employee recruitment, selection, training, and performance appraisal, continually stress your quest for quality. Employees who can deliver on the quality issue should be rewarded and visibly recognized.

Any subcontractors you hire must also meet your high standards. Be specific on what you expect. Otherwise their poor craftsmanship could destroy your business. This same suggestion applies if you're involved with a franchise or licensing arrangement. Since you're part of a total system, one weak link in quality control could hurt your sales badly.

To maintain high quality, you may have to make some additional investments. For example, more money may be needed for research and development, a bigger computer system, more phone lines, additional service reps, or more warehouse space for better customer delivery time. These are not easy decisions since the benefits may not immediately be apparent with more sales. Nevertheless, like many other marketing areas, the investment for better products and services becomes a wise budget decision instead of a nagging cost of doing business.

One last suggestion on your own quest for quality: Be careful if your business is growing rapidly. Sometimes shoestring marketers have problems with financial and managerial controls. They're expanding so fast that quality is sometimes sacrificed— knowingly or accidentally. They may have been successful because of their excellent reputation for high quality. They lose this one essential trait that made them so successful when they lose sight of their original goals. The moral: Don't push your business growth at the expense of lowering your high quality standards. It could even result in eventual failure.

In short, shoestring marketers of high-quality goods have more flexibility. They may charge relatively higher prices, keep customer loyalty, receive positive publicity, or attract more financial backing for expansion.

Further Resources

For more information or to keep abreast on current trends, contact:

American Society for Quality Control
310 West Wisconsin Avenue
Milwaukee, Wisconsin 53203

Through promotion, education, and research, this excellent international association focuses attention on important issues dealing with improving or maintaining excellent quality standards.

$

Restaging Products

Euripides, a 5th century B.C. Greek tragic dramatist, once wrote: "Leave no stone unturned." This age-old statement is certainly appropriate for marketers with shallow pockets.

There's an ever-present nagging challenge to sell and grow, even under limited financial conditions. But frugal sellers must condition themselves to find creative ways for increasing revenues while keeping costs down. How can you make additional money without major changes or investments within your current business structure? One excellent way is to spin off products (initially developed for your in-house use), by recycling the waste generated by your main product lines, or by thinking up a whole new use for the same old product.

Marc Goldfarb, a Los Angeles–based stockbroker, was looking for ways—other than selling stocks—to capitalize on his wide range of business contacts after the stock market crash of 1987. Having been quickly conditioned to look for opportunities resulting from crisis, he discovered that many apparel manufacturer clients of an investment banking firm he represented were suffering from a cutback in orders and excess inventory.

Goldfarb formed a trading group to act as a clearinghouse for unwanted inventory. His company finds new markets for excess apparel inventory that is not being pushed by manufacturers' reps.

"When a company has excess inventory there is no incentive for sales reps to solve the problem," says Goldfarb. This is especially true in the apparel industry where styles go in and out every few months. "Salesmen would rather push next season's lines because that's where the commissions are."

That's where Goldfarb comes in. Manufacturers would rather sell off the excess at a discount rather than chalk up a loss. Goldfarb finds a different distribution channel or alters the inventory and sells it at a profit. He charges a company that wants to recycle a product a 10 percent fee of the total cost of putting together the trade. For instance, he bought a large inventory of white denim Levi jeans at $5 a pair. The labels were removed, and Goldfarb farmed the jeans out to be tie-dyed. New labels imprinted with university logos or mascots replaced the old ones. Goldfarb sold the jeans to university bookstores for $10, and the bookstores, in turn, sold them to students for $30 a pair.

But companies with excess inventory don't necessarily have to go to a middleman to remarket a product. Often all it takes is a step back to look at a product in a different light. Sometimes a company can be too emotionally attached to a product and is not willing to deviate from its original purpose, says Goldfarb—a costly ego trip.

Restaging an old product is usually less expensive than trying to introduce a new one into the competitive marketplace because older products generally have acquired some name recognition. Often all that is needed is to update its image, make improvements, or create a spin-off.

Eveready Battery Company recently found a new distribution channel for its batteries by just changing the packaging. The batteries were imprinted with colorful designs of balloons, happy birthday greetings, and holiday designs. Eveready named its festive spin-off Gift Mates and found a new distribution channel in gift shops that normally do not stock batteries. The batteries are attractive enough to be placed next to gift wrap and greeting cards.

One way to create new uses for an old product is to pretend you have never seen it before. Let your imagination go and see how many uses you can come up with. Most will probably seem zany and impractical, but you may come up with one that is viable. It's not unusual for a spin-off to evolve into a separate business.

Here are some other illustrations of thrifty marketers who have broadened their offerings and increased revenues by spin-off and recycling.

• Entrepreneurs Babs Ryan and Joy Gowland, owners of a retail parfumerie, La Belle Epoque, in New Orleans, once paid $90 for four kaleidoscopes. Ryan and Gowland bought the toys to make a little extra money. If they didn't sell, they would at least entertain the men while their wives or girlfriends shopped for perfumes. The kaleidoscopes were an instant success, and people wanted to buy them instead of the perfume. As the perfume business declined, the partners expanded their kaleidoscope line, including opening up a second location, the Kaleido Shop. They now sell everything from a $3 cardboard model to a $3,000 hand-carved version. First-year sales were projected to be around $400,000, not bad considering that the original product intent was to make a few more dollars and possibly keep shoppers' companions from getting bored.[1]

• Film-Dallas Pictures, Inc., a small, independent movie production business, was developed from a seminar that its financial consultant founders gave on investing in motion pictures. The firm now makes "low-budget, low-brow, beat 'em up and get-out-of-town (Hollywood)" movies. The spin-off opportunities of cable TV, VCR rentals, and foreign opportunities also have encouraged Film-Dallas Pictures to become an independent movie producer. By analyzing investment opportunities and giving seminars, the founders identified a spin-off venture that became more profitable than selling their seminars on investing.[2]

• George Lutjem, consultant for the newsletter industry and president of his own firm, advises newsletter publishers to look for spin-off opportunities in the publishing industry. He advises his peers and clients to become the source of information in one's own field. In addition to newsletters, for example, publishers might seriously consider self-published books, industry directories, and nonsubscriber/subscriber surveys to build newsletter sales.[3]

• Neil Milner, executive vice-president and CEO of the Iowa Bankers Association, Des Moines, offers 100 ideas on how associations might increase outside sources of income. He says associations need to overcome dependence on declining membership dues. Some of his major suggestions in spin-off areas include insurance, travel, cooperative purchases, publications, magazines, resource centers, specialty items, printing, educational programs and conventions, rental income, computer services, consulting services, joint ventures, employee referral service, and financial advice.

However, says Milner, "If the service you provide your members ultimately does not do the job, you may defeat the very purpose of the service by decreasing not only your nondues income, but your dues income as well." He tells association marketers working with a tight budget to make sure that they have the professional and technical expertise to offer spin-off products.[4]

• James Ross, consultant for the University of Tennessee Center for Industrial Services, tells of one wood pine furniture milling company that started a business venture of recycling waste from narrow pine strips. From the strips, the company made small wooden baskets that were successfully distributed to craft shops, hospital gift shops, and department stores. "I think they were quite surprised with the success of this product," says Ross.

• One of the author's clients made wooden broom handles from his by-products of wooden pallets and crates. The broom handles provided a steady cash flow despite the small lumbermill's other cyclical sales.

• Many home builders also have a nagging problem of finding steady revenue opportunities. Their business, highly volatile, is dependent on the economy, as well as mortgage interest rates.

Some small home builders are now providing services in home improvement, equipment rental, educational courses for do-it-yourselfers, and cleaning and refurbishing home-related supplies, such as floor tiles, rugs and linoleum, and walls.

Why and when should low-cost marketers consider spin-off or recycled offerings? A major concern is to avoid spreading precious marketing resources and time too thin. Careful planning can help ease some of that concern. Overall, we think the pros of recycling and spinning off outweigh the cons. Spinning off and recycling can:

- Move sluggish inventory
- Make better use of waste
- Fill unused capacity/or time
- Help cash flow problems
- Cover overhead and fixed costs
- Test the waters for new customers or new product lines
- Develop employees or provide worthwhile management experience
- Improve efficiency within the business with spin-off ideas
- Satisfy current customers who may want additional products or services from the seller

On the other hand, marketers should avoid launching new projects for the sole purpose of making money, says Peter Quay Wright, senior account executive for Communicators, Inc., an association membership marketing and communication consultant in Rockville, Maryland. "Your primary objective must be to fulfill a need. Find out what your target markets really need and want that you can provide better or at less cost than anyone else."[5] Wright offers four important principles for a correct beginning:

1. Fulfill a need.
2. Think like an entrepreneur; be open-minded and innovative.

3. Start slowly. Build on current services.
4. Develop new and related offerings.

Spin-off ideas frequently are born when companies strive to improve their internal operations. Smart shoestring marketers constantly ask, "Do I seem to have a lot of waste? Is there something I can produce internally to improve my manufacturing, operations, and cost structure?"

From this self-analysis often come ideas for new business ventures. "Does this internal product [service] then have revenue potential for current or new customers? Are we already doing a task [e.g. new in-house computer knowledge-based systems to improve internal decisions] that may have sales appeal to external markets?" By having an open mind and constantly striving for improvement, shoestring marketers will uncover additional ways to invent and sell spin-off and/or recycled products.

According to one classic study of 152 spin-off ventures, services—rather than physical products—were the most common of all spin-off offerings. Some common services that were spin-offs were:

- Training and education services
- Product or process design and engineering services
- Marketing research and analytical services
- Physical and chemical testing services
- Computer and data processing services
- Personnel services
- Management consulting services[6]

It's understandable that services are popular spin-off ventures. In contrast to manufacturing and/or just selling physical products at the retail level, additional production or inventory costs are usually less—certainly relevant to marketers with shallow pockets.

Your own customers can help you discover new uses for your product. Ask them what kinds of products they think are similar to yours. Can you incorporate the uses of similar products into yours?

Review your distribution channels. Say you manufacture hosiery, and your only retail channels are department stores. Orders for your purple designer fishnet stockings, so popular last season, have dried up because the new rage this season is not purple fishnet but green. You're stuck with excess inventory of purple fishnet that your retailers wouldn't touch this season with a ten-foot pole. What do you do?

Why not try a different distribution channel? Discount the price of your excess inventory and sell it to some local grocery stores that would love to stock their shelves with designer stockings, even if they are slightly out of style.

Don't let the bottom line get in the way of being creative. Often it's the concern with the bottom line that prevents small-business people from thinking creatively about alternative ways of marketing their products.

Start with brainstorming ideas on what types of new services are attractive for bringing in more sales. Then you might explore opportunities to see if "waste" can be minimized or recycled for additional sales.

Remember, as shoestring marketers, "leave no stone unturned." You constantly need revenue-producing opportunities, and spin-off or recycled offerings may be one more profitable option.

$

Sales Letters

The latest technology in personal computers and office equipment offers low-cost marketers the opportunity to write sales letters. Low-price PCs allow you to personalize letters quickly and cheaply; no longer must your letters look as if they've been mass produced on some second-rate Ditto machines.

Sales letters can be powerful selling tools, especially in business-to-business markets. Once you overcome the initial writer's block, you'll be able to target your promotional pitch to certain individuals.

Sales letters are usually cheaper than sending out nonpersonalized mass mailings of brochures, fact sheets, product literature, and so on. Furthermore, readers like to receive material that is written for them instead of some "Dear Sir" clone and to see their name on an address label. Recipients of personal-looking letters are less likely to discard it as junk mail.

"Printed descriptive material is often necessary, yes, but the letter is your salesman," says Howard Shaw, a mail-order business owner. "The letter provides the human contact, the handshake, the personal influence to do business with you—and motivating push that closes the sale."[1]

Through sales letters you may seek new leads, provide product information, announce special sales, introduce new products, or actually make a sale. This correspondence is also effective in following up a sales call or saying thanks for an actual sale. (See Thanking the Customer.) With a letter, you can sell almost anything—a product, a service, an idea. Opportunities are unlimited, says Shaw.

When you compose sales letters, don't become bogged down with grammatical perfection, but your letter should be intelligible. With practice, writing does become easier. Proofread your letter several times for typos, and ask someone else to proof it too. That person may even have some suggestions for improvement. Eventually you'll be more at ease and will write with clarity and precision.

Many shoestring marketers lack confidence in their writing skills, losing out on a strong low-cost selling opportunity. Concentrate on tone—how the reader will feel when reading the letter. This approach often translates into a conversational style with everyday grammar and vocabulary. Write as if you were carrying on a conversation with a colleague. Be friendly but professional. Always keep the reader's viewpoint in mind. If you're appealing to well-educated, sophisticated business or professional clients, your syntax should be a little more upscale.

While keeping all this in mind, don't forget that you are writing a sales letter. Your letter should make the reader want to rush out and buy your product or service. When developing your strategies for an ongoing sales letter campaign, follow these time-tested guidelines:

1. Carefully direct your letters to the right audience. Do your homework about the people you are writing to so you know as much about them as possible. You can then specifically address some of the individuals' needs, concerns, problems, or potential benefits of buying your offerings.

In direct mail, for example, good marketers carefully break down names by major categories and subcategories. This task helps you construct very individualized letters. (In business-to-business markets, with fewer customers, this is somewhat easier.)

2. The introduction must spell out the benefits while attracting readers' attention. Some professional writers may experiment with thirty or forty trial openers before settling on one. The first few words are critical; a writer has to capture the readers' interest in the first sentence—or be banished to the garbage pail with all the other junk mail.[2]

The first paragraph of a sales letter should be no more than three lines. Galen Stilson, a direct mail expert, advises that the first paragraph be "brief, snappy, and strictly oriented to the interests of the reader."[3]

3. It's best to allow smoother reading by using short paragraphs, familiar words, sharp expressions, and short sentences. It's critical to adopt a "you" approach; put emphasis on the reader with words like "you" and "your"—not "we," "us," and "our."

4. Identify the advantages, as the consumer might see them, of your products. What do the readers care about? How well does your business meet their concerns? Clearly address these questions in your letters.

5. Appeal to the readers' emotions. Can your products help overcome fear, time pressures, money problems, stress, or anger? Tell why your products are competitively better in dealing with emotional issues.

6. Whenever possible, use supportive statements to back up your claims and selling points. You must establish confidence among the readers with such devices as certificates, company awards, expert endorsements, customer testimonials, warranties, reliable product literature, or unbiased but positive material. Readers especially like to hear about other people who had pleasant experiences with your business. Don't be modest about your accomplishments, particularly when they minimize consumer doubt.

7. While varying your sentence and paragraph length, be sure to repeat the benefits to your target audience. Some repetition is

acceptable because you want the reader to remember why your products are so needed. Also, repetition is required to improve memory and recall.

Postscripts are popular in sales letters. They help to repeat and summarize the essential reasons why the reader should buy from you. Point out the positive rewards for making a purchase; don't be subtle.

8. Close by encouraging some type of action. You may, for example, tell the reader to write or call for more information. Or provide toll-free numbers, postage-paid reply cards, sales reps' numbers, or self-addressed stamped envelopes.

To create direct action, you might try such popular techniques as:

—Offering a free sample
—Stressing the item's limited availability
—Giving a discount for a certain time period
—Making an ironclad money-back guarantee
—Using a tear-off stub on the order form

Most people are procrastinators. If given a chance to wait, your readers probably will never respond or will misplace your sales letter.

9. Send follow-up sales letters if you don't hear from readers. They could be busy or have merely forgotten about you. When receiving the first letter, some prospects may have had little use for your products. Eight to twelve weeks later, however, they might need your products.

Many direct marketers will tell you that three to five letters (impressions) are sometimes necessary before you get a sale. Some of your letters could be the goodwill type; others can be more direct by asking for the order.

Don't be discouraged if your earlier sales letters produce only minor results. They could be the good building blocks to getting sales from follow-up letters.

10. Despite your efforts, you'll never be sure of the full drawing power of a sales letter. Split-testing—testing sales letters against each other—is a common procedure. By coding different letters with different department numbers for each, you can

measure the response rate. Eventually you'll see which prospect lists, copy, envelopes, and the like have the best impact.

Almost every shoestring marketer can use sales letters. At first, the mechanics of planning and writing a letter seem time-consuming. But after writing a few, you'll find the words come easier. If they don't, assign someone on staff to write the letters for you.

Try to develop key repetitive paragraphs and phrases for different situations. You may also develop a solid nucleus of letters to use more than once. The letters may seem somewhat standardized to you, but new readers will find them personalized and original.

This promotional method is often cheaper than using some form of mass advertising that appeals to general markets. Today's word-processing software packages allow you the capability to mass produce letters that look as if you've typed them individually yourself.

To provide some additional help, here are a few other tips.

- Before writing the actual letter, write down the major purpose.
- Avoid technical or detailed language that confuses readers.
- Emphasize some key thoughts by using script, bold type, capital letters, or underlining or by setting them off with dashes.
- In long letters—say, more than two pages—use section headlines for easier reading. But try to keep letters as short as possible.
- Put your most important consumer benefits in the beginning.
- Be specific about benefits. You could write, for example, "You'll save an average of $10 per order. Here's how it works."
- Keep readers' vocabulary in mind.
- Express your thoughts in a precise, concise, and orderly manner, but don't worry about writing the greatest book on good grammar.

- Add a routing list at the top of letters to businesses to encourage forwarding to important buyers.
- Don't worry about having colorful and expensive graphics, layout, and typesetting. For shoestring marketers, a well-written, typed, personalized letter is more effective and cheaper.
- Create a time frame—"hurry up"—approach. Otherwise readers will forget and put it off (e.g., "limited time offer—buy now and save $20").
- Be persistent. A reader will finally buy sometimes after receiving three or more promotional letters.

Sales letters offer a wonderful opportunity to zero in on some good prospects individually. Compared with other promotional alternatives, you may really get your money's worth, yet this low-cost promotional technique is sometimes ignored. (Perhaps everyone thinks that letter writing is too time-consuming or is too worried about being criticized about the mechanics of writing.)

If you're considering using sales letters as a major part of your marketing efforts, start reading the column "Marketing Viewpoint" in *Direct Marketing* magazine. The column is written by sales-letter guru Dr. Luther Brock, otherwise known as the "Letter Doctor." He offers excellent tips for crafting effective letters.

$

Seminars

William Delphos knows a low-cost marketing tip when he sees one. He ought to—he founded Venture Marketing, Inc., a Washington, D.C.–based consulting firm, to help small businesses compete nationally and internationally on tight budgets. Delphos also knows how to market his own start-up firm's services on a tight budget. And he says conducting seminars is an effective and inexpensive way to draw clients.

Venture Marketing specializes in helping small businesses tap free and inexpensive government resources to help them compete overseas. Unfortunately, says Delphos, "the firms that need this help don't know where to begin to look for it." So instead of waiting for prospective clients to find out about his company, Delphos goes straight to the source. As an expert, he gives seminars on a subject his target market is interested in: competing internationally.

Delphos, who spent four years in a White House–appointed position with the Overseas Private Investment Corporation before founding Venture Marketing in 1985, decided to focus his seminars on one industry at first. He chose the electronics field because he knew the industry is highly concerned about international survival and is already competing abroad.

For less than $1,000, Delphos put together a humorous slide presentation using cartoons to illustrate the many services the government provides private companies to compete abroad. He then contacted a major trade association for the electronics industry to see if it would be interested in booking him to give a seminar to its members as part of the association's ongoing seminar series. The association has twenty-one councils across the country that are always looking for programming material of interest to groups of their members.

Delphos targeted several geographic markets where he was interested in attracting clients. The association did the legwork; it sent out a one-page flyer and wrapped the presentation around a luncheon meeting. "A lot of people make the mistake of thinking you have to start everything from scratch," he says. "We piggyback preexisting activities with a subject that would be of interest to members and let the association, as a part of its regular programming at each council, pick the time and the day, do the mailing, and charge what it wants to charge."

Venture Marketing does not make its bread and butter off seminars, however; Delphos conducts an average of only one seminar a month. He is more interested in clients he picks up as a result of the seminar.

Credibility plays a big role in attracting follow-on clients, says Delphos. "You're being ushered in as a featured speaker by an association that's representing the participants' interests. So, you walk in immediately with a credibility factor." At the end of the seminar Delphos makes it a point *not* to give out his business card—unless someone asks for it. He says he does not want to give the impression of trying to solicit business. Instead he sends all seminar participants a follow-up note, letting them know he enjoyed working with them.

"You get a real word-of-mouth selling capability by doing this," he says. "There may be only thirty-five members in an association, but it's amazing the power that as few as ten clients from an association can have when they turn into reference-selling multipliers." Of the first six seminars that Delphos conducted, he took on twelve new clients.

Don't worry if you're not always drawing a big crowd to your seminars. Delphos doesn't always think in terms of big numbers. "I get the same number of follow-on clients from a group of twenty as I do with fifty," he says. "Smaller groups give you the opportunity to get to know them and understand their products. The larger the group, the easier it is to be lost in the crowd."

Not every seminar you conduct may reap the results William Delphos has enjoyed. "To have a successful seminar you have to have the right topic, and you have to make sure you're talking to the right people," he says. You also have to have expertise in the field you're talking about.

To help draw the right kind of follow-on clients, Delphos advises being specific about your expertise, the content of your seminar, and the kind of audience you want to address when you're making arrangements with an association's seminar organizers. "If you're going to do this, you better have a very narrow cast expertise. That's the key. You've got to be perceived as being expert if you want follow-on clients."

Further Resources

For more information, see National Trade & Professional Associations of the United States listed in Part III—Further Resources.

$

Signs

"When I started my business, I was really working on a shoe-string," says Judy Greason, owner of the Bay Window Boutique, a women's specialty apparel and gift shop in Rye, New York. "Every time I would make a sale, I would run to the bank to cover a check that I had just written."

Greason's location—on the rear of a main street facing a parking lot—was a big marketing challenge. She had to be innovative to get customers to the back, off the traffic of the main street.

To overcome these obstacles, Greason put her resourceful, shoestring marketing instinct to work. First, she drew attention to her store by the power of inexpensive signage. In Greason's case, her signage was more than inexpensive; it was free. She retrieved a chrome sign holder that another merchant had thrown out and uses erasable ink to get the most use out of her laminated cardboard sign.

Greason crafts new, handwritten signs every few days, using tickler messages to pique the interest of passersby. WINTER WONDERLAND SALE—ALL ITEMS UP TO 80% OFF and MEN'S NIGHT ONLY are two ticklers that have helped lure customers into her shop as they walk through the parking lot.

For shoestring marketers, using festive and unique signs can be one of the most inexpensive ways to gain name recognition in the community. Most businesspeople overlook the effect that a good sign can have on increasing store traffic, especially if a business is off the beaten path. A sign says a lot about a company's goods and services and even its personality. It is the bait that can bring customers to your doorstep.

Lisa Renshaw used a giant 5- by 10-foot sign to attract business to her parking garage in Baltimore. The garage had been a failing operation with no name recognition until Renshaw took over its management. Her first order of business was to make train travelers at the nearby Amtrak station aware of the garage. (See Brochures and Flyers.) She renamed it Penn Parking to tie into the name Penn Station, the train depot serving Baltimore. The next step was to bring customers to her business.

Renshaw recalls that she "didn't even have enough money to have an [operating] budget, let alone an advertising budget," but she managed to scrape together enough money to have a sign professionally printed. She shopped around for small independent printers who were willing to negotiate the price of the sign and found a price that would suit her minimal budget.

"There's such competition out there in the printing market that you can get reasonable prices and get a professional look, too," she says. Marketers who use signs frequently to advertise sales and specials also should not overlook the proliferation of instant sign franchises around the country. They produce professional-looking signs in very little time for very little money.

Renshaw posted her bright blue sign with white lettering that read simply "Penn Parking—Fully Secured Garage" in front of the Amtrak station. She reinforced the sign by printing up pocket-sized coupon flyers, which she distributed personally to travelers exiting and entering the station. The flyer, printed with the same colors as the sign, included a perforated coupon for one free car wash after five visits to the garage.

"I tried to tie in as much as I could," says Renshaw. "Every different piece of advertising somehow tied into another. The garage sign tied into the flyers. And I thought if I could pick a name for the garage that would tie into the station, that's what I wanted to do," hence the name Penn Parking.

The signage and tie-in advertising has helped turn her business from a two-employee operation into a fourteen-employee, thriving business. When Renshaw started out, her garage's main competition was the Amtrak open-air parking lot. But her advertising and personal appeals at the station pulled so many customers away from the station's lot to her garage that she has since been awarded the management contract for the Amtrak lot.

Other innovative marketers are finding that signs do not have to be stationary to get attention. The American Trucking Associations reports that 10.1 million people see the average tractor trailer in a year. Local delivery vans make more than 16 million impressions on the community in a year, and 91 percent of the survey's respondents said they notice trucks that display words or pictures.

It makes sense. What better audience for your ad than motorists stuck in traffic with nothing to focus their attention on but your truck? And motorists driving down the interstate on a long trip—on long stretches of highway without billboards—are a captive audience for trucks with pictures or messages.

One midwestern food company researched the impact of mobile billboards and decided to use them as a major means of advertising. The company went to a local graphics firm to turn its tractor trailers into mobile billboards by silk-screening photographs of the company's products onto giant vinyl sheets with adhesive backing. The company's president reported overwhelming results.

Although the cost can be moderate to expensive, depending on the size of the illustration and technology required, advertising on your trucking fleet, otherwise wasted space, can be an effective way to permeate your target market area with your company's name or product—in big, bold letters.

The Transportation Department's Bureau of Motor Carrier Safety's rules permit full-scale ads on a truck so long as they do not interfere with its exterior lights, are not obscene, and do not create an optical illusion, such as stripes or circles that would make the truck appear smaller than it actually is. However, be sure to check local, state, and federal ordinances for updated rules and regulations on truck advertising before you turn your shipping fleet into giant billboards. And if you are planning to erect a stationary sign, check with your local government to ensure that you are not violating any local or state ordinances.

Your sign should say a lot about your company's products or services and its personality. Here are a few helpful hints:

- Include a logo, especially if it is used on other reinforcing items, such as flyers, brochures, and advertisements.
- Keep the wording brief. Too many words on a sign looks jumbled. Passersby generally will not take the time to read a wordy sign.
- Use the same colors as you do on other advertising, such as your business cards or company logo. You want prospective customers to associate particular colors on your logo design with your business.
- If you can afford it, try using illustration or photography on your sign. As the adage goes, a picture is worth a thousand words, and people remember visual images more easily than the written word.
- Type style should reflect the personality of your business. If you are an upscale jeweler, you don't want a homemade, folksy type of sign. On the other hand, if you're a country-cooking restaurant, you don't want your sign to be printed in sophisticated script.
- Discuss your goals, objectives, and exact budget with your printer. The more certain your printer is about your needs, the less likely you will end up with a sign that is overbudget and does not suit your needs.

Further Resources

American Trucking Associations, Inc.
2200 Mill Road
Alexandria, Virginia 22314

U.S. Department of Transportation
National Highway Traffic Safety Administration
400 Seventh Street, S.W.
Washington, D.C. 20590

American Council of Highway Advertisers
304 Pennsylvania Avenue, S.E.
Suite 300
Washington, D.C. 20003

Outdoor Advertising Association of America
1899 L Street, N.W.
Suite 403
Washington, D.C. 20036

Transit Advertising Association
1025 Thomas Jefferson Street, N.W.
Suite 502
Washington, D.C. 20007

Its members sell advertising in facilities of public transportation companies.

Signs Directory
American Business Directories
5707 South 86th Circle
Omaha, Nebraska 68127

Lists nearly 20,000 sign painters and printers nationwide. Published yearly.

Signs of the Times—Buyer's Guide Issue
Signs of the Times Publishing Company
407 Gilbert Avenue
Cincinnati, Ohio 45202

Lists more than 600 manufacturers and distributers of equipment and supplies for the sign industry; trade associations, consultants, trade shows, and other related organizations also listed. Published annually.

Signs of the Times—Sign Erection and Maintenance Directory Section

Same address as above. Lists more than 1,000 firms that install and/or maintain electrical signs. Published monthly.

$

Specialty Advertising

Specialty advertising is one way small associations and companies can boost membership, gain an edge on competitors, attract attention to a product introduction, or increase attendance at meetings.

All this from a coffee mug imprinted with a logo? Although the most common specialties—giveaway items imprinted with logos, slogans, or company or association names—are mugs, paperweights, writing pens, and calendars, associations and businesses can choose from more than 15,000 specialty items to fit any budget or objective, says H. Ted Olson, president of Specialty Advertising Association International.

Specialty advertising items are generally distributed free to customers, clients, or prospective association members. "The purpose is to incorporate them into a marketing strategy so that the items will be used often by the people you want to influence," says Olson. "As people use your specialty item, they will remember your association, company, or a particular promotion."

Among the sundry ways to incorporate specialty advertising items into a marketing campaign, many associations and businesses use them as envelope stuffers in direct mail campaigns. "It's a way to get your envelope opened," says Olson. With the proliferation of junk mail, the target audience often throws your message away before they even open the envelope, he says. "But when people receive an envelope that feels like there's something in it, natural curiosity will get them to open it."

Specialty advertising can also be used to generate sales leads. Williams Relocation Service in Tulsa needed dramatic results from a very small ad budget. The start-up operation, which helps transferred employees shop for homes, arrange for moving vans, and settle into new areas, needed to make a name for itself. To attract the business of fifty personnel departments of large corporations in three nearby cities, Williams Relocation chose a specialty ad campaign using a transplanting theme created by its ad agency to emphasize the care it gives uprooted employees. The company mailed empty flower pots imprinted with the phrase, "Official transplanting cost container." An attached card introducing the company's services said, "Employees are like plants; they'll flourish in the right environment."

On follow-up calls, salespeople delivered live plants for the flower pots. Of the fifty targeted companies, forty-five made appointments with Williams's salespeople to discuss the company's services. "That was really our purpose with the campaign," says Linda Brooks, relocation manager. "We were new and unknown. The program gave us a lot of name recognition in our target market."

Print advertising—at an estimated cost of $20,000—was prohibitive. "A year's advertising campaign in a small inflight magazine and a trade magazine was well over $200,000," says Brooks. The price for the "transplanting" campaign was only $5,300, which included 500 flower pots—50 of which were sent to prospective clients—and a fee of about $700 to the ad agency that handled the campaign. The company used the leftover items in an ongoing campaign.

Olson believes one of the greatest advantages of specialty advertising is the ability to reach a target audience. Regional associations and businesses can send their message to only those customers and members they want to reach. "Magazines, TV, and radio can reach huge audiences, but if you're only trying to influence a small segment of that audience, there is a lot of circulation waste," says Olson.

The Ohio Education Association went the specialty ad route during its membership drive in 1986. With the help of a specialty advertising distributor, they chose the theme "A + for Schools." They wanted to reach not only prospective members in the school system but boost morale of existing members as well. The association distributed bumper stickers to statewide members and gave apple-shaped lapel pins to faculty members at the association's leadership meetings. Lapel pins were also distributed to local chapter members. School secretaries received pens imprinted with the campaign theme, cafeteria employees received aprons imprinted with the theme, and bus drivers were given caps. Response was phenomenal. Membership increased by almost 3,000.

But specialty advertising may not work for everyone. "You have to have a good theme fit," cautions Olson. "And the item has to be appropriate for the people you're giving it to. You can't give tennis balls to golfers." Also a specialty advertising campaign should be unusual so it will stand out. That takes careful planning and deciding exactly what message to convey through a campaign.

There are more than 6,000 specialty advertising distributors (or counselors) nationwide who will help determine the objective you want to achieve through specialty advertising. The counselor suggests creative and useful items that best fit your budget and theme. Specialties can be ordered for a couple hundred dollars to thousands of dollars, depending on your objective.

Further Resources

For more information, you can find local distributors listed under "Advertising Specialties" in the Yellow Pages, or contact:

Specialty Advertising Association International
1404 Walnut Hill Lane
Irving, Texas 75038
(214) 580-0404

In addition, see *Incentive Marketing—Resource Guide Issue* listed in Part III—Further Resources.

$

Telemarketing

Telephone selling—taking customers' phone orders and/or making sales calls—is becoming an increasingly effective marketing tool. One of the fastest-growing marketing specialties, telemarketing accounts for more than $150 billion in yearly sales and should triple by 1990.[1]

"The telephone can be used to sell all manner of products and services, from encyclopedias to office decoration and maintenance services." says author James Porterfield. Although telemarketing can work for even the smallest operation, there is no single cookbook approach that will work for every organization.[2]

An average telemarketing operation can increase sales 10 to 20 percent; well-run programs can frequently double sales volume, says Richard L. Bencin, a telemarketing consultant and president of Bencin and Associates, of Cleveland. Effective phone calling can also help screen prospects for face-to-face presentation. One person, he says, can make about twenty calls per hour, completing five to eight of those calls.[3]

There are no specific estimates of telemarketing costs. The cost can range from fifty cents to $20 per call, depending on the nature of the conversation. The only agreement from telemarketing experts is that business-to-business calling is more expensive than calling on consumers.

Many small businesses use telemarketing to get leads, develop a prospect list for follow-up promotions, make goodwill calls to current customers or association members, service an account, or measure the degree of interest in the products or services of the caller's business or association. Cost depends on the complexities of the telemarketing objectives, products, and marketplace.

Don't think that telemarketing is only for large organizations. Most in-house telemarketing operations are actually developed by small businesses. In 1986 it was estimated that 140,000 companies were employing phone sales operations, and most of these were small businesses.[4]

You may use telemarketing for any number of reasons. The key is to decide on specific sales objectives. What do you want to accomplish through this powerful marketing tool?

In a survey in 1986 (published by the National Association of Wholesaler-Distributors), plumbing, heating, and piping firms were asked where telemarketing works best for them. Their response, in order of importance, was:[5]

Direct sales	40 percent
Inquiry handling	34 percent
Lead generation	14 percent
Cold call canvassing	9 percent
Other purposes	3 percent

Before starting or exanding a telemarketing operation, you must first understand a few basic realities and myths about telemarketing.

The first myth to discount is that consumers and businesses find phone calls a nuisance. Poorly trained and misinformed callers are a nuisance, especially if they call at dinnertime. But phone calls done correctly can provide good information, solve buyers' needs, and answer their questions quickly.

The reality is that telephone sales is an art with very few

magic formulas—despite the popular "ten telemarketing steps to $1 million in sales" mentality. You can learn some basic principles, but it's like learning to drive a car. You must practice and find what's best for your customers and your organization. You learn by doing.

Second, you should have a good concept of what will be covered. A canned script is not essential. If it's too contrived, it will turn off your listeners. No one likes to be "talked at."

Another misconception is that telemarketing is only for the hard or immediate sale. Inbound and outbound calls can serve other purposes, such as reinforcing other promotional efforts.

All kinds of products and services can be marketed by phone. It need not be limited to noncapital, small-ticket items. In fact, field salespeople of expensive equipment appreciate the good sales leads that are derived from a solid telemarketing program.

Forget trying to set up a boiler room operation; the number of calls you make is immaterial. It's how successful you are in achieving your goals with those completed calls.

Telemarketing is a tool that must be carefully planned and coordinated with your other low-cost marketing strategies. You must define your goals, hire the right callers, think about the message, carefully record the calls for market research information, develop a good data base system from the outbound and inbound calls, and analyze the program to improve future productivity.

Start this process by setting up a log report system. Log sheets may identify the date, time, contact, company, standard industrial classification, zip code, credit standing, credit limit, price quotes, promotional material already mailed, referral information, sales history, products previously sold, and type of follow-up needed. The range and type of information for the log sheet will depend on your own expectations.

Before making a telephone sales call, outline the key points you want to cover. Charles McNichols, a retired telemarketing executive near Nashville, Tennessee, recommends sending a letter, catalog, flyer, or promotional literature before making a sales call. "This mailing piece is in the prospect's hands, and you can use it as part of your script," he says. "It establishes the name of your company and yourself. Cold calls require more explaining and time."

After the phone conversation, you may decide to have someone make a sales call in person or send promotional material. Telephone log reports will ensure sound follow-through procedures. Once your form is developed, you'll find a wealth of information that aids the selling process. In fact, telemarketing is a quick and inexpensive way to get trends affecting your target market.

Field salespeople, advertising, direct mail, public relations, and telemarketing go together in communicating your business to the customers. Good timing of promotional and communication efforts will strengthen your telemarketing programs.

Telemarketing does take time. You shouldn't expect overnight miracles. Depending on the type of business, it may take six to twelve months before you see results. But be patient. After a certain point, sales should follow. Customer postservice outbound calls, for example, produce long-term results. They can generate favorable word-of-mouth recommendations.

S. Michael Zibrun, president and founder of a leading business-to-business telemarketing consulting firm, notes that when you start a program, 95 percent of its success depends on planning. Success depends on the people you select to make or take the calls.[6]

Motivating Employees to Sell Over the Phone

"The creative use of the telephone, organizing your calls before making them, and systematically recording the information sound very logical," says Charles McNichols, "but actually doing it is like trying to diet or stop smoking—neither of which many people are able to do."

Telemarketers, says McNichols, often prefer to take the easier inbound calls instead of making outbound calls. McNichols used to make each salesperson in his company spend one hour a day in a private room making a certain number of outbound calls.

TIPS: Successful Phone Conversations

John Franco, president of Learning International, Stamford, Connecticut, says that the first thirty seconds of an outbound sales call are vital. The caller should first acknowledge that the receiver's time is valuable and that the call may be an interruption. Good phone representatives know what to say in advance and have analyzed market data. In "The Trouble With (Some) Telemarketers," an article by Richard Bencin in the August, 1986 issue of *Business Marketing* magazine, Franco offers these six tips for a successful phone conversation:

1. *Set realistic call objectives.* Before calling, decide if you want to update your mailing list, qualify prospects, or close a sale.
2. *Ask the right types of questions.* Learn how to uncover customers' needs, problems, and concerns.
3. *Acknowledge what the customer said.* Don't talk *at* the listener. Talk *with* the person on the other end.
4. *Describe product features as benefits that are meaningful to the listener.* Follow a need-satisfaction selling method. Explain how you can solve the problems and needs of the listener.
5. *Recognize and handle attitudes.* Don't ignore any objections or negative attitudes that are voiced about your products.
6. *Know how and when to close.* Avoid the common error of talking past the close (that is, continuing to sell even after the customer has agreed to the caller's objective). This distraction may result in a new topic of concern by the customer.

Above all, think from the prospect's point of view. Surely you've been in the prospect's shoes at one time or another. Doesn't it bother you when a rude and persistent telemarketer calls just as you're sitting down to a rare dinner with your whole family together? Try not to call at dinnertime or early in the morning. Surveys show that consumers hate being bothered at these times.

Many consultants, trade associations, telecommunication companies, phone suppliers, universities, and government agencies are starting to offer low-cost training sessions in telemarketing for employees. AT&T has already circulated success stories about small businesses and entrepreneurs who have built their empires through phone services—from 800 to 900 numbers to collection of overdue accounts. You can pick up some timely insights for employee training from AT&T's reps or through the AT&T National Small Business Video Conference. (Call your local AT&T customer service for the latest on small business services.)

Every caller was also responsible for making quarterly follow-up calls on 100 accounts, identified as the 20 percent group that generated 80 percent of the firm's sales revenues.

Often all it takes to motivate employees are a few incentives. George Terzis, chairman of Santa Ana, California–based Candy Stripers Candy Company, gives daily cash motivators to the top-selling employees in his telemarketing department. He has even set up games in which the telemarketer who makes the sales within a certain amount of time gets to draw a prize.

Selling Quotas

How many calls can be made per hour, day, or week? A study in 1987 found that an effective telemarketer can make thirty to forty calls per hour.[7] Charles McNichols, on the other hand, says he averaged only ten calls per hour, which included recording the results of each call and reviewing the outcall form for the next call. McNichols believes that "four to five hours a day is all one person can spend on the phone and it's a very tiring operation."

The number of calls will vary by product and market. Test yourself on how many completed calls are reasonable within a certain time period; try one hour in the morning and one hour in the afternoon for a week, for instance. Make sure your self-test is long enough to be accurate. When you have a better picture, you can set the completed call quotas for you and your staff.

Without any specific quotas, calling will often be put off. Quota systems could be based on the number of dialed telephone numbers and calls completed, accounts serviced, and sales closed per day or week. Be sure your range of quotas is reasonable; otherwise you'll have personnel turnover, or your callers will come across as being terse.

Sources of Telephone Lists

Developing a telemarketing system is great, but who do you call? The following list may help you compile your own list of phone numbers:

- Yellow Pages directories (for business-to-business marketing)
- White Pages telephone directories (for locating consumers in a specific geographical region)
- Dun & Bradstreet credit reports
- *Directory of State Manufacturers*
- Trade association membership directories
- List brokers (usually located in the Yellow Pages under "Mailing Lists"). Brokers may charge anywhere from $20 to $200 per 1,000 names
- Trade show attendees
- Community, civic, or social organizations
- Current and previous customers or members (if you're an association)

Most of these sources charge only nominal fees—if any. Once your sales program is ongoing, you'll be able to test various lists to see which ones are the most useful.

Charles McNichols says that some updating of your lists is mandatory. Recent trends toward downsizing, reorganization, and mergers and acquisitions have caused many personnel changes in today's business world.

To ensure an effective and economic telemarketing effort, watch and control your costs. Analyze your results with the direct costs of doing telephone sales. This may include benefits such as the number of new accounts, volume, sales leads, type of inquiries, product information, or the number of inquiries handled. How do these benefits compare with other marketing efforts and your total operating budget?

Further Resources

For more information about telemarketing, contact:

American Telemarketing Association
104 Wilmot Road
Suite 201
Deerfield, Illinois 60015
(312) 940-8800

$

Thanking the Customer

In our big, complex, rapid, and global business world, customers often wonder if anyone appreciates their business. Everything often seems so impersonal. Once money exchanges hands, the customers feel they're forgotten. Although this may be untrue in your business, some of your customers may cling to this misconception.

One simple way to show gratitude is to thank your customers periodically for their patronage. By making it a common and standard business practice, it shows that you care about them. Employees should be constantly reminded to say "thanks" at the time of the sale. And then later, follow-up thank-yous can be expressed.

Joseph Cherry, president and founder of Cherry Tire Store, Maybrook, New York, started a simple policy of sending a personal thank-you note to each customer. Every evening he sits down to sign cards that read, "Thank you very much for calling Cherry Tire Service. We really appreciate your business." "Since each card goes right to the person I want to reach, it's better than newspaper ads," says Cherry. "And customers don't forget it."[1]

Some entrepreneurs even send personal handwritten (not

typewritten) notes after making a major sale. You can also call customers from time to time—such as on the anniversary of a big purchase—to see if they're still happy with the purchase and if there is anything you can do for them.[2]

A tickler file of purchase dates by customers' names is one low-cost way to remind you to send thank-you notes. Once you start, you should make it standard practice to send notes to *every customer;* otherwise some customers will wonder why they didn't receive any thanks. This is especially true in small markets where your customers interact with each other. If they haven't received an expected thank-you note, they'll wonder, "Are my purchases not important?" Be consistent—even during your peak and busy periods.

Some smart salespeople will periodically call customers to see if there are any problems or special needs. The main purpose is to say thank you, but if special problems or service requirements are needed, the requests are dealt with quickly.

When saying thanks, avoid the temptation of asking for more business. Some customers perceive this as tacky and question the sincerity of the thank-you note or call. Remember, the more opportunities you have to contact your accounts, the more they'll think of your business. Keep prospecting separate from the goodwill and thanks type of communication.

When there is good news for customers, share it with them. Perhaps you recently won an award, you're expanding, you're moving to modern facilities, you have positive revenue growth, or you've reached a business milestone. This is another chance to tell them thanks. Without them, this good news would not have been possible. You may even be able to pass along some of this favorable news through special parties, discounts, preferred customer sales, rebates, gifts, and so on. Some cooperatives, mutual companies, and franchisors provide dividends, discounts, and advertising allowances to show their appreciation. You too may say thanks with some tangible action.

Customers' birthdays may be another time to express your thanks. (See Kudos.) "We care for you . . . Happy Birthday!" is the title of a card that is sent to all of the patients of one small dental office. Colorful balloons are artistically printed on the cover. Inside the card is a statement, "All of us hope you had a wonderful and happy birthday. As always, thanks for your business."

Holiday periods provide additional opportunities to show your gratitude. One Tennessee veterinarian sends Christmas greeting cards to his customers' pets. Written inside the card is: "We appreciate having you and your pet 'Yankee' [customer's dog's name] as clients and wanted you to know we were thinking of you during this holiday season."

Whenever you send thank-you notes, be sure there is nothing included that could possibly offend any of your customers. For example, one successful Chicago mail-order photo-processing business included separate religious material with the developed

---

TIPS: Saying Thanks With a Gift

Some shoestring marketers like to express their appreciation with a gift. Paula Schauwecker, president and founder of Gift Search, a Dallas executive buying service, has some gift-giving advice:

- A gift should cement a good relationship, not try to create a new one.
- Aim for high quality. You can still find well-made items, such as letter openers or address books, for under $5.
- Reinforce your company image with the gift. For instance, a high-tech firm may give a small, streamlined calculator.
- Avoid potentially embarrassing personal gifts, such as personal clothing or hygiene items.
- Investigate your customers' background. Liquor, cigars, or ashtrays may upset some people.
- The safest gifts are usually food items; everyone can enjoy them, and they're usually inexpensive.

Source: Sharon Nelton, "It's Time to Say Thank You," *Nation's Business* (November 1987), p. 40.

film and thank-you cards. After a while, the founder decided to ask the customers to check a box with a self-addressed, stamped envelope if they no longer wanted the religious material enclosed. Some customers did specifically ask that this material be left out. Therefore, be careful of what you include; you never know who you might offend—even if you feel it's quite minor or innocent.

Sometimes your customers may enforce a policy of discouraging employees from accepting gifts from suppliers or vendors. You should find out if your customers follow this rule. Otherwise the employees will be disappointed by having to return gift items, and it could create some tension within your customers' organizations. This will hurt your future business in the long run.

"Thank you" is a powerful but low-cost marketing tool. It allows you to develop one of your most precious assets—your customers. No matter how busy, you should find ways in which you can show your appreciation. A tasteful and continuous practice of saying "thanks" is one of the basic rules of smart frugal selling.

Your appreciation will not only make your customers feel special but will keep them coming back. Too many marketers spend their time trying to attract new customers while neglecting to make sure their current customers are happy. It's much less expensive to keep current customers than to prospect for new ones.

$

Toll-Free Numbers

No doubt you've noticed that most mail order companies encourage you to use their toll-free 800 phone numbers to place an order. Direct mail marketers have long known the advantages of these numbers to spark potential customers into action. Now businesses of all types have discovered the benefits of toll-free calling. Eight-hundred numbers can be seen on everything from computer software packages to ice cream cartons.

In addition to increasing customer response, toll-free numbers present a helpful service image, speed the order process, offer personal contact with customers and suppliers, and can qualify sales leads immediately. According to a report by Cahners Publishing Co., 50 percent of toll-free inquiries lead to sales. Seven out of ten specialized business magazine readers use toll-free numbers, and nearly 90 percent wish more advertisers would offer toll-free convenience.

John Hines, cofounder and principal of Hines and Smart Corp., Boston, put in an 800 line as a customer convenience and a way to cut exorbitant phone bills. His company has been shipping live lobsters by air to restaurants and hotels since 1955. As the business grew through word-of-mouth referrals, direct mail advertising and publicity from in-flight magazines, Hines discovered his company's phone bill was growing too.

"A lot of the customers got into the habit of calling collect," says Hines. "Our phone bill was $3,000 to $4,000 a month." About that same time, AT&T was sending flyers with its monthly statements to advertise its 800 service. After receiving another hefty phone bill, Hines called the number—toll free, of course—on the flyer. An AT&T representative visited his business, analyzed his operation, and gave him a comparison figure of an 800-line phone bill to what Hines was paying. The difference was so great that Hines requested the 800 number; it has cut the cost of long distance calls just about in half. Although Hines cannot recall the exact amount of the initial 800 service hook-up, he says, "Whatever the cost was, I didn't consider it at all very much."

The 800 line, says Hines, "has helped us not only to retain our present customers, but also has helped us in securing new business." In addition to including his 800 number in direct mailings, Hines is listed in AT&T's *Toll-Free Directory*. The directory, which has both consumer and business versions, lists any business or organization with an 800 number. Hines paid $1,500 for his highlighted listing and considers the exposure worth the cost. "People do refer to it and use it," he says. "It's surprising how many people will look for an 800 number." (For information on how to advertise in this directory, see the sidebar at the end of this entry.)

"People like the 800 line; it's convenient for everybody concerned," Hines says. He also uses the toll-free number to encourage banks to call back on credit checks. "It comes in very handy when a customer whose credit line we are not familiar with wires us money," he says. "If we tell the bank to call us on our regular line to confirm the money wire, the banks don't like to spend the money. But they will call us on the 800 line and say, 'Yes we have a money wire for you.' So, we're assured that the customer we're shipping the lobsters to has paid us."

To find out whether your company or organization could benefit from a toll-free number, call several phone companies and ask for a brochure on their 800 service. Once you have an idea of what a toll-free number can do for you, call phone company representatives and ask for a free analysis. Compare the results of each, and choose the company you feel will give you the best service for the best price. AT&T, for instance, says its 800 Readyline start-up costs are about $100, and a monthly service charge is approximately $20 per 800 number. The price per call is based on the geographic distance and length of the phone call.

Most phone companies tailor the 800 number to suit your

Ad Rates for Toll-Free Directory

Ad rates for listing your company in the AT&T toll-free 800 business and consumer directories range from free (for a first-time listing that includes the company name, city, state, and phone number) to around $20,000 for a full-age ad on the outside back, inside back, or inside front of the directory's cover. Types of listings vary from boldfaced listings to fractional display ads to trademark listings.

A "Super Bold Listing" that prints "Joe's Garage" in large boldfaced type with a line separating Joe's listing from the ones above and below it and two lines of copy, such as "all major brands in stock" and "free catalog—discount prices" with a phone number, may run slightly more than $1,000. (Of course, prices change from year to year.) The directory does offer incentive pricing programs that can work with your budget and objectives.

For information about advertising in the directories, contact the authorized listing agent for AT&T Toll-Free 800 Directories:

M. Berry and Company
P.O. Box 6000
Dayton, Ohio 45401
1 (800) 562-2255

A representative will work with you to design a listing that best suits your needs and budget.

needs. For example, you can base the 800 calling area on your regional and seasonal needs. You pay only for the geographic coverage you want. If you prefer to receive calls only from the target markets of New York City and Chicago, for instance, you would pay a fee based only on those markets. Cost is further reduced by discounts for volume usage and calls placed on weekends and in the evenings.

Many companies and organizations are also using 800 numbers to cut outgoing calls made to talk with suppliers or conduct business. If you want to know whether a company or organization you're trying to contact has an 800 number, call the toll-free directory assistance line at 1(800)555-1212. The operator will look up the number for you and tell you whether it is a toll-free listing.

Further Resources

AT&T Toll-Free 800 Directory for Business
AT&T Company
550 Madison Avenue
New York, New York 10022

The first "official" directory of toll-free numbers. Cost is $14.95 for business directory. Also publishes a toll-free directory for consumers, $9.95. Free to 300,000 selected businesses and 1 million households with individual household incomes of more than $35,000. Ads accepted.

$

Tracking Your Competition

When was the last time you knew what your competition was up to? Most companies are pretty secretive about marketing strategies, especially in small market areas. But getting to know how your competition is positioning his product or service may help you spot new markets you may have completely overlooked—not to mention helping you redefine positioning strategies within old markets.

In today's increasingly competitive marketplace when marketing experts are constantly preaching that the only way to gain market share is to make your product jump out from the competitive pack, it helps to know how the competitive pack is planning to set itself apart from your product. If you're getting ready to launch a new product, for instance, you can save thousands of dollars and hours of research time trying to pinpoint the best markets by simply keeping track of your competition's positioning strategies.

One way to find out what your competition is doing—short of planting a spy in his operation—is to study his advertising. By compiling a clipping file of competitors' ads and publicity, you can better determine how you will plan your own positioning campaign.

When you are preparing your yearly advertising budget, it helps to know how much the competition is spending, where, how, and on what products the money is being allocated. Because you probably do not have time to read every publication your competition may be advertising in, subscribing to a clipping service can be an effective and efficient alternative. Clipping services also include tracking radio, television, and cable advertising and publicity, as well.

Burrelle's Press Clipping Service, Livingston, New Jersey, for instance, has a special division to provide advertising analysis of your competition. The service reads daily, weekly, and Sunday newspapers, as well as nearly every trade, consumer, and professional magazine. You tell the clipping service's representative your needs and objectives and who your competition is, and he or she will tailor a clipping program to suit your specifications. The service provides computerized reports on a monthly, quarterly, and cumulative basis that inform you of all you need to know about what your competition is up to. Cost depends on the frequency and concentration of the analysis.

By retrieving and analyzing your competition's advertising and publicity, you may find new markets and product benefits that you had not even thought about. You may also discover that they are cutting back their advertising in certain markets. With this strategic knowledge, you may develop a way to pick up where the competitor has cut back.

One marketing manager says that although he would arbitrarily leaf through magazines and clip his competitor's ads, until he hired a clipping service, he had no idea of all the different markets the competitor's products were in. He also discovered the trade publications the competitor most frequently advertised in—one indication (over time) of which publications offer the most reader feedback.

Some experts, however, think you should just go about your own business and never mind the competition, reasoning that if you worry about your competition, you never have time to do anything innovative yourself. On the other hand, knowing how your competitors are positioning their products, you might develop a better plan to distinguish your business from theirs. The key is not to see the competition as the intimidating enemy but as a source of innovative marketing strategies. Don't just look at what you traditionally have considered your competition. Related but noncompeting companies can be great sources of new marketing approaches too.

For more information about clipping services, flip through the Yellow Pages to the heading "Clipping Bureaus."

Further Resources

How to Find Information About Companies
Washington Researchers Publishing
2612 P Street, N.W.
Washington, D.C. 20007

Lists more than 1,500 state and federal government agencies, investigative firms, libraries, information services, computer data bases, trade association, labor unions, and other organizations that collect information on public and private companies. Published annually, $95.

$

Trade Shows

Trade shows (also known as sales exhibitions) can sometimes be a useful, cost-efficient marketing tool. Shows can reinforce your image, allow demonstrations, permit product sampling, lend credibility, attract sales inquiries, and even result in on-site sales.

In some industries, trade shows are almost a prerequisite for selling in certain markets. For example, machine-shop industries have a strong need to demonstrate their products. Trade shows allow these companies immediate, far-reaching geographical exposure and product demonstrations to key groups of prospects. The cost per demonstration plus set-up charges of the machinery could be far cheaper than making individual sales calls.

According to the annual survey of selling costs published in *Sales & Marketing Management*, the cost of one sales call is around $118 in consumer markets, $179 in industrial markets, and $162 in service markets. A 1985 study by McGraw-Hill, on the other hand, found that one sales call cost around $230, up 222 percent since 1975. Interestingly, McGraw-Hill notes that it may take 5.5 sales calls to get the order. The number of calls could easily result in a cost of over $1,200.

According to William Mee, president of Trade Show Bureau,

a trade show research organization, trade shows for small businesses offer the best marketing opportunity. You can reach more people in one hour than having a salesperson on the road for a week. He estimates the costs of getting one qualifying lead at $106.89. Mee notes that with a qualified trade show lead and sound follow-through with a telephone call or sales letter, it takes 0.8 sales call (cost of one sales call is $230 × .8 = $184) to convert one trade show lead. In short, it takes $106.89 plus $184 to obtain one sale. In round numbers, this amount is almost $1,000 less than getting an actual sale on the road (remember, 5.5 calls before your cash register rings).[1]

Although we may debate the exact costs for getting one order, trade shows do offer a viable marketing option for a shoestring budget, especially in the business-to-business markets. Mee states that a small company can accomplish a great deal with some creativity and pizzaz. Careful planning and a personable approach can help to ring up sales.

The International Exhibitors Association, Annandale, Virginia, publishes an excellent yearly budget guide for planning and controlling trade show costs. The guide's objectives are twofold: (1) to help in accurately predicting projected costs of doing business in the trade show exhibit industry and (2) to develop uniform methods for simplifying the annual estimation of your next year's costs. In this handy guide, a number of forms are provided that highlight four major and typical expense categories for participation:

1. Exhibit design and construction (e.g., construction materials)
2. Transportation (freight/drayage)
3. Show services (photography service, electrician's labor, furniture, and equipment rental)
4. Other expenses (presenters, air travel, hotel accommodations, and space rental)

The guide also contains a survey of "estimates of anticipated changes" as reported by the industry suppliers who offer the goods and services that go into the cost of trade show participation.

Tradeshow Week (Los Angeles) publishes *Annual Survey of Labor Rates*. For example, in 1986, riggers had the highest nationwide hourly average rate ($36.20) of the nine labor categories surveyed, while security guards had the lowest hourly rate ($8.04). This outstanding guide also conveniently gives the index of labor rates for forty-two major trade show cities.

As you can see, there is a wealth of trade show data, which can prevent you from busting your marketing budget.

Some people believe that sales exhibitions are only for the rich or big organizations. Yet in some cases—especially in foreign trade or in high-technology/industrial domestic markets—trade show participation is a sure way to achieve credibility and make smart selling gains.

To succeed as a trade show participant, you should follow four basic rules:

1. *Define your trade show objectives.* Some well-thought-out objectives are essential. You may, for instance, want to introduce one new product; identify 100 new qualified prospects from the projected 2,000 registered visitors; or write $50,000 worth of sales or identify and eventually sign up $100,000 of subcontracting business. However, do not forget the major purpose. Trade shows should have a direct or indirect impact on making sales and bringing in revenues. This multibillion-dollar industry and marketing tool is serious business. It's not merely to have fun, garner a free trip, or combine pleasure with business. You should use trade shows to induce revenue.

2. *Select a trade show.* Two major sources about specific exhibitions are *Tradeshow Week Data Book*, which tracks over 2,500 major shows, and *Exhibit Schedule*, which gives more than 10,000 shows, many of them small. Your own trade or industry associations should also have practical information on which shows may be worthwhile. Vendors and suppliers, distributors, sales agents, and other business associates can often provide some suggestions on which shows would be best.

Before making your decision, see if the trade show organizers can provide an audit (verifying the number of attendees) or a survey (audience profile) from previous shows. Was this audit or survey done by the organizer or an impartial independent outside source? Some organizers may even provide information on those who preregistered for an upcoming show.

In your preliminary investigation, ask sponsors if they can supply you with some names of people and similar businesses who previously exhibited their products. You can contact them too for evaluation purposes.

If doubt still persists, sign up as a registered attendee and check out the professionalism of the show plus the makeup of the audience. This transitional step is cheaper, and it gives you some useful data on industry and competitive trends. If impressed, you can become an exhibitor the next time.

One low-cost tip is worth mentioning: Do consider regional shows, especially if you lack the distribution and marketing capabilities to expand beyond a certain geographical distance. There are many fine regional trade shows that can provide powerful revenue opportunities.

In your decision-making process, consider: (1) the mix of attendants and visitors, (2) your own market targets, (3) which products to show, and (4) the finances needed to display your products. Your task is to pick the shows that will meet your trade show objectives at the most reasonable cost.

3. *Generate traffic using preshow promotion.* Without proper planning and good incentives, you may miss some key prospects or be disappointed with the actual traffic volume at your booth. Time is so precious during the show that you must manage it carefully. From our experiences, we all overestimate how much can be accomplished at a show. After, we're disappointed that we didn't spend as much time with certain people as we had hoped. Good planning of contacts and preshow promotion will minimize some of these time pressures.

Letters, phone calls, mailers, news releases, and ads about your participation are sometimes needed to generate interest and traffic flow. Sales promotion gimmicks, such as drawings, contests, free prizes, special events, or a preshow brunch, could be prudent. Remember, it's worth an extra couple of hundred dollars if it brings the right prospects to the booth. Make sure, however, that these are bonafide prospects. You may attract the wrong people to your booth, in the process distracting and discouraging good potential customers.

Get some idea if the potential attendees are truly solid prospects. Some qualifying and preshow screening will enhance your chances during the show. Just telling people you will have a booth is inadequate. You must capture their attention and interest.

4. *Decide what you will do during the show.* The Trade Show Bureau and National Association of Exposition Managers will provide vital advice on determining booth size, booth design, staffing, ideal number of people to have in your booth, product demonstration procedures, and how to work the booth.

You need a well-trained person to staff your booth. Don't assume that you or your sales personnel are automatically the most qualified. Mee observes that business women—not models—are extremely effective as booth representatives. Visitors want answers to their questions, which models can't always provide. Mee recommends that staffing people smile, never sit down, and never send out negative signals via bad body language.[2]

Sometimes booth visitors are technicians who enjoy talking with their peers in the seller's business, called "opposite numbers." If your association or small business does not have a technician on the staff, look to your trade association, professional temps, nearby college professors, and suppliers for help.

If you're participating at a foreign trade show, the retired president of Porelon, Inc., Art Langlois, who is quite experienced with planning overseas trade shows, advises the business owner or chief executive to attend the exhibitions. Since many business owners and chief executives of foreign firms attend international shows, they expect and demand to speak with top executives and owners, their counterparts. Sending lower-level managers creates a personal affront. Langlois says that if your own rep comes from the country where you are exhibiting, you should have this agent, licensee, distributor, or vendor in your booth.

Whether in foreign or domestic shows, keep four basic rules in mind when working the booths:

1. Be sure to display the company name, product literature, and promotional materials.
2. Avoid mass merchandising your literature, brochures, and the like. They're too expensive to be given to curiosity seekers or poor prospects.
3. Be cautious of giving out your trade secrets; rest assured that your competitors are in attendance.
4. Always remember what you are trying to accomplish at the show. Sometimes design your own lead cards. These can be filled out by the visitors and will enable good follow-up for making concrete sales calls, mailings, or phone calls. Although trade show sponsors have lead cards about the attendees, they are usually too general. Design your own to fit the market information you need.

Returning from a trade show may make you physically and mentally tired. From being away, your filled in-basket and many catch-up projects will compound your busy schedule. These conditions could prevent your quick response with vital contacts you made during the show.

In their promotional pamphlet "180 Marketing Tips," the Milford, Ohio, consultants TechneGrowth suggest writing an immediate letter—dated the last day of the show—to all the booth's visitors thanking them for their interest in your organization. Soon after, you can put priorities on the most viable prospects to contact. This procedure, according to the consulting firm, demonstrates that you are a class organization. For a very small enterprise, even a one-person business, a quick follow-up letter shows solid professionalism.

How do you know if the sales exhibitions are worth their marketing costs? A successful shoestring marketer will try to measure a show's value against bottom-line results. Trade show effectiveness, according to Gary C. Young, University of Massachusetts at Boston and sales exhibition researcher, has not received the type of research needed as compared to other media. He notes that a study of the actual size and quality of attendees will help exhibitors plan for future shows. Performance measures are sales-lead generation, attendees' buying practices, or how the exhibits influence buying plans and awareness.[3]

In evaluating trade shows, one caveat should be given. We know of incidents whereby two or three years may have passed before a major sale can be traced to a show. A specific exhibition is frequently the seed or initial contact to a sale. Your patience and limited budget may be taxed. A solid judgment call requires a fair time frame. This longer time lead is especially true with high-tech or capital equipment industries. Recognize this limitation when doing your postshow evaluation. Don't be premature.

When operating on a low budget, be sure to contact local, state, and federal government economic and community development agencies. Many of them provide some excellent low-cost or free services for trade show participation.

To illustrate, the Mid-South Trade Council (MSTC) is an international trade development consortium in the mid-South region, encompassing Alabama, Arkansas, Mississippi, Tennessee, Louisiana, and the World Trade Center in New Orleans. On a regional basis, MSTC provides services to businesses interested in pursuing export opportunities. One of its goals, giving maximum exposure in foreign markets for member state businesses, is implemented through a series of catalog shows, trade fairs, and promotional events in the principal marketing regions of the world.

For a very modest cost, you can register your business and have state officials help give information about your services at various foreign trade shows. (The costs vary for each state.) Check with your own state economic agency or local government representative to see if your state has a similar service (most do) with a regional consortium.

Individual states also carry out certain programs to help businesses—especially small ones—sell their wares. Tennessee, for example, sponsors catalog mission products shows through the

Tennessee Office of Export Promotion. At no cost, the state sponsors companies at a catalog booth during a U.S. products show in a foreign region or country. The business must provide product literature; a brief description of trade show objectives, such as locating an agent or getting leads; and a reply to government staff members about any product promotion questions; and it must agree to respond promptly to any leads or inquiries garnered at the show.

Leigh Wieland, a Tennessee export consultant, notes that although participation in trade shows is usually limited to a certain number of companies, at times there are problems in getting businesses to participate even though the costs are zero. In spite of success stories from catalog mission programs, businesses just don't take advantage of the low-cost services offered by the state. Moreover, government officials often get excellent leads for some participating firms, but they fail to follow through on leads or quotation requests or they wait too long and the trade show attendee loses interest. Some companies that are committed have reaped the benefits, says Leigh.

In short, trade shows are a possible low-cost option for your business. To control costs, you might even share the booth with business associates or someone who has a similar but noncompeting product line, or try government-sponsored booths.

In certain industries, trade show participation is almost mandatory for acquiring respectability or getting accounts. If you are still unsure about the benefits, try some of these alternatives:

- Contact your own trade associations.
- Visit some sales exhibitions as an attendee.
- Contact the Trade Show Bureau and the National Association of Exposition Managers (NAEM), which offer excellent advice, checklists, budget guides, display rules and regulations, and an introduction to solid literature on trade show marketing.

NAEM publishes *Inform-a-Grams*, which offer tips for displaying your products. You can get its Publication Catalog by writing to its office at 334 E. Garfield Road, P.O. Box 377, Aurora, Ohio

44202. These sources provide an excellent foundation on effective trade show marketing. They can also help in limiting your expenses while still getting big results.

Further Resources

Meeting News—Directory of Sites, Suppliers and Services Issue
Gralla Publications
1515 Broadway
New York, New York 10036

Lists hotels, halls, convention bureaus, and suppliers of meeting/convention products. Annual, $4.

Meetings and Conventions—Gavel International Directory Issue
Murdock Magazines Division
News Group Publications, Inc.
One Park Avenue
New York, New York 10011

Details more than 4,000 halls, hotels, suppliers, speakers, entertainers, incentive travel houses, and sources for sports stars for meetings and conventions. Annual, $10.

Trade Show and Convention Guide
Amusement Business Division
Billboard Publications, Inc.
Box 24970
Nashville, Tennessee 37202

Information covers 14,000 conventions and trade shows worldwide up to seven years in advance. Also includes companies near trade show sites that supply support services like photography, exhibit design, hotels, and halls. Annual, $65.

$
___

Trends

How do some companies seem to know what's going to be in vogue before anyone else does? Their specially tailored products are the first in the market and get the biggest slice of market share pie. Do these companies have some direct line to a trend-predicting guru?

Big corporations actually do spend millions of dollars on consultants and market researchers to track consumers' buying trends to find out what products will be in in the future. But you don't have to spend millions to foresee the future. You can be your own trend-tracking sleuth, says Faith Popcorn, founder and CEO of New York–based BrainReserve, Inc. She ought to know; she's helped giants like Pillsbury Company spot changing values, needs, and life-styles that make consumers favor one product over another.

There really is no mystery to predicting trends, she says. By observing consumer attitudes and actions, small-business people can tailor their products and services to meet changing needs—even before consumers realize they have them. And all they have to spend is a little time, she says. Here are a few of her trend-tracking techniques:

- Read every current publication you can.
- Watch the top ten TV shows—or tape them and watch at your leisure. "They're an indicator of consumers' attitudes and values and what they're going to be buying," says Popcorn.
- See the top ten movies. They also influence consumer behavior.
- Talk to at least 100 to 150 consumers a year about what they're buying and why. "Do one-on-one interviews at supermarkets, on the street, wherever you find consumers," Popcorn advises. "You've got to go beyond your own structured marketing research, because reports are distorting. You've got to talk to consumers yourself."
- Talk to the top ten smart people in your life. Listening to observations of people whose opinions you value can give you another perspective of where the future is headed and how your business fits in.
- Talk to your children. "It's very important to understand what your children are doing, what they're believing, and what they're watching on TV," says Popcorn. "They can be tremendous guides for you." Also talk to their friends, who might be more honest with you than your children, she says.

Working the Trends You've Observed Into Your Marketing Plan

Make a list of the trends you have spotted. Write a brief description of your product's benefits and its positioning in the marketplace. Moving down the list, see where your product matches the trends and where it falls short. For example, you see an increase in microwave foods with a gourmet image and low-sodium content. But your company makes frozen gourmet entrees packaged in aluminum-foil containers, and sales are quickly declining.

Where you see your product falling short of meeting trends,

develop ways to bring it more in line. "If you see your product falling away from too many trends, you've got to either change your product or dump it, because you know you're going to have a failure," says Popcorn.

Your entrees fit the upscale, gourmet image but fail to meet the trend toward convenience and microwave cooking. They also fall short in the health category because of their high salt content. To put some life back into sales, consider changing your packaging. Aluminum foil cannot be used in microwave ovens. By eliminating the aluminum, you will open your product to a whole new market. And to appeal to the health conscious, you might cut the sodium content. Bring this to their attention by printing "lower salt content" on the package label.

"Every company that has made it, has followed this process," says Popcorn. Take Ben and Jerry's Homemade, Inc., an ice cream franchise in Waterbury, Vermont. "They matched on about ten out of ten trends," she says. The product met several trends: Having a person behind the name (Ben and Jerry), premium value (indicated by its premium price), and complication of product (it is not simply vanilla, chocolate, strawberry). And by listing a toll-free phone number on its product's package, the company presented the image that it cares about customers' opinions (trend toward integrity and humanization).

Spotting the Difference Between a Fad and a Trend

"You'll know a particular activity is a trend when you see it in many different categories, and you'll start to see it printed in some of the more far-out presses," says Popcorn. "With constant monitoring, you just get a feeling that this is something important."

The difference between a fad and a trend is longevity and "how many people are doing it." The typical life cycle of a fad is six months to two years. A trend emerges over many years. This is a difference that small-business people need to be particularly aware of.

Businesses should look for life-style changes that are years in the making, like convenience-minded, two-income families or entrepreneurial women. A successful company will customize its product or service to make their lives better or easier in some way.

Trends Carrying the Country Into the 1990s

A new trend called "cashing out" is emerging, says Popcorn. The materialistic yuppies of the '80s are trading in higher salaries for lower-paying jobs they find more fulfilling. "Under that trend there is an increase in charity hours and trying to find integrity and religion," she says. Companies wanting to cash in on cashing out may find that sponsoring charitable activities is a way to boost public awareness of their products or services.

Popcorn also sees a trend toward cocooning, which means "people are staying at home [after work] and feeling protected because they can't handle what's going on in the outside world."

While some people are cocooning, others will be falling into the fight-back trend. "Consumers are getting angry when they're not getting what they want when they have been promised something," says Popcorn. Examples of the trend toward fight-back is the increase of television talk shows like Oprah Winfrey's and Phil Donahue's, as well as an increase in 800 numbers and firing off complaint letters to corporations. Following up on complaint letters may be one way companies can win customer loyalty.

The trend of going back to traditional values, getting married, and having children also continues to grow, she says. One result of this trend will be an increase in entrepreneurial women. "Women are going to be the big business owners of the 1990s," predicts Popcorn. "Forty-nine percent of entrepreneurial businesses will be owned by women by 1990. They're going home again to have their kids, and it seems like the perfect side thing to do is open a business."

Businesses that spot market changes, such as aging baby

boomers, and tailor their services and products to meet the market's needs are the ones that win long-time consumer loyalty. Open your eyes. Trends are evolving all around you. Do you see any that can help your company gain an edge in the marketplace?

Further Resources

American Demographics, Inc. sponsors a number of conferences on target marketing and demographic changes for businesses and nonprofit organizations. For more information and a conference schedule, contact:

American Demographics, Inc.
P.O. Box 68
Ithaca, New York 14851
1 (800) 828-1133

$

Universities

John Elkins had built a small but respectable wedding and portrait photography business in Durham, North Carolina. In ten years of business, he saved enough money to open a studio in a basement office area of a local shopping mall, and he booked enough weddings to keep himself busy every weekend. But he found he wasn't turning as much profit as other photographers in the area.

To expand his business, Elkins wanted to attract more clients for the commercial photography side of his trade. But to do this he would have to change his image. His $140,000 annual revenues afforded him an advertising budget of only a few hundred dollars—not enough to include the kind of market research it would take to carve a new market niche in the Research Triangle area of North Carolina.

In 1987, however, Elkins learned about an organization that could conduct the market research he needed and make recommendations about how he could break into new markets. The organization's fees: absolutely nothing. The organization? The Small Business Institute program (SBI).

Funded by the Small Business Administration, there are more

than 500 SBIs across the country, as well as in Guam, Puerto Rico, and the Virgin Islands. They are housed in universities and colleges and provide intensive management assistance by teams of qualified college students in business disciplines.

Throughout the school year, students meet with local small-business owners who want to expand their product lines and markets but cannot afford to contract expensive professional management consultants. After months of conducting market surveys, management analysis, expansion feasibility and strategy studies, and even product line diversification and exporting analysis, the students put together a written detailed case report on their findings and their suggestions for improvement. The findings are presented to the client.

The SBI that helped Elkins is based at Duke University in Durham. His project was assigned to several students from Duke's Fuqua School of Business. They first asked him to prepare a report on his company's background, samples of his past advertising, lists of competitors, current and past clients, and companies he would like to recruit as clients.

Duke's student consulting group is made up of more than 100 MBA candidates and is supervised by Ted Wolf, a retired management consulting partner for Peat, Marwick, Mitchell & Company. He screens applicants who have been in business for more than one year, have a good track record, "but can't afford the professional fees of $50 to $100 an hour," says Wolf. "We also work with local associations," like the Durham Arts Council and Goodwill Industries.

Elkins's case is typical of projects the consulting groups takes on, says Wolf: "More than 50 percent of our activities is in developing new products, finding new territories and niches and advising them on what type of marketing they should be doing."

After several months of talking to Elkins's competitors, current and past clients, and prospective clients in the field he wanted to expand into, the students made an oral presentation to Elkins, followed by a written report of their findings and recommendations.

"They found that ad agencies, real estate developers, and architects who hire commercial photographers to take photos for their brochures, reports, and advertising look for quality first, then the ability to meet tight deadlines," says Elkins. "They also found that if you can do the quality work and turn it out on time, they don't mind paying extra for your service."

The students told Elkins that his clients considered him a general photographer and were not likely to hire him for big commercial projects. Their first recommendation was for him to change his business cards, emphasizing the commercial side of his business for these customers. "They said I'd be in better position to charge higher fees if I presented the image of specializing in commercial photography," says Elkins. "But I still use my other business cards emphasizing general photography for my wedding and portrait clients."

Now when Elkins goes to trade fairs to make contact with big corporations, he knows what they are looking for in a commercial photographer and presents that image. "I no longer stress my great location or camera equipment because I now know they really don't care about that," he says.

Another way small businesses can receive expert management assistance is through Small Business Development Centers. There are forty-nine of these centers located in forty-two state capitals. The center offers small business services through a network of subcenters and satellite locations, usually universities, community colleges, vocational schools, chambers of commerce, and economic development corporations.

Unlike the SBIs, services are donated by experienced individuals recruited from professional and trade associations, the legal and banking community, academia, chambers of commerce, SCORE (Service Corps of Retired Executives), and ACE (Active Corps of Executives), as well as other volunteer organizations.

The SBA funds 50 percent or less for the operation of each state Small Business Development Center. The small businesses receiving their services pay the rest. Often, however, matching funds are provided by contributions from state legislatures, private sector grants, state and local chambers of commerce, state-charted economic development corporations, and universities.

Services range from research assistance on all aspects of small-business management, financial, marketing and technical counseling, how-to export and import advice, and venture capital formation, as well as advice on how to participate in small-business incubators. A business incubator offers start-up businesses a common location, such as an office park or building, on-site management assistance, and shared support services, such as clerical and janitorial. Many universities and established businesses actively support incubator programs because they bring new companies into the community and provide a demand for their services as well. (See the National Business Incubation Association listed in Part III—Further Resources.) All these services are available to any person interested in going into business or expanding an existing small business.

Further Resources

For more information on Small Business Development Centers and Small Business Institutes, contact the nearest SBA office listed in the telephone directory in the "U.S. Government" section. You may also try contacting local universities to see if they have such programs or:

U.S. Small Business Administration
1441 I Street, N.W.
Washington, D.C. 20416
(202) 653-6668 or 6330

Or call toll-free (800) 368-5855 for a list of SBIs and SBDCs in your area.

In addition, see Distributive Education Clubs of America and Service Corps of Retired Executives listed in Part III—Further Resources.

$

Visual Merchandising

You are a store owner. Imagine that you are new in town and are window shopping. Is your store's appearance appealing enough to lure you in and keep you coming back?

Using visual treatments to make your store exciting can be critical to business, depending on your product or service. If you, as a store owner, are not excited about the way merchandise is presented, how can you expect customers to be intrigued?

A store's atmosphere can be a drawing card for repeat business. Justin Moreau and Robert Hanfling, who founded Star Magic, a futuristic, space-age gift store in New York and San Francisco, have refined the art of dazzling their customers. At a 1988 National Retail Merchants Association convention, Moreau illustrated his stores' success by giving a few tips on merchandising.

"Cheap effects are sublime if done creatively," he says. "Use all available space, not just the walls and floors. Hang [merchandise] from the rafters to give depth and perspective." He strongly encourages store owners to create a memorable shopping experience for customers by entertaining them, by being theatrical.

"You know you're a success when you see their eyes pop and their jaws drop as they walk in."

The use of lighting and music can be inexpensive ways to create a certain ambience and mood. Moreau uses floodlights, neon, and slide projectors to highlight different areas of his store. For stores that are very small, he advises using particular colors and mirrors to create a spacious, streamlined look. For stores that play music, Moreau suggests tunes that do not demand attention. The music should suit the mood of the store, and managers should be selective of music for their clientele. Moreau says synthesized, celestial music works well in his stores.

Even companies that have a seemingly boring product can create an exciting image. Barbara Fine, who owns and runs the Map Store in downtown Washington, D.C., uses innovative window displays to pull customers into her store. Her displays express her company's personality, and they have become a powerful and inexpensive marketing tool for the business.

"One thing about windows that I think people don't realize is that it's space you're paying for, and if you've got a decent location it really pays to bother dressing it up," says Fine. Making maps and guidebooks exciting has been a great challenge, she says. "Maps, being so one-dimensional, can be very boring and static looking even though the maps themselves can be very exciting," says Fine. "But the general public generally doesn't think so. So, I always try to think in three-dimensional terms when I design a display."

One April, Fine created an arrangement of French maps and guidebooks under brightly colored umbrellas for an "April in Paris" theme. The display was eye-catching, says Fine, because "we were putting something three-dimensional with something flat and boring." She also places items at different depths in the window to make the most use of her space and draw customers' eyes to each item.

The key, no matter what business you're in, is to "catch people's eye, make them think, make them laugh," says Fine. "If there's an important international event, we try to emphasize that." For the Winter Olympics, Fine displays a scoreboard with

TIP: Creating Effective Window Displays

Here are hints from Barbara Fine on designing window displays:

1. Decide how often you want to change the display. Based on frequency, plan a display schedule on a calendar, lining up holidays and special promotions to coordinate with specific displays. Planning ahead means you will have plenty of merchandise for the display and for your customers.
2. If a display remains in a window for more than two weeks, keep it clean, replacing faded items as needed. A dusty, faded display can detract customers just as a fresh display will attract customers.
3. Borrow props from other businesses. By placing a "courtesy of" sign with the display, you are not only giving other stores some free advertising but are saving a lot of money by not having to buy expensive props.
4. Divide large windows, the most difficult to deal with, into smaller display areas by grouping merchandise. A fabric store, for example, may break its window into three separate arrangements of fabric with different notions or craft items at the base of each. Keep enough space between the displays to maintain the integrity of each grouping. If they are too close, the window looks jumbled. Or dramatically fill the entire space with big props.
5. Balance form, shape, and color in the display. Check your local library for introductory books on art.
6. Try to avoid putting everything you sell in the display area. A window filled with a clutter of merchandise can often leave the passerby with no impression at all. Focus on only a few items.
7. Visit stores that employ professional window dressers to note what they are doing, in both windows and in the store as well. Imagine your merchandise in the display. You can do the same by flipping through interior design, fashion,

and trade magazines. Advertisements are also a great source of design ideas.

8. If you are really at a loss for window design ideas but still feel the need for good window displays, ask an employee if he or she would like to work on one. Or contact local high school or college art departments to see if any art students might be interested in creating some displays for you.

9. Check your local toy, paper product, fabric, and five-and-dime stores and florists for inexpensive props: toys, dolls, stuffed animals, model airplanes and cars, lace, ribbons, fresh and silk flower arrangements, potted plants, sphagnum moss, posters, prints, maps, wooden crates, umbrellas, baskets, rented mannequins, old books, confetti, colored tissue paper, balloons. Also check art supply stores for inexpensive display stands.

---

the maps of participating countries beside each event. Each day Fine puts a check mark in the boxes indicating whether a certain country received a gold, silver, or bronze medal the previous day. Fine says people will make a special point of walking by the window to keep track of who is winning the Olympic events.

"A lot of people stick their heads in the door and say, 'Like the window this time,'" says Fine. The media also have noticed Fine's displays. Her store has been mentioned in *The New York Times*, *The Washington Post*, the *Museum and Arts* magazine, and several regional publications. "It's reaching a point where our customers and the people who go by the store feel as though they have to comment on the window display. They'll tell us whether they like it or not." A traditional favorite is the Thanksgiving display when Fine fashions turkeys out of maps of Turkey.

While Fine is particularly artistic and innovative, most store managers or owners don't have the time or the creativity to fashion eye-catching displays. For the less imaginative, Fine suggests seeking out creative employees to design the window. When Fine is too busy to put up the display, which may take anywhere from thirty minutes to two hours, her employees put their creative juices to work. Sometimes they team up and stay after work to tinker with the display. It's a good way for employees to get to know each other better and feel as if they're contributing to the overall appeal of the store, says Fine.

One way to keep up a continuous stream of window display ideas is to put on a contest periodically for employees. The one who comes up with the best idea gets a small bonus or reward. You can extend the contest to your customers, giving a discount or a free sample to the person who comes up with the winning idea.

The cost of Fine's window displays "can vary from almost zero when I'm working with just the product to well over $100 depending on what kind of props I'm buying," says Fine. "If I'm putting in a formal flower arrangement, which has to be changed four times in the course of two weeks to keep the flowers fresh, I'm looking at something close to $200."

To keep costs down, Fine borrows a lot of her props from other stores in the area. For an American West display, she borrowed a saddle, spurs, and cowboy hat from a nearby western store. "Most companies are glad to lend material as long as you have something in the window that says the items are courtesy of that particular store. It helps us; it helps them." The Map Store also lends maps to other stores for their displays.

Fine usually has to give the store manager a deposit for the amount of the items she borrows. "But as long as you return the items in their original condition, they hand your check or credit card receipt back to you." Many of Fine's more than 200 suppliers will also send free promotional displays for her to put in the window.

In the fifteen years Fine has been running the store, she never has been robbed of a display. But there are certain items Fine says store owners should not place in a window display—jewels, for instance. And depending on the location of your store—particularly if you are in an urban area—you may not want to display bottled liquor. For St. Patrick's Day one year, Fine contemplated putting an Irish whiskey bottle filled with colored water in her display. But she realized it might be too tempting for some potential troublemakers late at night. "I didn't feel like paying to put a whole new window in," she says.

Most store owners don't give their store windows much consideration one way or another. They tend to leave their window displays in too long or incorporate the window space into the showroom display. "When you change the image of your store from the outside people notice," Fine says. "If it stays the same, after a while people just don't notice it." If a display stays up for longer than three weeks, the items start to fade, get dusty, and lose their appeal. Fine changes her display every two weeks, cleaning it out and washing the windows with each change.

With all the time and trouble that designing window displays can sometimes take, Fine says she can understand why more shop owners don't want to bother very often. "Yet when you do it consistently, it really does pay off. People write to us, saying, 'We saw your display and we want to know about that map in the window.'"

No matter what you sell, there are possibilities for exciting, interesting, and amusing displays. It is through a display of particular items that you can get a better feel of customers' reactions to certain products.

Further Resources

For more information, see National Retail Merchants Association, listed in Part III—Further Resources.

Word of Mouth

They told two friends and they told two friends and so on and so on and so on. . . . This is word-of-mouth marketing.

Associations and entrepreneurs who work hard to please their customers greatly benefit from word-of-mouth marketing—usually at no extra cost. They know that they can't simply buy their customers' loyalty; they have to earn it. And after they have earned their customers' satisfaction, they can encourage customers to tell their friends.

An article in the *Journal of Marketing Research* about a small piano-tuning business illustrates that word-of-mouth communication can have a dramatic impact on expanding a solid customer base. The findings, though limited to this particular business, are applicable to other small businesses and low-cost marketers.

The piano tuner developed a thriving business from referrals by a local music store and former customers. Other additional business—via word-of-mouth advertising—came from the piano tuner's personal social network—neighbors, church and social club members. These people would suggest the piano-tuning service to their social and professional acquaintances. Individuals associated with the piano tuner produced 1.43 new referrals per individual, with an additional .23 new clients coming from each music store customer.[1]

This study shows the powerful pyramid impact of word-of-mouth advertising. One person, association member, or business customer could be directly or indirectly responsible for attracting ten, twenty, or thirty new customers. No one can really imagine the true geometric impact of word-of-mouth endorsements.

Once a shoestring marketer is aware of the need for referrals, he or she must then try to create a culture and program that cultivate a vote of confidence in the marketplace.

Bill Brannen, author of *Advertising and Sales Promotion* (Englewood Cliffs, New Jersey: Prentice-Hall, 1983), says the good word doesn't spread by itself. You have to help it:

1. Give customers something to talk about.
2. Ask customers to talk about your business, especially when their complaints have been handled well.
3. Make it easy for customers to talk about your business.

"A referral card system that offers some small gift or bonus to the present or new customer is one method of giving some momentum to word-of-mouth advertising," says Brannen.

Roger Ford, director of the Entrepreneurial Center at James Madison University, Harrisonburg, Virginia, and a former owner of three successful small businesses, actively worked a word-of-mouth advertising campaign. He started by creating a clean and neat environment for customers. When Ford and his wife owned a retail liquor store in upstate New York, he says, "We had a strong fetish for keeping the place clean." Employees dusted the displays, fixtures, and inventory three times a day.

The Fords carefully hired employees with pleasing personalities and warm smiles. "We sought employees who wanted public interaction and had a positive, upbeat attitude," says Ford. "That way customers knew we appreciated their business."

Additional services were added for customers' convenience: free delivery within a seventy-five-mile radius, free gift cards and boxes, free holiday foil gift bags, and opportunities to taste various products before making a purchase. "We didn't want some-

TIPS: Proactive Image Building

Specialty Advertising Association International decided to deal with an ongoing identity problem. Based on some marketing research, a number of key image-enhancement strategies were suggested (although some terms may be different, the steps and suggestions are also relevant to small businesses and other shoestring marketers):

1. *Identify the relevant publics,* who have a bearing on the success and recognition of membership (sales revenue for small businesses).
2. *Evaluate current image,* using interviews or questionnaires.
3. *Identify your image strengths and weaknesses,* including how each public group perceives your association.
4. *Develop an agenda* dealing with the perceptions of desired image.
5. *Design strategies* to correct image misconceptions or negative perceptions.
6. *Develop communication programs* to reach your relevant programs.
7. *Implement strategies.*
8. *Conduct follow-up studies.* Ask yourself questions like: Are positive attitudes being spread through word-of-mouth channels and negative ones being eliminated?

The SAA International notes that the proactive image program can increase new membership, create a more active membership, improve relationships with new clients, recruit qualified employees, result in fewer complaints, and generate more pride in the industry.

Source: "Tips for Proactive Image Building," *Association Management* (July 1987), pp. 47–49.

one to buy a product—especially certain types of wine—and then be disappointed," he says.

The Fords developed a file system for their key customers, making note of special requests, likes and dislikes, and when a customer might need his inventory replenished. They had three theme parties for customers to sample wine, cheese, and special liquor brands—many supplied free by the vendor.

By developing a positive image, the word-of-mouth advertising network naturally grew. "Our immediate goal was to achieve $100,000 [in sales] a year," says Ford. The word-of-mouth advertising helped the couple realize their goal much sooner than they expected. The Fords have since sold their store at a handsome profit.

Consumers obtain most of their purchasing information from other people. Advertising and sales promotion create an awareness for your product and service, but word of mouth may be a major catalyst for more sales. This is especially true of intangible services that are sometimes difficult to compare in quality.

Carol Colman, a partner in the marketing firm Inferential Focus, says that word-of-mouth advertising begins because people need to socialize. She believes that people like to share their experiences with each other.[2]

Many experts advise marketers to identify the influencers (also called opinion leaders)—the people who try a product or service and then tell others about it. Because some people want to be associated with a certain social class, they often copy the leaders. Try to spot the opinion leaders in your target market. It helps to ask customers how they heard about your business or who recommended your business. Aim some of your selling efforts at the influencers.

Small-business owners and association managers should be active in social, community, and civic organizations. Affiliations frequently are powerful in attracting influencers and also cultivating other forms of word-of-mouth advertising. Without ignoring your daily operations, you should carefully choose the clubs and associations that give you the most visibility and allow you to contribute your expertise.

As far as we know, there is no trade association specializing in word-of-mouth advertising. However, the American Society of Association Executives, Washington, D.C., may refer you to a particular association.

Work with your own trade and professional associations, as well as your customers' associations. Not only will they offer advice, but they may even be the influencers in many cases.

$

X-Ception

For the small-business owner or association director, time is a precious asset. It seems there are just never enough hours in the day to accomplish everything they set out to do. Hence, there is a need for management by exception—that is, carefully selecting (or X-ing or checking off) what you need to do yourself and what can be done by others.

Nadine Gramling, chief executive officer of Southeastern Metals Manufacturing Company, Inc., a metal construction materials firm, advises entrepreneurs and managers to learn how to plan and conserve precious time. Gramling says small-business owners worry if employees are doing everything correctly. Entrepreneurs especially feel that no one knows how to run the business as well as they do. While certain tasks can't be delegated, the entrepreneur simply can't do everything singlehandedly, says Gramling. "That's one of the hardest things about running a business that grows in sales from zero to $30 million—you've got to learn to delegate, to turn loose some jobs because you should be planning for the future," says Gramling.[1]

Deciding when to get involved and when to delegate is diffi-

TIPS: Identifying and Avoiding the Biggest Time Wasters

R. Alec MacKenzie, author of *The Time Trap* (New York: AMACOM, 1972), lists his universal time wasters in the business world.

1. Lack of planning
2. Lack of priorities
3. Overcommitment
4. Management by crisis
5. Haste, urgency, and attempting too much
6. Paperwork and reading
7. Routine and trivia
8. Visitors
9. Telephone
10. Meetings
11. Indecision
12. Lack of delegation

Business writer Michael LeBoeuf lists his top ten time wasters ranked by sales representatives:

1. Telephone interruptions
2. Drop-in visitors
3. Lack of self-discipline
4. Crisis
5. Meetings
6. Lack of objectives, priorities, and deadlines
7. Indecision and procrastination
8. Attempting too much at once
9. Leaving tasks unfinished
10. Unclear communication

As frugal marketers, you may identify with these two lists. Analyze your own situation and carefully decide which scenarios demand your attention. Time is an irretrievable, inexorable, and inelastic element for shoestring marketers. You can't afford to waste one minute.

Sources: R. Alec MacKenzie, *The Time Trap* (New York: AMACOM, 1972); Michael LeBoeuf, "Managing Your Time, Managing Yourself," *Business Horizons* (February 1980): 42.

cult. There's a natural tendency to become a hands-on entrepreneur or manager because resources are so scarce. You may fear that mistakes will occur without your input. And some mistakes can be fatal to a small enterprise. Yet, to grow, the founder must learn to let go and do some delegating.

Since time is a precious commodity, you must practice some "management by exception." In other words, you must deal with only those issues that need your coverage. Don't be enamored with everything; otherwise, you'll have less time to serve your customers and no creative time in which to sell your business concept to many interested parties.

Some marketers believe that as a business grows, the owner or CEO must do less operational work and more strategic planning. But James Koch, founder and CEO of the Boston Beer Company, believes that more entrepreneurs and shoestring marketers must get more involved with selling. Although selling is fundamental to a business, it's a devalued skill. "Tell people you're a salesman, and they act like you've got crumbs on your shirt," says Koch. "However, I first don't need a computer, a desk, or an office. What I first need is a customer."[2]

With the CEO doing some selling, the rest of the employees of a small business will know where the priorities are, says Koch. "Even today, running a $7 million company with twenty-eight employees, I spend about two-thirds of my time selling beer. When people ask me why I don't even have an office, I tell them it's really very simple: I can't sell beer to a desk."

Whatever your own feelings, in delegating and managing your time, be sure your organization primarily remembers the customers, competition, and the goal of creating solid products and services that are demanded in today's tough market milieu. Your management by exception should always include attention to your customers and the correct selling strategies.

As a business develops—especially during rapid-growth periods—it can frequently become bureaucratic and sloppy. Suddenly it sells shoddy products or services, forgets customers' needs, and assumes that it's indestructible in the marketplace.

Too often, at the expense of their customers, the entrepreneurs or managers devote time and resources for bigger facilities, more computing power, excessive modernization, relocation, or hiring more administrative staff. In addition to incurring runaway overhead costs, the business loses sight of what allows it to prosper in the first place. Be sure you overcome this common but misguided strategy.

On the other hand, trust your subordinates and give them worthwhile projects—known as delegation. R. Alec MacKenzie says time is a unique resource that cannot be accumulated like money or stockpiled like raw materials. You must learn to have faith in your subordinates' capabilities.

Naturally some mistakes will occur. But with proper training and instruction, the subordinates can do operational tasks. You can then concentrate on Koch's suggestions: studying your customers, finding ways to improve your offerings, and increasing sales to enhance the bottom line. In simple and brief terms, our true feelings for carefully placing the Xs (management by exception) for shoestring marketers are: stay close to the marketplace and sell, sell, sell the organization to customers, suppliers, creditors, bankers, and the community at large.

$

Yellow Pages

If you had to sink all your marketing dollars into one ad for an entire year, most likely it would be in a Yellow Pages directory. Not only is it a fairly inexpensive way to advertise, but it is also one of the easiest ways to reach prospective customers. Unlike placing one-time ads in newspapers or magazines—which are frequently overlooked by readers—a listing in the Yellow Pages reaches a captive audience—repeatedly. A person who opens up the Yellow Pages is ready to make a purchase. In most cases, you don't need to do a thing but be polite if a person calls for directions or asks for a price.

But how do you get your listing to stand out? If your company's name does not begin with "A" the next best thing is an eye-catching listing or an ad to incite a potential customer to call or come to your store.

Cyma Carn, for example, placed a large boxed ad in a Pages Plus Yellow Pages directory serving metropolitan Detroit to attract customers after she relocated her store to a site that offered lower overhead but less visibility. The ad included an illustration of Carn with her arms "reaching out" to potential customers, as well as a map. "I'm at 222 E. Harrison and even people in this suburb don't recognize it," she says. The ad is a great conversation piece in addition to attracting business, says Carn. "That ad comes up so much in conversations with my customers that I'm astonished." But it's no wonder. Carn reinforces her directory listing in other advertising by telling customers to look up her Yellow Pages ad for directions.

Creating an off-beat directory ad is one way to draw the attention of people ready to spend. Bob Bly, a New Milford, New Jersey–based copywriter who specializes in direct response advertising, offers some techniques for getting more responses from your ad:

- Put a heavy dashed border around fractional ads. This creates a coupon-like appearance, which tends to stimulate response.
- Offer free information in the ad, such as a booklet, brochure, catalog, or price list. The ad can even serve as a discount coupon if a line of copy says to mention seeing the ad for $1 off any item or 10 percent off any service, for example. The idea is to stimulate response to your ad, not only to track its effectiveness but to keep it in the phone book for repeat usage.
- Give your free literature a title that implies value. "Call for a free 'product guide' sounds better than 'catalog,'" says Bly. And "planning kit" sounds better than "sales brochure."
- Offer a free item in your ad—a product sample, free analysis, consultation, estimate, demonstration, seminar, or free trial.
- If you offer a discount coupon in the phone book's coupon section, indicate this in your directory listing. Make the coupon large enough so that there is room for prospects to write in their names and addresses. When customers turn in their coupons, you will have follow-up information for direct mailings.

By modifying existing ads using these techniques, advertisers can increase response to their ads by 20 to 100 percent without destroying the basic concept and theme of their campaigns, says Bly.

Some other points to consider including in your directory ad are the number of years in business, experience and scope of your firm, awards, certification, and trade association memberships to present a credible image, suggests L. M. Berry & Company, sales rep for the AT&T Toll-Free 800 Directories. You might also choose to stress your advantages over the competition, unique selling features, and market positioning statements in your headlines.

Provide all the information that might influence the caller, and remember that if the caller does not see products or services listed in your ad, he might assume you do not offer them. You might list trade and brand names available, inventory availability and delivery information, prices, financing plans such as credit cards and discounts, as well as catalogs and guarantee or warranty policies.

Most important, make sure your phone number—especially if you have an 800 number—is large and easy to read. Also include hours to call, local contact numbers or special customer service lines, and local branch addresses. However, the more information you include in your ad, the more it will cost. Try to provide only the information that your target market will consider to be the biggest influence to call your company over the competition.

Which directory should you advertise in? Today directories are segmented to target specific consumers. There are Yellow Pages for senior citizens, ethnic groups, women and minorities, businesses, as well as local and regional directories. There is even a phone book of companies and organizations offering toll-free numbers. By advertising in one of these segmented directories, you are more likely to reach the audience who will buy your product or service. Usually segmented directories' ad rates are less expensive than those of the larger directories.

But you are not reaching as wide an audience with your ad. Use a segmented directory if you have pinpointed a certain target market for your product. A gerontologist, for instance, can save money on ad rates and reach only his target market by advertising in a phone directory for senior citizens.

You can find the various Yellow Pages directories listed in the "Advertising—Directory and Guide" section of your regional Yellow Pages directory. Call the phone number listed for an advertiser's packet, which will give you ad rates, deadlines, and requirements for placing an ad. A representative will also help you create the listing that best suits your needs.

Most directories offer a variety of space listings and typefaces (styles of type, such as bold face), which allow for varying amounts of information to supplement a business's name, address, and phone number.

If you are interested in placing ads in, say, twenty different directories throughout the country, a Yellow Page directory service—listed in the same section as Yellow Pages directories—will make the arrangements and consolidate the billing so that you will receive one bill instead of twenty. These agencies are compensated by the directories' publishers. You, the advertiser, pay no fee to these agencies for this service other than the cost of the ad.

Further Resources

National Yellow Pages Service Association
Advertising Bureau
888 West Big Beaver Road
Suite 414
Troy, Michigan 48084

$

Zeroing In on Your Markets

You can't please all of the people all of the time. That adage rings especially true for businesses with limited resources. They simply cannot afford to offer something to everyone. When they do, selling efforts and dollars are spread too thin, wasted, and directed at small, unprofitable markets.

As a shoestring marketer, you must follow one of the most important fundamental rules of successful marketing: Identify unmet needs within select groups, study the competition, and then create good competitive products and services desired by the groups you've spotted. In a nutshell, you must learn to zero in on key customer groups. You can't afford an expensive shotgun approach; instead, a rifle marketing approach allows you to hit your bull's eye. (In marketing terminology, this process may often be called market targeting, segmentation, or market niche.)

Although this is the last entry in this encyclopedia, the concept of zeroing in on your well-defined markets is a vital first step for smart shoestring marketers. Before embarking on any glitzy campaign, identify people and organizations with common characteristics that have a strong need for your business. Instead of trying to sell to anyone and everyone, picking and aiming for specific markets is easier, cheaper, more profitable, faster, and safer to the well-being of your business, association, or nonprofit organization.

Here are a few simple examples to illustrate the concept of zeroing in on specific market segments:

- A local builder decides to build homes for the smaller, more affluent market.
- A small law firm has successfully specialized in the health-care industry within the Florida market.
- A new publisher produces and sells only inexpensive romance paperback novels to the teenage market.
- A small independent retailer cameos high-priced jewelry for professionals within the country club set.
- A local pizza business goes after people who live within a seven-mile radius.
- A new association decides to attract members who have a major interest in robotics.
- A small rent-a-maid service goes after the two-career couple household employed by government agencies in Washington, D.C.
- To aim at sport enthusiasts, a small manufacturer produces neckties in the form of fish, golf clubs, and baseball bats.

Examples of target marketing are endless because so many businesses, associations, and nonprofit organizations have increasingly used the niche approach to survive and compete.

Market holes are areas where existing sellers have not responded to a need, says Walton Chapman, founder of a Santa Fe, New Mexico, building business. Because buyers were having problems finding affordable homes, his firm identified a strong need for good middle-price-range housing in the Santa Fe area. "If you can solve the problem that creates the hole, you've got an exclusive grip on a nice piece of the market," says Walton. "When you start small, as we did, with a little capital or land, the market hole strategy is a good way to go."[1]

When dividing the total or mass market and looking for profitable holes, look for small groups of potential or actual consumers who have common traits. This enables you to serve better the interests of the submarkets while pinpointing your selling opportunities in each one.

There are two general markets: (1) households and (2) organizations, such as manufacturers, wholesalers, retailers, government, professional service firms, and nonprofit organizations. The second group is often known as the intermediate-industrial market. You may have a business that serves both markets, which isn't unusual.

In analyzing your selling opportunities, see if your market targets meet certain conditions. Otherwise you're wasting your precious resources by zeroing in on the wrong market targets. To give you some focus and direction, Worksheet 8 points out some key factors to consider. By objectively answering the questions, you can decide which consumer groups may be the best to go after.

Worksheet 9 gives you some ideas on how you might even classify your individual markets. The worksheet illustrates the degree of detail that is feasible in breaking down the total population. Of course, one of your markets may have more than one common trait (e.g., a certain occupation, location, and income could be one of your market targets).

The process of classifying and analyzing markets will help you in deciding the best way to spend your marketing dollars. It's not simply an academic exercise that is never used. After studying who your customers are and who you want to attract, you can develop sound marketing strategies. Marketing segmentation helps in answering such essential questions as the ones listed on page 333, below Worksheet 9.

WORKSHEET 8

Planning Market Targets

Customer/Organization ————————— Date ————

Address ———————————————————————

Type of Business ————————————————————

Previous Customer: ——— Yes ——— No ——— Not Sure

	Potential business—How Favorable?			
	Excel- lent	Some- what	Poor	Not Sure
1. Size	——	——	——	——
2. Growth rate	——	——	——	——
3. Captive customer	——	——	——	——
4. Interest	——	——	——	——
5. Willingness to buy	——	——	——	——
6. Economic ability (enough income)	——	——	——	——
7. Attitude toward us	——	——	——	——
8. Profit opportunities	——	——	——	——
9. Repeat business	——	——	——	——
10. Ability to meet their needs	——	——	——	——
11. Bring in other customers	——	——	——	——
12. Easy to reach	——	——	——	——
13. Flexible on terms of sales	——	——	——	——
14. Positive cash flow	——	——	——	——

WORKSHEET 9

Different Ways to Segment a Market—
How Attractive and Useful for Your Business?

Classification	Very	Some-what	Not at All	Not Sure
I. Household Consumer Market				
A. Demographics (age, sex, income, occupation, etc.)	___	___	___	___
B. Geographic location (block, city, county, state, etc.)	___	___	___	___
C. Method (cash vs. credit customers)	___	___	___	___
D. Timing of purchase (daily, weekly, monthly, etc.)	___	___	___	___
E. Size of market (who buys greatest or least amounts)	___	___	___	___
F. Purchasing influences (child, parents, grand-parents, friends, etc.)	___	___	___	___
G. Personality	___	___	___	___
H. Benefits received from product/service (eco-nomic, convenience, security, status, etc.)	___	___	___	___

(Continued)

WORKSHEET 9 (*continued*)

Classification	Very	Some-what	Not at All	Not Sure
I. Total life-style (i.e., total sum of all characteristics including demographic—must really know your market to use this one)	____	____	____	____
II. Government				
A. Federal	____	____	____	____
B. State	____	____	____	____
C. County	____	____	____	____
D. Local/city	____	____	____	____
III. Selling to Other Business by Industry				
A. Agriculture	____	____	____	____
B. Forestry	____	____	____	____
C. Fishing	____	____	____	____
D. Mining	____	____	____	____
E. Type of manufacturer (e.g., steel, automotive, machinery)	____	____	____	____
F. Public utilities	____	____	____	____
G. Retailers	____	____	____	____
H. Wholesalers	____	____	____	____

Classification	Very	Some-what	Not at All	Not Sure
I. Transportation	____	____	____	____
J. Services (insurance, banking, hospitals, etc.)	____	____	____	____
K. Professional services (doctors, dentists, lawyers, etc.)	____	____	____	____
IV. International Markets	____	____	____	____
V. Not-for-Profit Organizations	____	____	____	____
VI. Education (public schools, colleges)	____	____	____	____
VII. Other Markets				
A. _____	____	____	____	____
B. _____	____	____	____	____
C. _____	____	____	____	____

- What products to sell?
- Where to advertise?
- How much to charge?
- Where to locate my business?
- Who should I call on?
- Why do people buy?
- When is the best time to sell?
- Should discounts be offered?

These few questions are not complete, yet they show the importance of first defining your markets. If you haven't already done it, develop your own current customer profiles to see which traits seem to be prevalent. Are there noncustomer groups you should be serving? Is it too expensive to serve certain segments? What can be done to get more sales from current targets? Is your market changing and will some segments become more important? As noted, this whole process will enable you to make better decisions on where to get the most benefits from your marketing dollars.

In sum, target marketing is a major step to smart selling. Here are a few dos and don'ts to enhance your own methods for hitting the "bull's eye."

Do	*Don't*
Match your products with your market targets. Is there a good fit?	Assume all markets are the same and that one strategy will work for all of them.
Watch and gauge the successes and failures of serving different market groups.	Ignore your competitors' actions in different market segments.
Make sure you have the resources to go after certain market targets.	Forget that markets change and some profitable groups may become less important in the future.
Qualify your market targets with sound marketing research procedures.	Concentrate only on the actual buyers while ignoring people who may influence or actually make the decision to buy the products (such as children or teenagers).
Continually find ways to pinpoint key customer groups	Go after markets that are beyond your resources and end

and accurately describe their behavior.

up causing severe financial problems. Don't assume that all your market segments cost the same to serve and bring in the same profit margins.

PART

III

FURTHER RESOURCES

$

Further Resources

At the time of this writing, the following addresses as well as sources listed throughout this book were accurate; however, you may want to check association directories and the *Directory of Directories*, found in most libraries. It is not uncommon for addresses to change or small associations to go defunct.

Academy of Marketing Science
Box 248012
Coral Gables, Florida 33124

Sponsors and supports grants for both the advancement of the teaching of marketing and research in marketing.

Advertising Agencies Directory
American Business Directories, Inc., a division of American Business Lists, Inc.
5707 South 86th Circle
Omaha, Nebraska 68127

Lists 21,000 agencies. Annual (published in January), $175.

Advertising Council
825 Third Avenue, 25th Floor
New York, New York 10022

A nonprofit organization of volunteers who conduct advertising campaigns for the public good.

Adweek Directory of Advertising
A/S/M/ Communications, Inc.
820 Second Avenue
New York, New York 10017

Lists agencies, clients, and the media the agencies use. Separate editions per region. $25 per edition.

Adweek Portfolio
A/S/M Communications, Inc.
820 Second Avenue
New York, New York 10017

Lists agencies in five volumes: commercial production, creative services, design, illustration, and photography. Listing includes artists, suppliers, agencies, and other companies whose products or services are related to advertising. $25 per volume.

American Economic Development Council
4849 North Scott Street
Suite 22
Schiller Park, Illinois 60176

Once part of the Chamber of Commerce, the AEDC is a tax-exempt, incorporated organization of professionals active in promoting economic development.

American Management Association
135 West 50th Street
New York, New York 10020

American Marketing Association—Membership Roster
and Buyer's Guide to Marketing Services
American Marketing Association
250 South Wacker Drive
Chicago, Illinois 60606

Available at a cost of $75.

Auctioneers Directory
American Business Directories, Inc.
5707 South 86th Circle
Omaha, Nebraska 68127

Lists more than 9,600 auctioneers across the country. Annual, $90.

Bradford's Directory of Marketing Research Agencies
and Management Consultants in the United States and
the World
Bradford's Directory of Marketing Research Agencies
Box 276
Fairfax, Virginia 22030

Lists 1,600 marketing research agencies. Annual, $48.

Brand Names: Who Owns What
Facts on File, Inc.
460 Park Avenue South
New York, New York 10016

Lists 750 firms and their 15,000 brand names. $65.

Business Organizations, Agencies and Publications Directory
Gale Research Company
Book Tower
Detroit, Michigan 48226

Lists more than 22,000 organizations and publications whose products or services are beneficial to business. Includes trade, commercial, and labor associations, government agencies, stock exchanges, U.S. and foreign diplomatic offices, regional planning and development agencies, conventions, fairs and trade organizations, franchise companies, banks, newspapers, information centers, computer information services, and research centers. Biennial, $265.

Business/Professional Advertising Association—Membership Directory and Yellow Pages
Business/Professional Advertising Association
205 East 42nd Street
New York, New York 10017

Lists advertising agencies, marketing communications consultants. Ads accepted. Biennial, $25.

Chamber of Commerce of the United States
1615 H Street, N.W.
Washington, D.C. 20062

Department of Commerce of the United States
14th Street between Constitution Avenue and E Street, N.W.
Washington, D.C. 20230

Branches of particular interest to small business include: National Technical Information Service, Bureau of the Census, Economic Development Administration, International Trade Administration, Patent and Trademark Office, and Minority Business Development Agency.

Direct Marketing Association
6 East 43rd Street
New York, New York 10017

Direct Marketing Marketplace
Hillary House
1033 Channel Drive
Hewlett Harbor, New York 11557

Lists 5,000 direct marketing companies, service firms, suppliers, as well as creative and consulting services in the field of direct mail, radio, and TV marketing. Annual, $75.

Direct Selling Association
1776 K Street, N.W.
Suite 600
Washington, D.C. 20006

Members are manufacturers and distributors who retail products door to door, by party plan, and other means of personal selling directly to the consumer.

Direct Selling World Directory
World Federation of Direct Selling Associations
1776 K Street, N.W.
Suite 600
Washington, D.C. 20006

Lists thirty direct selling associations focusing on person-to-person and party-plan selling. Annual, $40.

Directory of Directories
Gale Research Company
Book Tower
Detroit, Michigan 48226

Guide to more than 9,000 business and industrial directories, professional and scientific rosters, directory data bases, and other list and guides of all types.

Directory of Mailing List Houses
B. Klein Publications, Inc.
Box 8503
Coral Springs, Florida 33065

Lists more than 3,000 mailing lists brokers, compilers, and managers. $30.

Distributive Education Clubs of America
1908 Association Drive
Reston, Virginia 22091

Members are mostly students who are concerned with distribution, marketing, merchandising, and management. DECA students typically attend school part time and work part time.

Export Licensing, Attn: Electronic Submission, U.S. Department of Commerce
P.O. Box 273
Washington, D.C. 20044

For information about submitting an export licensing application via computer, call (202) 377-8540. For guidance on licensing requirements for the Commerce Department's exporter assistance staff, call (202) 377-4811.

Free Money: For Small Businesses and Entrepreneurs
John Wiley & Sons
605 Third Avenue
New York, New York 10158

By Laurie Blum. Contains more than 300 sources of providers of start-up capital, research grants, expansion funds, operating assistance, and others. Regional listings by state. Also outlined are funding opportunities for minority enterprises, including ventures run by blacks, Hispanics, American Indians, or women. $12.95.

Incentive Marketing—Resource Guide Issue
Bill Communications
633 Third Avenue
New York, New York 10017

Covers more than 1,000 specialists and suppliers of promotional products and services for incentive marketing campaigns, such as sweepstakes and contests. $3.

Information USA
Viking Penguin, Inc.
40 West 23rd Street
New York, New York 10010

By Matthew Lesko. Reference book to hundreds of free and inexpensive government sources. Copyright dates 1983, 1986.

International Directory of Marketing Research Houses and Services
New York Chapter, American Marketing Association
420 Lexington Avenue
New York, New York 10017

Covers more than 1,200 marketing research consultants and suppliers of marketing research needs, including a list of computer programs for market reseach. $50.

International Directory of Market Research Organizations
MacFarlane and Company, Inc.
One Park Place
Suite 450
Atlanta, Georgia 30318

A list of more than 1,300 market research firms in the United States and abroad. $90 plus shipping.

International Directory of Published Market Research
MacFarlane and Company, Inc.
One Park Place
Suite 450
Atlanta, Georgia 30318

Lists nearly 400 firms that have published more than 10,000 studies of specific worldwide markets. $69.75 plus shipping.

Mail Advertising Service Association International
7325 Wisconsin Avenue
Suite 440 West
Bethesda, Maryland 20814

Members are producers of direct commercial mail and list brokers.

Mail Order Association of America
2550 M Street, N.W.

9th Floor
Washington, D.C. 20037

Mailing List Users and Suppliers Association
322 8th Avenue
12th Floor
New York, New York 10001

Manufacturers' Agents National Association
P.O. Box 3467
Laguna Hill, California 92654

Market Access Reports
International Trade and Marketing Association
4010 West 65th Street
Minneapolis, Minnesota 55435

Lists business opportunities in developing countries, including large construction projects and equipment purchases planned for funding but not yet released for public bidding. Twenty publications focusing on different regions. $295 per issue.

Marketing Agents for Food Service Industry
111 East Wacker Drive
Suite 600
Chicago, Illinois 60601

Marketing Communications—Directory of Special Agencies Issue
Media Horizons, Inc.
50 West 23rd Street
New York, New York 10010

A list of about 175 specialized marketing and sales promotion agencies with expertise in direct mail, couponing, dealer incentives, media buying, meetings and conventions, sampling, sweepstakes and contests, and trade shows. Annual, $5.

Marketing Research Association
111 East Wacker Drive
Suite 600
Chicago, Illinois 60601

National Association of Display Industries
419 Park Avenue South
3rd Floor
New York, New York 10016

Members are manufacturers and distributors of fixtures and displays.

National Association of Women Business Owners
600 South Federal Street
Suite 400
Chicago, Illinois 60605

National Business Incubation Association
Ohio University
Innovation Center
One President Street
Athens, Ohio 45701

National Mail Order Association
5818 Venice Boulevard
Los Angeles, California 90019

National Retail Merchants Association
100 West 31st Street
New York, New York 10001

Publishes many helpful how-to books on operating, merchandising, and marketing retail operations.

National Trade & Professional Associations of the United States
Columbia Books, Inc.
1350 New York Avenue, N.W.
Suite 207
Washington, D.C. 20005

O'Dwyer's Directory of Public Relations Firms
J. R. O'Dwyer Company, Inc.
271 Madison Avenue
New York, New York 10016

Annually profiles more than 1,700 public relations firms nationwide. $90.

Package Design Council International
Box 3753, Grand Central Station
New York, New York 10017

Members are industrial and graphic design consultants specializing in package design and brand name development.

Packaging Institute International
20 Summer Street
Stamford, Connecticut 06901

Promotion Marketing Association of America
322 Eighth Avenue
Suite 1201
New York, New York 10001

Members are premium users, manufacturers, consultants, and ad agencies.

Public Relations Society of America
33 Irving Place
3rd Floor
New York, New York 10003

Service Corps of Retired Executives (SCORE)
1129 20th Street, N.W.
Suite 410
Washington, D.C. 20036

Nonprofit organization of retired executives of all fields who volunteer their management expertise and advice to small businesses.

Small Business Administration
Imperial Building
1441 L Street, N.W.
Washington, D.C. 20416

With regional and district offices in every state, SBA services of particular interest to small business are Minority Small Business-Capital Ownership Development, Business Development, and Office of Women's Business Ownership.

Small Business Sourcebook
Gale Research Company
Book Tower
Detroit, Michigan 48226

Covers trade associations, federal and state government agencies, sponsors of educational programs, publishers of reference publications, sources of equipment and services and statistical and marketing data, venture capital firms, and other companies that offer assistance to small business. $140.

Standard Directory of Advertising Agencies
National Register Publishing Company, Inc.
Subsidiary of Standard Rate and Data Service, Inc.
Macmillan
3004 Glenview Road
Wilmette, Illinois 60091

List of more than 4,400 advertising agencies across the country. Annual, $109.

Standard Rate and Data Service—Co-op Source Directory
Standard Rate and Data Service, Inc.
Macmillan
3004 Glenview Road
Wilmette, Illinois 60091

Lists more than 3,700 cooperative advertising programs offered by manufacturers. Semiannual, $124 per copy.

Standard Rate and Data Service—Direct Mail List Rates and Data
Standard Rate and Data Service, Inc.
Macmillan

3004 Glenview Road
Wilmette, Illinois 60091

Lists 55,000 mailing lists composed of businesspersons and firms, general consumers, cooperative mailings, and package insert programs. Details include list title, address, phone number, method of delivery, schedules, price, restrictions. Bimonthly, $70; or $170 a year with semimonthly update bulletins.

Typesetting Services Directory
American Business Directories, Inc.
5707 South 86th Circle
Omaha, Nebraska 68127

Lists more than 9,000 typesetting firms nationwide.

$

We'd Like to Hear From You!

If you think your business or association has had great success with a particularly innovative and inexpensive marketing strategy, we'd like to hear about it. We may include your example in updated volumes of this book.

Please send a brief description of your marketing strategy, the results you've seen, and a phone number where we can reach you. Address your letter to *The Frugal Marketer*, 854 Forest Drive, Cookeville, Tennessee 38501 or 11968 Heathcote Court, Reston, Virginia 22091.

Notes

Part I

1. Edward McKay, *The Marketing Mystique* (New York: American Management Association, 1972).

3. Controls: Cash Flow and Costs

1. "Internal Financial Strategies," *Venture* (September 1985), pp. 65–72.
2. Ted Frost, *D&B Reports* (January–February 1987), pp. 28–29.
3. James Howard, *D&B Reports* (January–February 1987), pp. 19–23.
4. Arnold Goldstein, *Starting on a Shoestring* (New York: Ronald Press, 1984).

Part II

Advertising: Budget Stretching

1. David Ogilvy, *Ogilvy on Advertising* (New York: Crown, 1983).
2. Tom McElligott, "Face-to-Face," *Inc.* (July 1986), pp. 31–38.
3. J. Donald Weinrauch, *The Marketing Problem Solver* (New York: John Wiley, 1987).
4. David Ogilvy, *Confessions of an Advertising Man* (New York: Atheneum, 1980).
5. "Sales Calls + Direct Mail = Super Sales," *Sales & Marketing Digest* (February 1988).

Advertising: Co-op Advertising

1. Stephen Greyser and Robert Young, *Cooperative Advertising: Practices and Problems* (Cambridge, Mass.: Marketing Science Institute, 1982), pp. 82–105.
2. Ibid.

Advertising: Media and Message

1. "Print Ads Need to Grab, Hold Reader," *Sales & Marketing Digest* (February 1988), p. 7.

Advertising: Miscellaneous Notes

1. Sandy McGlashan and John Clausen, "Is It Time for an Ad Agency?" *Nation's Business* (October 1987), pp. 74–75.
2. Ibid.
3. Alec Benn, *The 27 Most Common Mistakes in Advertising* (New York: AMACOM, 1978).

Business Cards

1. "Does Your Business Card Mean Business?" *Entrepreneur* (August 1987), pp. 83–85.
2. "Use Business Cards to the Best Advantage," *Sales & Marketing Digest* (May 1987), p. 10.

Customer Relations

1. "More Than a Third of Michigan Consumers Have Been So Burned That They Shy Away From Some Business," *Marketing News*, April 24, 1987, p. 20.
2. Ray Considine, "Readers Respond," *Direct Marketing* (October 1987), p. 6.
3. Stanley Modic, "Unhappy Customers," *Industry Week*, August 10, 1987, p. 36.
4. Carol Gold, *Solid Gold Customer Relations* (Englewood Cliffs, N.J.: Prentice-Hall, 1983).
5. Laura Liswood, "Once You've Got 'Em, Never Let 'Em Go," *Sales & Marketing Management* (November 1987), pp. 73–77.
6. Philip Zweig, "Banks Stress Resolving Complaints to Win Customers' Favor," *Wall Street Journal*, December 8, 1986, p. 31.
7. F. G. Rogers, *The IBM Way* (New York: Harper & Row, 1986).

Downturns

1. Bruce Posner, "How to Stop Worrying and Love the Next Recession," *Inc.* (April 1986), pp. 89–95.
2. Robert Allen and H. John Altorfer, "Pulling a Company Out of a Tailspin," *Marketing Practices Quarterly* (Spring 1986), pp. 6–9.

3. Bruce Posner, "Hidden Perils in a Volatile Economy," *Inc.* (March 1986), pp. 113–116.
4. Kurt Benz, "Making Sick Companies Well Again," *Advantage* (October 1982), pp. 43–46.

Exporting

1. "Removing the Obstacles to Export," *D&B Reports* (May/June 1987), pp. 48–49.
2. "Made in America Sells Abroad," *In Business* (September/October 1987), pp. 30–32.
3. *A Basic Guide to Exporting,* U.S. Department of Commerce (Washington, D.C.: U.S. Government Printing Office, 1986).
4. "Exporting: Creating an International Market," *Small Business Report* (February 1987), pp. 20–23.
5. "Made in America Sells Abroad," op. cit.
6. Eric Wiklund, *International Marketing: Making Exports Pay Off* (New York: McGraw-Hill, 1986).
7. Peter B. Fitzpatrick and Alan S. Zimmerman, *Essentials of Export Marketing*—American Management Association Management Briefing (New York: AMACOM, 1985).

Home-Based Businesses

1. Marion Behe, "Homebased Basics," *Entrepreneur* (December 1987), pp. 123–125.
2. Phoebe Hawkins, "Going to Work by Staying Home," *Insight,* July 21, 1986, pp. 44–45.
3. Ibid.

Kudos (Tickler File)

1. "In-Store Stuffers," *In Business* (January–February 1988), p. 21.

Location

1. Donald Hauck, "Location, Location, Location!" *Venture* (April 1987), p. 100.
2. Jose DeCordoba, "Location, Location, Location," *Wall Street Journal,* May 15, 1987, p. 20D.
3. Bill Logan, "First Places That Work," *Venture* (December 1984), pp. 92–100.

Manufacturers' Reps

1. Bert Casper, *NTMA Journal,* December 1, 1983.
2. "Uproar in Rep-Land," *Sales & Marketing Management* (November 1986), pp. 64–68.
3. J. Donald Weinrauch, *The Marketing Problem Solver* (New York: John Wiley, 1987), p. 223.
4. Casper, op. cit.

Marketing Research: Focus Groups

1. "Listening, the Old-Fashioned Way," *Forbes,* October 5, 1987, pp. 202–204.
2. Richard A. Zeller, "In a Productive Focus Group, Participants Talk to ach Other," *Marketing News,* May 8, 1987, p. 35.
3. Robert Inglis, "In-Depth Data: Using Focus Groups to Study Industrial Markets," *Business Marketing* (November 1987), pp. 79–82.

Names and Logos

1. *The Naming Guide: How to Choose a Winning Name for Your Company, Service, or Product* (Dallas: The Salinon Corporation, © 1987, 1988), pp. 2–7. The Salinon Corporation is located at 7424 Greenville Avenue, #115, Dallas, Texas 75231. For a copy of the complete guide, please call (800) 722-0054 or (214) 692-9091.

Pricing Decisions

1. David Ogilvy, *Ogilvy on Advertising* (New York: Random House, 1985).
2. Ibid.

Prospecting for Gold

1. "Let Your Non-Sales Employees Assist in Generating Leads," *Sales & Marketing Digest* (December 1987).

Quality

1. "The Push for Quality," *Business Week,* June 8, 1987, p. 134.
2. Ibid., p. 136.
3. Ibid.
4. Thomas Peters and Robert Waterman, *In Search of Excellence: Les-*

sons From America's Best-Run Companies (New York: Harper & Row, 1982).

5. Robert D. Buzzell and Frederick Wiersema, "Successful Share-Building Strategies," *Harvard Business Review* (January–February 1981), pp. 135–144.

6. John Ryan, "Quality Is Making a Comeback," *Association Management* (October 1987), pp. 42–45.

7. Nora Goldstein, "Quest for Quality," *In Business* (July–August 1986), pp. 50–51.

Restaging Products

1. "A Kaleidoscopic Business Idea Sells," *Venture* (June 1987), p. 10.

2. "Indies Boffo; Nix Hollywood," *Venture* (November 1987), pp. 75–80.

3. "Becoming the Source of Information in Your Industry," *Hotline*, October 19, 1987—newsletter issue, pp. 2–3.

4. Neil Milner, "100 Ways to Generate Nondues Income," *Association Management* (August 1987), pp. 127–129.

5. Peter Wright, "Increasing Nondues Income," *Association Management* (August 1987), pp. 118–121.

6. "Spin Off Products and Services," Report 613 (New York: The Conference Board, 1976), pp. 1–32.

Sales Letters

1. Howard Shaw, "Super Sales Letters," *In Business* (March–April 1987), pp. 24–25.

2. Howad Shaw, "Keeping Letters Alive," *Direct Marketing* (April 1987), pp. 68–73.

3. "Selling Strategies," *In Business* (January–February 1987), p. 14.

Telemarketing

1. "Ringing Up Sales," *Business Week*, June 22, 1987, p. 118F.

2. James Porterfield, *Selling on the Phone: A Self-Teaching Guide* (New York: John Wiley, 1985).

3. "How to Start a Business-to-Business Telemarketing Program," *Marketing News*, March 16, 1984, p. 8.

4. "New Laws Take Toll on Telemarketers," *Inc.* (June 1986), p. 20.

5. *Win-Win Telemarketing for Wholesale Distributors* (Washington, D.C.: National Association of Wholesalers-Distributors, 1986).
6. Michael Zibrun, "Business-to-Business: A Value-Added Service to Build Opportunity," *Marketing* (December 1987), pp. 67–76.
7. "Telemarketing: Part 2," *Small Business Report* (September 1987), pp. 66–72.

Thanking the Customer

1. "Marketing: The Personal Touch," *Inc.* (January 1988), p. 85.
2. "Old Customers Mean New Business," *Success* (April 1986), p. 21.

Trade Shows

1. Carol Riggs, "Trade Shows Deliver Sales," *D&B Reports* (September–October 1987), pp. 22–49.
2. Ibid.
3. "Talking Turkey on Trade Shows," *Business Marketing* (March 1987), pp. 94–103.

Word of Mouth

1. Peter Reingen and Jerome Kernan, "Analysis of Referral Networks in Marketing: Methods and Illustration," *Journal of Marketing Research* (November 1986), pp. 370–378.
2. "The Best Kind of Advertising," *Forbes*, April 20, 1987, pp. 91–92.

X-Ception

1. Del Marth, "Women of Steel," *Nation's Business* (February 1988), pp. 85–86.
2. James Koch, "Portrait of the CEO as a Salesman," *Inc.* (March 1988), pp. 44–46.

Zeroing In on Your Markets

1. Chris Miller, "Filling in the Holes," *Nation's Business* (October 1986), pp. 85–86.

Index